The Wild Edge

The Wild Edge

Life and Lore
of the
Great Atlantic Beaches

SECOND EDITION

by
Philip Kopper

Illustrated by Anne E. Lacy

The Globe Pequot Press

Chester, Connecticut

Library of Congress Cataloging-in-Publication Data

Kopper, Philip.
    The wild edge : life and lore of the great Atlantic beaches /
Philip Kopper : illustrated by Anne E. Lacy. — 2nd ed.
      p.   cm.
    Includes index.
    ISBN 0-87106-319-0
    1. Seashore biology—Atlantic Coast (U.S.) 2. Beaches—Atlantic Coast
(U.S.) 3. Atlantic Coast (U.S.)—Description and travel. I. Title.
QH92.2.K66 1991
574.974—dc20
                91-14943
                CIP

Manufactured in the United States of America
Second Edition/First Printing

For
Mary née Carll
naturally

Contents

Preface to the Second Edition

Times change. Tides turn. A dozen years have passed since I did the major reporting for this book. Then, the Cold War was in a state of constant smolder, Carter was president and American hostages were held in Iran. Now the Cold War is over, and, as I write, American forces are at war with Iraq. But this book is about the beach, and the beach remains—perpetually the same and newly changed with every wave.

The past dozen years have seen Hurricane Hugo, the separation of uncounted sand spits into islands, the ghastly development of condominium communities in sight of surf—nay, in reach of the next high tide that's driven even higher by storm winds. Stretches of the Eastern Seaboard have been occupied by forces as aggressive as armies invading captive nations. Those forces, needless to say, include people I know, people like me. Yet the fact remains that the beach endures.

So much has changed along the shore from Maine to North Carolina since the previous edition was written that I was tempted to write an entirely new text. This book was born of the 1970s, that puzzled, in-between period spawned by the riotous sixties and then obliterated by the "Me Decade" with all the spite that spoiled adolescents reserve for doting parents. Rereading the original text, I found it naive in some respects, idyllic in several passages, and somehow hopeful throughout—young, in a word, as I was younger then.

This book appeared before anyone heard of finding medical wastes on far-flung beaches, let alone of wearing shoes in the sand for fear of stepping on used hypodermic needles. It was written before anyone except scientists thought about global warming and greenhouse gases. Written when I was a bachelor, it is far more sanguine and positive than anything I would write now as a middle-aged husband and father. But a book, like a son, has a life of its own and a right to enter its teens without being given a new character at its progenitor's will or whim.

So instead of starting from scratch, I have updated the book. I have corrected bald errors—facts that have been overtaken by time, names of organisms that have been changed by scientists and even (truth to tell) some things that I got wrong in the first place. Beyond

corrections, I have reordered some chapters, made judicious cuts
here and there, clarified passages, expanded a few others and written de novo to reflect a few recent events and new experiences. I
tried to avoid "revisionism," however; incidents and opinions remain if they were genuine in their time and what changed was me
alone.

I endeavored to let this revised edition reflect its origin as a
book of curiosity and wonder, the book I wrote because I couldn't
find one to explain all the things I wanted to know about the beach.
You see, I have changed more than beaches have. Yes, sea level has
risen in the past dozen years. Delaware and North Carolina have
allowed some absolutely horrendous development to take place.
But the beach persists! With no further fanfare whatsoever loggerhead sea turtles are returning in greater numbers to nest along the
Outer Banks. Brown pelicans have returned to Virginia. The osprey
has returned to Martha's Vineyard.

This book was never meant to be a travelog. Though I've done
considerable traveling both to write and to revise it, you'll not find
many tips about where to stay or what to eat. It is an apolitical work,
though allusions to political stupidity and social insanity appear.
Nor was it ever meant to be a nature guide—though I hope it may
introduce new readers to aspects of a world that they haven't seen
in quite the same way before. It is what it is, a book that I hope may
inform, intrigue and amuse some readers for another dozen years.
You're as welcome to it as you are to the beach itself.

Sea oats along the Outer Banks

Prologue: The Whys of This Book

The road *best* traveled has a thousand names and one destination: the beach. Depending on where you start, it may point anywhere on the compass, though it usually wends an easterly way in the territory I frequent—Mid-Atlantic America and New England. Most often the Beach Road ends on an island, for beaches in these parts are almost always on islands. Go beaching from Maine to the Outer Banks and you'll leave the mainland, perhaps unawares, since so many of eastern America's islands are linked to land by bars, isthmuses or man-made causeways. New England's coast is a virtual archipelago, the legacy of glaciers; then starting along New York's Long Island, sand spits and sand piles are the rule, all of them boasting the rubric "barrier island." By one count, some 121 major "coastal barriers" comprising 365,372 acres and stretching 1,104 miles mark the eastern seaboard as far south as South Carolina. (So tidy an enumeration is deceptive. What about the place I reached with dry shoes one morning but then was stranded on for half a day by a frigid infusion from the Gulf of Maine? It was an island at high tide, a peninsula at low.) Whatever the numbers, let us concentrate on the beach itself.

Between surf and turf lurks a bewildering complex place, one we take for granted. The seashore is like sex: easy to enjoy without knowing much about how it works. And mysterious as it is, sex might be the simpler to understand, as it comprises just two major elements: anatomy and emotion. The beach involves many more particulars: rocks, plants, animals, weather, climate, water, physics—all tangled together like a surf row of seaweed, spider crabs and tidal lint in the wide-meshed net of natural science. The only constants are energy and change in this ribbon of a region where old land meets the kinetic ocean. This shoreline is the manifestation of movable objects meeting resistible forces—sand and stones versus water in waves. (The ocean is presently winning as its level rises inches a century, and global warming is picking up the pace dangerously. But stick around long enough and I can promise you another ice age, I think.)

I first took the Beach Road far longer ago than I can cogently recall; suffice it that my earliest memories involve summers beside salt water—seasons filled with sand-castle fantasies and alive with horseshoe crabs, unforgettable creatures when you're barely twice their size.

More than twenty years later I began driving the Beach Road for myself. By then I had become in turn a newspaper reporter, an editor, then a freelance writer tackling targets of journalistic opportunity: the social lion of the moment, the ideal flow of traffic through an automotive shop, the ebb and flow of life and death in a hospital emergency room. After writing stories like these I'd seek a natural place that nurtured fundamental things, where I could watch the tides turn and listen to ghost crabs. Back at the beach it was retreat and renewal in endless succession; there was either overwhelming peace or natural fury—violence without malice. Back at the beach it was predation as usual and reproductive life. Thoreau wrote, "I love nature partly because she is not a man but a retreat from him. None of his institutions control or pervade her; there a different kind of right prevails. . . . He is constraint; she is freedom for me. He makes me wish for another world; she makes me content with this."

I took his meaning and became benignly addicted to beach trips. At the beach were mysteries, yet their solutions seemed accessible. In order to plumb them I began researching the beach like a reporter. First I turned to books, the field guides, of course. Perhaps they'd at least name all the birds, beasts, shells, shrubs, trees, animal tracks, marine mammals, edible plants, fishes, crabs, coelenterates, minerals, meiofauna and more. Soon my purportedly portable nature library grew too large to tote, even in an L. L. Bean bag. Each book became more encyclopedic than the last. Every memoir reported a species or behavior pattern I'd never seen but failed to mention what I encountered yesterday. I read impressive anthologies about the titanic and intelligent whales, but I found little that was intelligible about whiffets (by definition "small or insignificant" animals).

Outer dunes: beach grass, sea rocket and sand

Something as important as the beach, I decided, a place so complex, dynamic and perpetual, deserved better press, and this book was conceived. I set out to write the single volume I would have liked to pack along in the beginning of my beachings. It would be an anthology of sorts; a compendium of the several natural sciences encountered along the edge of the land where the Atlantic Ocean makes the shore. These sciences per se are not natural, of course, but man-made. They are the categorized results of man's awkwardly systematic rummagings to explain to himself what the starfish and osprey take for granted. They are the unravelings of the practical, physical mysteries that surround us. Look around. Every object, organism, sprig or stone raises a question. How does the tide move? When does a lobster mate? Where do jellyfish go in winter? What does beach grass need to grow where nothing else can survive? What makes sand build into seemingly stable dunes?

Consciously looking around became a compulsive task. Instead of packing a library to the beach, I'd take an empty pack and return with it full of shells, rocks, bleached branches, bones, seaweeds, unidentifiable litter and an occasional corpse. (Often a live specimen would go astray on the drive home and end up hiding under the bucket seat while the Mustang spent a few summer days parked on a city street. More than one common crab and whorled whelk gave up a fulsome ghost to haunt my car for weeks.) A reporter by training and a writer by trade, I'd explored several scientific realms before, one at a time. This job was different. So many scientific disciplines apply to the beach: botany, ornithology, ichthyology, geology, animal behavior, tide mechanics, invertebrate biology, barrier island dynamics, human physiology, and more. It would take a lifetime to explore each cul-de-sac of every disciplinary subdivision.

In desperation I got a big Jeep to cover more shifting ground. It extended my range. Like any vehicle it served as an effective bird blind. It offered shelter when I was too lazy to pitch a tent, even provided a place to read and write at a makeshift desk. It took me the lengths of islands and to the outermost ends of peninsulas. But a Cherokee Chief is not a guru and my enlightenment remained a dappled thing, like the surface of the sea when the moon starts breaking through a hurricane sky. In libraries and on the beaches I finally realized why all the books fail to contain all answers. Because no book can articulate every question about each thing we see, let alone what we can't see: objects hidden by time or distance—the oceanic birth of a skate from its batlike egg case or the once-a-year matchmaking shivaree of terns on remote islands.

By design then, this book is not intended to tell everything about anything, such as the sex life of the oyster (though some intimate details are bared). To tell all would require the patience of Job for every reader and leave me no space to say anything about a sea rocket's succulence or the gemstones in sand. My chosen task is to examine the obvious, the commonplace, the apparent and often-encountered: such things as birds, grasses, crabs, clams, flotsam, jetsam, algae, empty shells, fetid fish, hazards to human health, marine delicacies and prime movers of the beach itself. The goal became to describe the visible tips of disciplinary icebergs and to outline the different scientific glaciers that spawned them. T. S. Eliot warned, "I will show you fear in a handful of dust." I wanted to tell how to find life in a hatful of sand. Dylan Thomas remembered among his Christmas presents in Wales "Books that told me everything about the wasp except why." I set out to describe the things most commonly encountered along a natural beach; readers must guess many whys for themselves and come up with more answers than mine.

As finally born, this book is a hybrid. It owes something to the great clans of field guides and something to didactic scientific monographs. While it attempts to discuss some important biological matters, it ignores obfuscatory terminology. What's sauce for scientific method can be souse for simple clarity and the nonspecialist's understanding. While I have tried to be as accurate as possible, I've not split every hair of biology's luxuriant pelage nor outlined every bone of scientific contention. I chose to use common, popular names for beasts and vegetables while also indicating the latest in Latin. Call a spurge a spurge, but call it *Euphorbia polygonifolia* as well in case someone wants to pursue the scientific literature.

The layman is often seduced into believing that painstaking science has an answer to every question. That notion—which more laymen infer than most scientists imply—is false. The natural world, even that corner of it found along the littoral, is too complex for total human comprehension. One can grasp many pieces of the puzzle, learn their shapes and patterns, even put some of them together. But the whole picture is too huge to articulate completely. Don't worry about it. However elusive total knowledge may be, it isn't a prerequisite for comprehensive appreciation. Let it be enough, somehow, to get glimpses and continue wondering. Only a know-it-all knows it all. Study what you can; look; then let intuition leap and in passing, perhaps, nod courteously to the Beach Goddess, whoever she might be.

This volume describes a ribbon of a region running from the pug nose of Maine to the sandy underbelly of the Outer Banks—

1,200 miles as some shorebirds fly but nearly 20,000 if one walked
every mile of the convoluted littoral. It does not explore every cove
and bay along the coast. It will, I hope, open doors to many rooms
in the *oikos*, the Grecian house we leased to build the scientific and
humane theater called ecology. Part horizontal field guide, part
anthology of the natural sciences, it surveys the many constituent
parts of the beach, which have been broken down for the convenience of scientists and beach strollers alike.

Take it as a given: Scientific inquiry has always been a ponderous cart behind the horse of simple human curiosity. At its
worst, science can become a more blinding opiate than the most
parochial dogma. At its best, it is an avenue for exploring places and
things that antedated our interest and will survive our passing. One
compelling attraction of the beach is the certainty that it will be
there long after us. Physically the beach will remain, as dynamic as
ever, long after *Homo sapiens*, with its cerebral subspecies of poets
and physicists, has become extinct. But for as long as we can,
people will continue visiting this partially hospitable place. It draws
us for as many reasons as there are human beings. When I get fed
to the teeth with petty politics, grand opera or argumentative scientists, I visit a stretch of coast to encounter the ineffable. When
Wilbur and Orville Wright wanted to fly, they went to the Outer
Banks. William Blake, in all his internal and external wanderings,
sought

> To see a World in a Grain of Sand,
> And a Heaven in a Wild Flower,
> Hold Infinity in the palm of your hand
> And Eternity in an hour.

My real reason to go beaching is recreation—or re-creation.
But I've learned why beach grass hurts in early summer and gotten
a peek at its miraculous regenerative ways. I've gained a fond respect for the horseshoe crab, which has the engaging habits of
eating with its shoulders and swimming upside down after dark. (I
haven't wantonly killed one in years, except to eat—and once was
enough.)

To each his own along the shore.

If science couldn't reveal all, neither would nature. Each time
I walked another stretch of beach to the farthest point seen from the

starting place, I found new frustration—or so it seemed. I secretly kept hoping that beyond the next point of sand or rocky head the littoral would offer up all the answers, that windrows of knowledge would be washed ashore to explain what the books didn't. Instead there'd be just another cove alive with seaweed and raucous birds— or utterly empty, provoking another question. And there would be another dim point in the distance. So I'd go away again, back to the city, the libraries, the laboratories, the museums, the typewriter, knowing one thing for certain: While I'm gone and when I return the beach will be there, still shifting, changing, mystifying, reassuring, continuing.

Driftwords: The Longest Meal

The tide rises along a narrow, empty island's shore; the sun slides down behind the continent. This place—for the miles I can see in any direction—is mine alone. It was a willet's when I arrived, but the bird fled, flashing its chevrons and complaining prettily.

Pour a shot over the last ice and break out peanuts. Quick, tidy up the Cherokee before the light goes completely and find that shell book among the tackle and oilskins. Do it now; it's easy enough to pitch the tent after dark on a clear, calm night like this. Light the safari lamp and study a bird guide, learn field marks for tomorrow; the sandpipers all looked alike today. (No more peanuts. Buy peanuts next time you see a store.) Set up the stove, heat the soup, choose the entrée—canned hash or the fish that didn't bite? A good old Carolina boy said the fishing will be bad for days after this onshore wind. "It makes the water mulky." *Mulky.* We spoke at noon and I haven't seen a brace of people to talk to since. The word lingers.

(Will you please pitch the tent and roll out the bag so it's ready when you are? All right.) When that chore's done, the soup's ready. Then take a walk to clear the palate; go see what the tide dragged in . . . nothing to write home about yet. Whet the knife, chop an onion, sauté in butter with four twists of fresh pepper, start the hash. (Buy no more hash! Tiresome hash.) While it's browning, sort the day's crop of sprigs and shells: *Quercus virginiana* (live oak from a hummock near the marsh) and *Atrina serrata* (a pen shell from the swash). R. Tucker Abbott's field guide shows how to tell the pen shells apart by internal muscle scars. He says the critter's edible, like a scallop. Or was. Mine's dead, an empty shell, but one fragile half is intact. A lucky find. Alive it grew narrow-end down, anchored by byssus threads like a mussel. The external scales helped hold it and provided attachments for barnacles, oysters and worms. *Seashells of North America* reports: "Within the mantle cavity of this bivalve a small crab, *Pinnotheres* receives protection and feeds upon surplus food particles." Elsewhere I've read that *Pinnotheres ostreum*, in particular, inhabits oysters commensally, too, doing them no harm. Those pea crabs, no bigger than lima beans, are said to be delicious.

Abbott does not say pen shells are rare; they are southern

animals with thin, fragile shells. I've found only fragments before. (Save it in a jar filled with water as a cushion.) "The brittleness of the shell is due in part to the very large size of the prismatic crystals, which can be easily seen with the aid of a hand lens." (Where the devil has the lens gone?) That can wait. The hash is crusty. (Crack a beer and bring Thoreau to dinner.)

In *Cape Cod*, Thoreau tells of a place a thousand miles back and a dozen decades ago. He walked its length more than once, lodging with local folks and lighthouse keepers—an interesting way to travel. (Today all the lighthouses—even several standing from his time—have signs warning the public to stay away.) One of the first things he sees is the new wreck of the British brig *St. John* on Grampus Rock off Cohasset. Shipwrecks were common in the 1840s; scores of immigrants drowned. (Put on your editor's cap and punctuate the leagues-long sentences of his transcendental sermon.)

> Why care for these dead bodies? They really have no friends but the worms or fishes. Their owners were coming to the New World, as Columbus and the Pilgrims did. They were within a mile of its shores. But before they could reach it they emigrated to a newer world than ever Columbus dreamed of. Yet one of whose existence we believe that there is far more universal and convincing evidence—though it has not yet been discovered by science—than Columbus had of this: not merely mariners' tales and some paltry drift-wood and seaweed, but a continual drift and instinct to all our shores. I saw their empty hulks [their bodies, he means] that came to land. But they themselves, meanwhile, were cast upon some shore yet further west, toward which we are all tending, and which we shall reach at last. It may be through storm and darkness, as they did. No doubt we have reason to thank God that they have not been "shipwrecked into life again." The mariner who makes the safest port in Heaven, perchance, seems to his friends on earth to be shipwrecked, for they deem Boston Harbor the better place. . . .

Clean-up is fast and easy. Wash the pot, pan, cup and plate in the swash. Flatten empty cans to pack them out again. Close up the car. Brush the teeth. Do the little that one can to help a rising tide. Check the stars again while coffee water boils. Open a can of fruit. (Save half for breakfast, damn it. Stop nagging.)

There's dew enough now to wipe the salt off the windows. Walk the berm with the six-volt flashlight pinning ghost crabs that flee, then cower in the beam. (Never heard of anyone eating a ghost crab, anywhere). Oh hell, nearly midnight; you have a date with a fish at dawn. And so to bed. Crawl in. Zip up. Lights out. Pray for a shifting wind and the wit to fool a flounder. (Good night.) Nice party. Thanks. (Good company.) I hate eating alone.

PART ONE

The Zoological Beach

The shore—from surf across swash zone, foreshore, berm, barrier dune and swale to marsh and bay—supports what's arguably the most varied visible fauna of any habitat in the temperate world. This is the place marine turtles and ancient arachnids seek to lay their eggs in summer sand. Birds abound here at every time of year: spring and autumn migrants, winter residents and summertime brooders. Predatory fishes hunt within reach of well-cast bait, while biting crabs lurk in shallow water and stinging jellies drift aimlessly. An occasional whale strands itself. Hundreds of different crustaceans go about their business sideways. Carnivorous mammals leave the maritime forest to scout the littoral for food, rodents ply the grasses, snakes slither down to the swash from time to time and mollusks by the millions inch about on both sides of the land. This place is alive; its denizens are easily seen by anyone who comes here and cares to watch.

CHAPTER ONE

Family portrait of crustaceans: lady crab, barnacles, hermit crab, lobster

The Crabs—True, Blue and Otherwise

At the outset of this first chapter on common beach creatures, a few words on terminology are mandatory. Take it as a given: Among the familiar animals in general (and crabs in particular) misnomers and confusing repetitions are the first rule. Confusing duplications are the second. The Atlantic blue crab is mostly green. Horseshoe crabs aren't crabs at all, zoologically speaking, but members of another general category of critters. Further, the barely edible horseshoe crab goes by the alias "king crab" along some stretches of the Atlantic coast while in the Pacific Northwest the same words signify a long-legged delicacy. Thus "king crab" may refer to an East Coast cousin of spiders or to a proper decapod from the wrong address. Clearly, common nomenclature can be confusing. But the scientific idiom has shortcomings, too, superficially at least, because few folks speak Latin with any ease. (Ask your friendly neighborhood fishmonger, "How's your *Callinectes sapidus* today?" and he's likely to take it amiss.) The scientific names are unfamiliar and unredeemingly polysyllabic—though frequently mellifluous when untangled properly. More important, they have the advantage of being particularly specific while also indicating some basic relationship between organisms.

Before anyone's enthusiasm curdles in the face of the Latinate, consider the background. The terminological ball game played by biologists today was kicked off by an eighteenth-century Swede whose own name most often appears in its Latin form: Linnaeus. Carl Linné (1707–1778) was so slow as a boy that his father nearly apprenticed him to a shoemaker, according to one account. A more laudatory biographer says the curate's son was so fond of flowers that he was dubbed "the little botanist" at the age of eight. In either event he became famous in his own time as a trailblazing botanist and, incidentally, an explorer as well, though he trained as a physician. In the days when modern science was in its confused and adventurous infancy, a medical diploma provided entree to every corner of the scientific world. The ambitious man of science was surrounded by field after field of uncharted territory; the natural world was so haphazardly known that a kind of anarchy reigned. Linnaeus brought some order to it.

Having successfully practiced medicine and taught at the university in Uppsala, he switched professorial chairs and published landmark works on the classification of plants and methods of classification. Of paramount importance, he was "the first to enunciate the principles for defining genera and species and to adhere to a uniform use of the binomial system for naming plants and animals." He called his system "a concise methodical and ingenious synopsis whereby a mineral, a plant or an animal could be referred to a definite place within the system and associated with a name." The legendary eleventh edition of the *Encyclopaedia Britannica* opines, "He made many mistakes [in actual classification]; but the honor due to him for having first enumerated the

principles for defining genera and species, and his uniform use
of specific names, is enduring." In recognition for his scientific
preeminence, he was admitted to the nobility and given the
honorific "von." Curiously, he offered one revolutionary hypothesis that caused little hoopla at the time. In the tenth edition of
his *Systema Naturae*, published in 1758, he placed man among
the other primates. But when Charles Darwin expanded similar
ideas in his *Origin of Species* 101 years later, he scandalized the
world.

Linnaeus' system depended on Latin, then the accepted international language, which survives to this day as a kind of *lingua
franca* among biologists of every tongue. Like any good cataloging
system from the phone book to Dewey Decimal, it is essentially
open-ended and infinitely expandable. As new groups of flora and
fauna were studied during Linnaeus' lifetime and after, his system
found room for them. They might not always be accommodated
with alacrity, but the method worked; a species could be put in its
place and retrieved at will if further research showed it had been
misplaced originally. The barnacle, for example, because of superficial appearances was long assumed to be a kind of mollusk and was
so classified. But after its life cycle and anatomy were examined
more closely it was reclassified as an arthropod, one of the jointed-
legged animals like crabs and insects.

This points out one of the traps of attempting absolute scientific accuracy: Many biological truths have a certain transience. One
reputable taxonomist says, "Every authoritative text is obsolete by
the time it gets to the printer," because ongoing research constantly reveals newer information and prompts revisions. Over the
years there has been a great deal of pulling, stretching and occasional downright unpleasantness among taxonomists. A generation
ago the International Commission on Zoological Nomenclature,
which keeps tabs on things, was moved to issue a declaration "on
the need for avoiding intemperate language in discussions on zoological nomenclature." But then Linnaeus himself, the father of
taxonomy, died after a fit of apoplexy.

Nonetheless, the system he invented evolved into a complex
matrix within whose cubbies taxonomists continue to work and
wrangle. It depends on an "Obligatory Hierarchy of Ranks" in a
declension from the general to the specific (literally), which runs as
follows:

Kingdom
   Phylum
      Class
         Order
            Family
               Genus
                  Species

But that's just the bare bones of it. As the life sciences became increasingly sophisticated, these categories proved insufficient to accommodate all the distinctions and commonalities that were perceived. Hence a variety of interlinear classifications came into being so that today the full classification of an organism can stipulate its membership in each of the following groups and more: kingdom, subkingdom, phylum, subphylum, superclass, class, infraclass, cohort, superorder, order, suborder, superfamily, family, subfamily, tribe, genus, species and subspecies. Think of it all as an unspeakably big family tree. The closer you find two leaves on a twig, the closer their kinship; branches of the same limb are related in ways that other branches are not, but everything originally came from the same stem. Yet, like a family genealogy commissioned by a social climber, any branch of it may be of dubious legitimacy. One expert may prove an organism's place in the scheme of things to his complete satisfaction and another may challenge it. Eventually the case is settled in the court of taxonomic opinion by other descriptive biologists as one hypothesis or the other is generally accepted— if only pro tem.

   Climbing down out of this hyper-ramified baobab (i.e., from the specific to the general) one can trace a lineage of sorts for a crab that turns up in Cape Cod lobster pots. I've heard it called both the rock crab and the Jonah crab, but the Latin name specifies: *Cancer irroratus*. Along with one other species in coastal Atlantic waters it represents the family Cancridae, which in turn fits into the infraorder Brachyura or true crabs, a group that also includes blue crabs, spider crabs, calico crabs, ghost crabs, etc. They all constitute one of five groups in the suborder of decapods (Decapoda). These ten-footed creatures share the distinction of belonging to the class Crustacea. In turn this class belongs to the phylum Arthropoda, which comprises all animals with jointed legs and segmented external skeletons.

It bears mention that Linnean categories are not of equal size; the tree is not evenly pruned, to continue the botanical metaphor. Class Crustacea for example, contains 30,000 species, while another class contains more than a million insects. By the same token, many species have numerous cousins of the same genus, yet some species are the only surviving members of the genus and family; still others may be considered biologically isolated as far back as the order level.

After finding something's phylum, there's nothing left but its biological kingdom, a choice between animal and vegetable for larger life-forms, though many smaller organisms manage to keep a foot in each field.

There are—ready or not—five kingdoms, three of which succor a variety of microscopic organisms such as the viruses, bacteria, some algae, molds and fungi (which occupy an entire taxonomic realm of their own). Most larger members of the world's biota belong to either the kingdom Metaphyta (plants from the true algae on up) or the kingdom Metazoa (higher animals), which has been rent into two subkingdoms. One is devoted to sponges. The other, the subkingdom Metazoa (just to obscure things), contained twenty-seven phyla by a recent count that itself is subject to revision. In any case, all but one of these phyla belong to invertebrates. (The remaining phylum, Chordata, includes the subphylum Vertebrata, class Mammalia, order Primatae, suborder Anthropoidea—as opposed to the Prosimii like lemurs and such—family Hominidae, genus *Homo*, species *sapiens*. *Homo sapiens*, modern man, is the only extant member of the hominids.)

Thus, the living world by scientific tradition is divided first into kingdoms and then into phyla. One of those twenty-odd invertebrate phyla is phylum Arthropoda. It contains three subphyla. The first is for sea spiders and the second has classes for horseshoe crabs on the one hand, plus mites, spiders, ticks and pseudoscorpions on the other. The third subphylum, Mandibulata (whose members have similar mouth parts), includes the class Insecta and the class Crustacea. Kenneth L. Gosner writes with authority that "Crustaceans are so diverse an assemblage that, beyond defining them as arthropods with mandibles and two pairs of antennae, a useful yet concise statement of their collective traits is impractical." Suffice it that they all stem from the same branch of the phylogenetic tree; in generally Linnean and Darwinian terms, they share a common ancestor and thus are taxonomic cousins. Alas, "the classification of higher Crustacea has had a tortured history." They are now distributed among eight subclasses which comprise everything from the wood louse and fairy shrimp to the barnacle and lobster.

More to the point, the class Crustacea includes four superorders, one of which comprises the order Decapoda, or ten-legged animals that are now considered arthropods. Within this order are five infraorders including Brachyura, the true crabs, and we are back (terminologically speaking) where we started. Obviously it is easier to speak of true crabs than brachyurans. But if one jumps the binomial fence into the field of common names one finds a number of commonly visible creatures called crabs even though they aren't, e.g. horseshoe crabs. On another hand some noncrabs have much in common with the Brachyura since they are fellow crustaceans, notably the lobster and barnacle. For the sake of the reader's convenience (and the writer's sanity), this chapter will deal with animals that share two obvious unscientific traits. Crabs in name or in fact, they have shells that they molt (unlike the mollusks), and they live along the Atlantic littoral. People plying those beaches are likely to see these creatures, dead or alive.

Consider their outstanding common characteristic first. A crab, like every arthropod, has an exoskeleton. This exterior structure serves the same purpose as our internal skeleton: It's a solid framework for flexible muscles. It also serves as the animal's primary defense. The crab's shell is composed of chitin, a polysaccharide that in and of itself is soft and flexible. Calcium salts and/or the formation of links between protein molecules harden the shell into effective armor. But unlike other kinds of body covering, i.e. human skin, the crab's exterior is composed of rigid plates that don't grow apace with the inner animal. Rather, growth occurs in seemingly abrupt stages that are triggered by hormones.

When a crab grows too large for its shell, it bursts at the seams, crawls out and proceeds to grow a new, larger shell with plenty of room inside for muscle and organ growth. The process of the actual molt is called ecdysis, a Greek word H. L. Mencken borrowed to coin the term ecdysiast for the exotic dancers of Baltimore. While the crab's molt is a most dramatic event—far more so than a stripper's peel—the animal is actually in a constant state of preparing for or recovering from ecdysis, just as an adolescent boy is constantly growing out of and into his clothes. "Immediately before and after the casting of the old exoskeleton, water is taken into the animal to expand the soft new cuticle," according to A.P.M. Lockwood, lecturer in biological oceanography at the University of Southampton. "The consequent increase in size is sometimes loosely referred to as 'growth' but strictly the process is only one of expansion. True growth, the incorporation of new tissue, occurs during the later stages of the cycle."

Before an existing shell is shed, an inner skin covering the muscles begins absorbing calcium from the existing outer shell. Softened as a result, the outer shell splits and the animal faces the arduous business of getting out of it. This is a far worse struggle than a balding veteran wrenching his way out of the twenty-year-old uniform he managed to squeeze into for the Memorial Day Parade. In lobsters a claw or leg may be lost in the convulsive process of shedding a too-small shell. Figuratively speaking, if the animal can't get out of a sleeve, it sheds that part of the suit. The beast will then grow a new appendage, which will be clearly smaller than its opposite number until it catches up in size and appearance two or three molts later. Its overall growth will be slowed, but it can survive the loss.

Exposure to sea water hardens the new exoskeleton, typically in a matter of days. When it has hardened to become a functional shell, excess water is expelled from the muscle tissue, which shrinks, leaving room for actual growth inside. But molting is a perilous process at best. First there are the mechanical problems of getting out. Then there is a period of defenselessness when the soft-bodied, often immobile animal is easy prey for any carnivore. In addition there is the biochemically tricky business of extreme changes in tissue- and cell-fluid composition as water is absorbed and expelled.

Some arthropods may double their body weight with the pre-molt absorption of water. Many expand one-quarter in size with each molt. Typically the decapods split open at the rear of the carapace, or upper body. This means a lobster opens around his belt line, backs out of the front part of the shell and shucks the rest like sweatpants, more or less. Shrimps eat their cast-off shells, apparently as a handy source of the calcium they need to harden their new shells. After molting, the process of true growth resumes—until things tighten up again. Components of the old shell begin to be reabsorbed, the shell softens, and the cycle begins again. The true crabs, exemplified by the European *Cancer pagurus*, go through the following cycle, according to Dr. Lockwood's timidly-titled *Aspects of the Physiology of Crustacea*. This is a fair model for all marine arthropods.

Stage One: The newly molted animal seems a miracle of incompetence and vulnerability. It can't eat. Often it can't even walk. The new exoskeleton is initially so soft that the crab's limbs won't support its weight, and it gains weight alarmingly fast as muscle tissues absorb water in large quantities. Water content of the whole animal reaches a high of 86 percent. *Stage Two:* The new shell calcifies and a new layer of shell is secreted. Water content declines. *Stage Three:* Feeding resumes and major tissue growth occurs. This stage lasts for more than two-thirds of the cycle. Metabolic reserves accumulate as tissue growth concludes. Water content falls to 60 percent. *Stage Four:* Calcium from the existing exoskeleton is absorbed as outer layers of the subsequent shell begin to develop. Calcium reabsorption continues and the shell cracks, admitting water which the muscles begin to absorb. *Stage Five:* The animal, instinctively alerted to find the safest possible place to hide, struggles out of the old shell and absorbs water rapidly, preparing to create a new exoskeleton.

And so it goes, all over again.

The cardinal prerequisite for biological success is reproduction (should anyone wonder why zoologists are so interested in procreative methodology, e.g. sex). Crustaceans lay eggs. Most protect them one way or another. Typically the female carries them until they mature, which accounts for the "berried" lobster or "spongy" crab carrying a mass of roe beneath her. After an egg hatches, the larva develops through a series of remarkably dissimilar body shapes in the course of several molts. These changes can be more distinct than Dr. Jekyll's metamorphosis into Mr. Hyde. Gosner puts it this way: "Morphological differences between larva and adult and between successive larval stages may be so great that one would not guess them to be consecutive manifestations of the same ontogeny." In other words, a baby crab don't look like pa.

True Crabs

Atlantic Blue Crab (*Callinectes sapidus*)

A popular prototype, the common and justly famous Atlantic blue crab is green on top and whitish below. The female's claws are tipped with red, while the male's have bright azure highlights. Gender (and in the female, maturity) can also be told by the shape of a structure on the bottom shell called the "apron" by diners or the "abdomen" by biologists. The male's resembles the stem of a champagne glass, its foot aligned with the back edge of the shell. In the virginal female, or "she-crab," the apron resembles a rounded isosceles triangle. The sexually mature "sook" wears a semicircular apron with a small triangular point during the last stage of her life.

"No other crab has been fished so intensively and thus observed so much," writes William W. Warner in his elegantly entertaining natural history of the animal and its human pursuers, *Beautiful Swimmers*. This crab's generic name, *Callinectes*, translates into Warner's title, while *sapidus* means tasty or savory; it is as delightful at the table as it is nimble in the water. Its swimming ability results from the flattened, oarlike shape of its fifth pair of legs, which enable it to dart reasonable distances as fast as a fish or to leisurely cross the Chesapeake Bay at will. The fourth, third and second pairs are walking legs. The first pair is armed with sharp, quick claws that bite painfully. The broad body has sharply pointed sides that may be useful defensively, since it usually moves sideways.

This outstandingly belligerent and sharp-sighted animal willingly attacks people—or so it seems. They'll go for a tired sailor's toe dangling from the back of an anchored boat, I can assure you, with an alacrity that seems purely malicious. Reputed to be largely creatures of estuaries, they regularly seek the ocean, as when the spent female goes offshore to die after shedding her last eggs and when the larval and intermediary "megalops" stages drift far out to sea. (Some summers these mites become beach pests, unpopularly called "sea fleas," that cling to swimmers and leave rashes of bites.) By far the largest live specimens I've encountered were caught by a boy in a pond that drained barely 50 yards into the Atlantic across Martha's Vineyard's south beach. They were nothing special, he said, the fruit of twenty minutes' wading with a crab net and bucket in hand. Both were wider across the back than my binoculars, which measure 7½ inches.

Economically important, blue crabs are marketed in two stages. The "hardshell," or "steamer," is the more common. The more expensive "softshell" is the same beast in a state of exoskeletel undress right after ecdysis. Before molting, the soon-to-be vulnerable crab hides in shallow bay waters among eelgrass. When commercial crabbers catch a "peeler" with its characteristically pliable shell, they set it aside in a floating pen until it sheds. The pens must be checked frequently because crabs in captivity cannibalize each other, though there's no evidence that this occurs in the wild. Aggressive and sly, crabs actively hunt minnows and small crustaceans. Burrowing in sand or mud, they lie in wait buried up to their stalked, compound eyes, which have almost a 360-degree ken.

Blue crabs usually mate in fall at the time of a female's final molt. Following an active courtship dance, the male carries his chosen mate through the water, cradling her beneath him for a matter of days until she casts her shell. Warner writes:

> Protection is afforded the female by the male's urge to find good cover and, when the female's moult begins, his habit of standing guard over her by making a cage with his walking legs. He does this very patiently, since the moult may consume two or three hours. When at last the female lies exhausted and glistening in her new skin, he allows her some moments to rest and swallow the water that is necessary to fill out her weakened stomach and muscle tissues. This done, the male gently helps the female turn herself about—she may well have gotten impossibly oriented in the final throes of ecdysis—until she is on her back face-to-face beneath him. It is a most affecting scene. You cannot possibly mistake these actions for anything other than lovemaking. . . . When the female blue crab is ready, she opens her newly shaped abdomen to expose two genital pores. Into these the male inserts his pleopods or two small appendages underneath the tip of his elongated abdominal apron. When all is in place, the female so extends her abdomen that it folds around and over the male's back, thus effectively preventing any risk of coitus interruptus. Truly, blue crabs are locked in love's embrace. They remain so, blissfully, for from five to twelve hours. Daylight or night, it makes no matter.

The female may brood two batches of eggs—2,000,000 at a crack—before her swan song. After shedding her eggs in spring, it's deep water curtains for her; she cannot molt again. Perhaps two from each batch reach maturity after going through as many changes in metamorphic rank as a Mason. An individual that starts life measuring ¹⁄₁₀₀ of an inch goes through seven, sometimes eight larval stages. Each zoeal form has a functioning tail, huge eyes and varying numbers of appendages. Then comes the intermediate "megalops" stage which normally lasts less than two weeks. But if water conditions aren't right, the potential crab may remain in this premature limbo for three months before becoming a recognizable crab the size of a pinhead. By November, when it buries itself in mud for winter, the crab will measure an inch or two. Having once molted every three to five days, it now goes for periods of more than a month. In all, a blue crab may molt more than twenty times in addition to its larval changes. Mating typically occurs at the end of an individual's second summer.

Calico Crab (*Ovalipes ocellatus*)

A close cousin of the blue crab, the "lady" or "calico" crab has a rounder body speckled with pink or lavender dots. A member of the same family (Portunidae) as the blue crab, the lady crab is also euryhaline; it survives wide variations in water salinity. But it frequents ocean shallows more often than its relative and consequently is found more often on Atlantic beaches.

The lady crab ranges as far north as the Gulf of Maine and, despite her name, is as pugnacious as the blue. This trait gets the animal into frequently fatal trouble. A portunid would rather fight than flee under almost any circumstances. Attacked by a lobster, it will take a boxer's stance and snap back, first losing one claw to its larger antagonist, then the other, and finally its life.

Green Crab (*Carcinus maenas*)

Some individuals of the species are very well named—they're very green indeed, though others may be orange or brick red. Regardless of color, *Carcinus maenas* looks a lot like other members of the portunid family, the blue and calico crabs, with quick claws and nimble, gracefully pointed walking legs. It lacks the broadly flattened rear pair adapted for swimming, however.

Common along the littoral from New Jersey to Maine, green crabs are easily found at low tide hiding under rocks and among beds of seaweed.

Jonah Crab (*Cancer irroratus*) and Rock Crab (*C. borealis*)

Although the Cancer crabs share the northern part of the blue crab's range, they are not likely to be confused with the portunids because of their rounder shape and more passive behavior. Caught in a trap, they won't try to bite their captor, but will cower instead. In the wild, this craven manner helps the rotund animals survive, if their shells happen to be thick enough. Attacked by a lobster, a Cancer crab tucks its appendages tight beneath its body and sits things out rather than putting up its dukes and getting them bitten off one by one.

The two species, which grow to 5 or 6 inches across the carapace, differ in the sculptured edges of their shells. In the rock crab each "tooth" of the shell's edge has several tiny points and notches; its body margin looks like an irregular hacksaw blade. In the Jonah each tooth along the body edge has just one low-angled point.

Steamed *C. irroratus* are delicious—sweeter than blue crabs, though not as meaty and harder to make a meal of. The claws of large individuals are marketed; however, this is an economically insignificant species compared to its Pacific Coast kin.

Spider Crabs (Family Majidae)

Several members of this family frequent the littoral. Their common name derives from the fact that they look like long-legged spiders. Their bodies may grow as big around as tennis balls. *Libinia emarginata* has nine bumps in a row down the middle of its back. *L. dubia* has six bumps in that row. Their adult bodies are quite round, while *Pelia mutica* and the two species of the genus *Hyas* have oval bodies. *Pelia* has a two-pronged nose, *Hyas* has a simple pointed nose.

This may be the most lethargic clan of the entire order, or so I thought before meeting Alta VanLandingham, a seashell seller of

1. Green crab (*Carcinus maenas*); 2. Rock crab (*Cancer irroratus*); 3. Spider crab (*Labinia emarginata*); 4. Lady or calico crab (*Ovalipes ocellatus*); and 5. Blue crab (*Callinectes sapidus*)

Ocracoke. Her living room was filled with huge aquaria, one of them the domain of Lady, a spider crab she'd raised from infancy. When Mrs. VanLandingham entered the room, Lady scampered delicately over rocks and mollusks to the near corner of the aquarium to greet her mistress and only her mistress, who reached down into the water. The crab would cling to the woman's fingers—hoping to be fed, no doubt—with the eagerness of a spoiled spaniel.

Spider crabs are commonly found on beaches tangled in bundles of seaweed and lost nets. On land they seem like sluggards, but this may simply be because they're out of their element and dying for water. They recover quickly enough when put back in the wash. Caught in a dredger's net and tossed back overboard, they sink like so many stones because they lack flattened rear swimming legs.

The spider crab uses camouflage to conceal itself on the sea bottom, whether for offensive or defensive reasons. It takes bits of algae, sea lettuce or eelgrass and fastens them to the hooked hairs on the top of its carapace. The algae will grow there until the crab looks like a local rock. Of course after ecdysis the crab must put on new makeup.

Ghost Crab (*Ocypode quadrata*)

Sharing the land with us, ghost crabs are among the most easily observed crustaceans. But it still takes some patience because of human ways and crab's natural caution. The dry upper portion of Atlantic beaches as far north as Delaware is this spry

Ghost crab (*Ocypode quadrata*) outside its burrow

animal's natural habitat, but the first problem is to find a beach sufficiently natural to nurture the critter. Many resorts clean their sands with huge machines that scrape up the surface and sift out anything much larger than a matchstick. These beaches are certainly clean—to the point of sterility; a self-respecting ghost crab can't eke out a living on them. So to see *O. quadrata*, find a moderately wild beach, look for a stretch of sand marked with holes the size of a nickel or larger, then sit still and wait.

Though some generally reliable texts say ghost crabs are strictly nocturnal, I've seen these whiffets busying about beaches from Delmarva to the bottom of the Outer Banks at every time of day. Their business includes carrying sand out of their yard-deep burrows and finding food both dead and alive. They eat carrion when they find it. They also hunt beach fleas, sand crabs and almost anything else smaller than themselves. (The body of a full-grown adult may be 1½ inches wide, but the span of their legs just about triples their apparent size.) Whether gray, white or tan, they are about the color of the sand they inhabit. They have smooth, squarish bodies and nimble legs that carry them sideways at such brisk speeds that they're known as "the rabbits of the Crustacea." They spend a great deal of energy keeping out of larger creatures' way by scurrying down their burrows.

Descended from a marine ancestor, they have not become entirely terrestrial but must return to the shallow swash several times a day to wet their gills. Like most crustaceans, they have stalked eyes but, oddly, not very acute vision. Austin Williams, a crab expert with the National Marine Fisheries Service, says they cannot perceive sharp images—only shadows and moving objects. Flipping the stalked eyes up in the manner of spasmodic windshield wipers, they peer over sand ridges or the rims of burrows like doughboys using periscopes to scan the enemy trenches.

O. quadrata which is alone in our range, represents a genus containing a score of species worldwide. Its family also includes the fiddler crabs found in the muddy marshes and backwaters.

Crabs Other Than True

Hermit Crab (Superfamily Paguroidea)

Though the hermit crab molts, the shell you see is not its own, but the recycled remains of a mollusk. In fact it lives in a stolen shell, walking around the ocean floor like a turtle with a short lease. The true exoskeleton (as opposed to the borrowed shell) that the hermit crab sheds is composed of softer material than a true crab's. Only the hermit crab's head and claws are heavily calcified—so it seeks the protection of a borrowed shell for its soft parts. When it molts and outgrows one borrowed shell, it seeks out another that fits. A venerable hermit crab that started out in the remains of a periwinkle may live to plod around in the cast-off shell of a moon snail.

This decapod begins life as a free-swimming larva that lives on plankton and is barely visible to the naked eye. After several metamorphoses it takes on a curiously asymmetrical appearance. The naked adult looks something like a shrimp-sized lobster gone wrong, with unequal claws that are characteristic of each species and two well-developed pairs of walking legs. But it's rarely seen naked. When attacked in its borrowed shell (by a man or other predator), it hangs in there so tightly with its last two pairs of highly modified legs that usually it can't be removed in one piece.

It appears that three families of hermit crabs comprising a dozen species inhabit the western Atlantic. In coastal waters are the left-handed hermits (Diogenidae) and the right-handed hermits (Paguridae). Another family, the Parapaguridae, live in deep water—as much as 3 miles deep. Some of the shallow-water species tolerate extreme variations in salinity and may be found in marshes; I've even found a few scavenging in the dune grass in Virginia, though they do not survive very long out of water. Snorkeling off Cape Poge, I've seen them by the score, burrowed in the sand up to their eyes and waving their antennae shyly.

Sand Crab (*Emerita talpoida*)

Not a true crab, the gregarious Atlantic sand crab is the single local member of the family Hippidae. It burrows in shoals of thousands where waves break on sandy beaches from Cape Cod south to

Sand crabs (*Emerita talpoida*)

Hatteras and beyond. Each wave tumbles the animals and surface sand around; before the next wave breaks, the sand crabs bury themselves back into sand again up to their antennae. They use these delicate appendages to sift food particles from the backwash. As tides and storm surges come and go, these misnomers migrate up and down the summer beach, always staying in the active surf zone. In winter they evidently seek out deeper water. Since these animals live on plankton and are themselves prey for a host of larger animals from blue crabs to bass and shore birds, they are a key link in the food chain.

Sand crabs are very easy to catch in hat or hand. Absolutely harmless—they tickle your palms while burrowing in a handful of wet sand—they're good momentary pets for small children, especially squeamish tots who are afraid of animals. Shaped rather like moles or minute armadillos, they behave more like terrified bunnies.

The female of the species grows larger and lives longer than the male. About ½ inch long, the little males cling to husky mates during summer breeding seasons and soon die. The inch-long females often survive a second winter.

Barnacles (*Subclass Cirripedia*)

Louis Agassiz, the great nineteenth-century naturalist who urged his students to "study nature not books," described the barnacle as "a little shrimp-like animal standing on its head in a limestone house and kicking food into its mouth." That may sound absurd, but it fairly states the case. The barnacle is a catholic and successful creature that has adapted in myriad ways. Its subclass comprises 1,000 species around the world. More than a dozen are found in Atlantic coastal waters; five of these are goose barnacles, and the rest belong to two acorn barnacle families. The latter in particular are the common animals that foul boat hulls and cover tidal rocks with thousands of individuals per square yard.

Typical barnacle eggs mature and hatch within a parent's shell before the larvae, armed with three pairs of legs, swim free. After several molts and a complete metamorphosis, the animal looks somewhat like a bivalve mollusk. In this form it settles head first on a hard surface—a ship's hull, dock piling, rock or the epidermis of anything from a whale to a horseshoe crab to another barnacle. (Different species prefer different surfaces.) Glands on its antennae excrete a cement to anchor the animal before it undergoes a final metamorphosis into the adult form, which has neither eyes nor sensory appendages. The shell, composed of six plates to form a rough cone, was responsible for barnacles being considered mollusks for so long. It is secreted by a highly modified version of this crustacean's carapace. The adult's six pairs of legs have become "cirri," which the animal projects like feathery fans that wave rhythmically in the water to catch plankton and other minute food particles. In a falling tide, the barnacle retracts its cirri and closes the plates of its shell, sometimes with an audible click, to avoid drying out before the tide returns.

Barnacles are typically hermaphroditic. While self-fertilization can occur, the animal usually mates with a neighbor in its closely packed colony by means of a slender sperm tube that reaches into a nearby shell.

A goose barnacle looks rather like its acorn barnacle relatives atop a wormlike extension cord. The nether end attaches to some hard surface while the lightly shelled business end waves at the top of the flexible neck. Along the Atlantic beach these are most often found attached to driftwood or fishnet floats that wash in from deep water after a long time at sea. Both in ancient Greece and Britain, folk myth held that this kind of creature spontaneously spawned various geese. Hence, in parts of Catholic Europe, goose could be eaten on traditionally meatless fast days—because it was sired by an aquatic animal. Pope Innocent IV put a stop to that in medieval Europe. Religious doctrines aside, people in some parts of the world eat the larger species of barnacles.

Horseshoe Crab (*Limulus polyphemus*)

Upwards of 600 million years ago, before the Devonian age of fishes, before the advent of sharks or insects, an ancestral arachnid inhabited the Precambrian seas. This creature produced the prolific trilobites, which dominated marine life for millennia, but it became extinct along with the kindred sea scorpion, which presumably used its spike tail as a weapon. In time—according to widely accepted but unproven theory—some of its descendants crept onto the land to evolve into spiders, ticks, mites and terrestrial scorpions. One group that has remained marine and essentially unchanged for some 200 million years is the horseshoe crab. Four species of this once-cosmopolitan class remain, curiously, only on the western sides of the great oceans. The only individual that inhabits our waters is *Limulus polyphemus*, a crab in name only, a recognized "living fossil," and a beast that deserves far higher esteem than it usually receives along our shores.

Ponderous when coming inshore to breed, the horseshoe crab is agile in the water. For example, the shape of the shell apparently functions like a hydrofoil. When it swims(!)—usually at night and upside down at that—the shell shape forces the flow of water to keep the animal up off the ocean floor. By day, as the animal walks right-side up against a current, water passing over its shell presses the creature down against the sand. Walking locomotion is provided by five pairs of walking legs; swimming power is provided by five pairs of "book gills" (so called because they resemble pages in a book), which riffle, so to speak, when the horseshoe crab swims.

However familiar it may be on a sheltered beach in early summer, *Limulus* looks bizarre—something like a rusty antique helmet with a plate to guard the nape of some Tartar's neck and a sharp spike hanging out aft. A 2-foot-long horseshoe crab doesn't use its tail aggressively, but only as a self-righting device when it's capsized—either accidentally or when the animal settles down after an inverted swim.

The location of its book gills—behind the legs—is unique. So is its eating apparatus. The mouth is located between its paired legs, which are equipped with short-spined grinders. Mollusks and worms pulled from sea-bottom burrows with tweezerlike pincers are "chewed" by the animal's "shoulders" and passed into the mouth. Consequently *Limulus* can't eat while standing still. But if it lacks manners by dining on the run—or the crawl—it is a certified blueblood. Like some crustaceans and mollusks, the horseshoe crab's blood has a blue tinge due to the copper it contains instead of iron to carry oxygen. This blood is invaluable in medical research since it will not support the growth of bacteria. The animal's nervous system, which functions like our own but is much simpler, also provides food for scientific thought. In 1968 Haldan K. Hartline of Harvard won a Nobel Prize for describing how our optic nerves transmit photoelectric impulses. His investigations depended largely on horseshoe crabs as neurological guinea pigs.

The animal's four eyes are rather special, too. One pair is compound, the pair that looks like caricatured "Dragon Lady" eyes at the front corners of the shell. When *Limulus* molts, these eyes are shed with the old shell; the animal grows new compound lenses. Solar engineers have proved that the special shape of these components—a slightly rounded cone with a blunt end—is the

Horseshow crabs (*Limulus polyphemus*) come ashore to mate.

most efficient light-gathering form imaginable. Its second pair of eyes is the two small black dots on either side of the median line near the front edge of the shell. These are sensitive to ultraviolet light and may be the secret to the animal's navigational competence.

Living on the ocean floor and often rummaging around the surf zone like a snowplow with its front edge scraping under the surface of the sand, this whiffet can startle an unsuspecting wader by moving underfoot. But it's not known to strike anything in anger (or hunger) much larger than a marine worm. Alive, horseshoe crabs come ashore only to breed, yet their inanimate shells wash up from one end of the year to the next. Though they appear to be whole animals, these are husks, not corpses, that result from molting. Unlike the crustaceans, which typically crawl out of a shell backwards (more or less), the horseshoe crab splits the forward edge of its outgrown shell and walks straight ahead. Then the shell often seals shut again before ending up on the beach. Find a shell that's still split and you can see the compound eyes still transparent and intact.

Horseshoe crabs start crawling ashore in early summer and a female may return ten times a season. Perhaps she's making up for lost time, having molted sixteen times before reaching maturity at the age of nine. She scrapes out a depression in the sand just below the high tide line and lays 1,000 eggs at a crack with her mate in tow, literally, semi-piggyback style. He holds on to her shell so tightly that the boxing-glove–shaped claspers on his first pair of legs may leave dents in her shell. The female, which is larger than the male (and has five identical pairs of pincers), drags her mate across the nest while he deposits sperm. The next wave or tide covers it all with fresh sand. About 1/10 inch in diameter, the round, light-green eggs hatch in a matter of weeks and tailless "trilobite larvae"—so called because they resemble those extinct oddities that once ruled the Precambrian seas— crawl out and head for the water. Needless to say, not all the eggs hatch; many are eaten by fishes, crabs and migratory shore birds, for whom this roe is an essential food source during their long spring odysseys.

Aboriginal Americans are said to have used the animals' tails (or telsons) as spearheads and to have feasted on *Limulus*. In parts of the Far East horseshoe crabs are considered a delicacy today—

though one Pacific Ocean species is said to be poisonous to man. English colonists reportedly sneered at them as human food. Having considered the possibility for some time, I steamed a fresh horseshoe crab like a blue crab and sampled it as Fourth of July hors d'oeuvre. The taste resembled lobster—tainted by a rank beach at low tide.

Lobster (*Homarus americanus*)

Lobsters copulate in the "missionary" position, face to face (as near as they can manage). For the female that supine coupling, which occurs soon after a summertime molt, is the onset of an astonishing dedication. She carries the live sperm for anywhere from a month to a year until underwater conditions trigger ovulation, which is independent of her molt/mating calendar. She turns over on her back to stand on the tripod of claws and arched tail. The eggs emerge from small openings at the base of the second pair of walking legs and pass over the seminal receptacle between the last pair of legs which releases the stored sperm. Her swimmerettes (the pairs of small, flat appendages under the tail) beat rhythmically to pass the fertilized eggs along the underside of the tail, where they are secured to hairs on the appendages by a sticky secretion.

Right-side up again, she will carry the eggs for as long as another year with her tail curled beneath her to cradle and protect them as they ripen. During this period her active swimmerettes will keep them supplied with cleansing and oxygen-rich water. At first the eggs are black; as they mature, they become golden brown and microscopically highlighted with the iridescent eyes of the embryos within. When the eggs are fully ripe and water conditions dictate, the female walks straight into a current high on her legs while vibrating her tail and swimmerettes to shake loose larvae as they hatch. She starts this one evening at twilight, apparently to give the larvae as much protection of darkness as possible, since the clouds of young attract foraging fishes. She may have as many as 100,000 eggs, which are hatched in several batches every night for as long as two weeks.

As the larvae leave the eggs they float toward the surface. During their early stages of life, they are planktonic and drift at the mercy of the currents. Eaten by a variety of larger organisms, the lobster larvae themselves eat whatever they encounter, including each other. After the fourth molt, when the nascent lobsters have gained some power of locomotion, they settle toward the bottom where they will live the rest of their lives. After the fifth molt they look and act like lobsters.

The mature lobster hunts by night, haunting the bottom for mollusks, worms, crustaceans and fish. Evidently it prefers live prey to carrion. By day the lobster seeks shelter in crannies or under rocks, wedging itself backward into an impregnable lair with its claws guarding the entrance. In water with clay bottoms, the animal will even dig burrows to hide in. When threatened in the open it may fight or retreat, its long antennae feeling the way behind it. And it can swim backward with quick spasms of its powerful tail.

Juvenile lobsters molt two or three times a year as they outgrow their shells. Curiously, a molted individual returns to its aggressive ways hours after it has cast its shell—before the new exoskeleton has hardened completely. In fact it may still be somewhat vulnerable, but its manner belies this and the bluff apparently works in the wild. Large lobsters may molt only every two or three years. They live for fifty years or more; lobsters weighing about forty-five pounds have been caught and creatures estimated at fifty pounds have been sighted by divers.

The lobster mates for the first time when it is four or five years old, after the female molts. The sex of a lobster can be determined externally. The female's first pair of swimmerettes is feathery and soft; the male's is hard and grooved to carry sperm into her seminal receptacle. An active courtship dance prior to copulation may last half an hour, though the act of mating is over in a minute. Today lobsters are taken legally in large numbers before they've grown large enough to mate. Hence the breeding stock is being removed from seabed to table. Another problem that threatens their future is pollution. Minute amounts of petrochemicals in the water raise havoc with the lobster's navigating ability. (While young ones stay close inshore and don't travel far, large lobsters have been captured 100 miles away from the deep canyons where they were tagged.)

Driftwords: How Old?

The "big bang" kicked off the universal ball game on the order of fifteen billion years B.P. (Before Present), say Nobel Prize-winning physicists Arno Penzias and Robert Wilson. According to the *Scientific American*, which keeps track of things a little closer to home, earth didn't emerge until 4.6 billion years ago, and it took another billion years (plus or minus 200 million) for the first living material to get organized. By 3.4 billion years ago, the fossil record suggests, blue-green algae had arrived. Multicellular organisms appeared one billion years or so ago, and things biological began accelerating. Vertebrates arrived 530 millions years back, the first mammals half that long ago, and Neandertal man was certainly lurching around Europe about 100,000 B.P. So what? These staggering figures don't amount to much that's conceptually useful.

Look at it another way. Let the standard unit of time be the traditional biblical lifespan of three score years and ten. L = 70 years. That puts the publication of this book only 28 L into the C.E. (Christian Era). Today we are about 1,400 L away from Neandertal man. This means that if all my college classmates had appeared on this earth sequentially (instead of virtually en masse), the valedictorian might have been the first man to carry a torch in prehistoric times.

The first mammals appeared 2,857,142 lifetimes ago, and the numbers become incomprehensible again. But stay with me a little longer. Earth began sixty-four million lifetimes ago. And if the universe began with a bang C. 15,000,000,000 B.P., that was 214,285,714 L ago—just about the number of lifetimes laid end to end as there were Americans when this book first appeared. The great whales' ancestors wriggled back into the sea about 900 L ago. The number of lifetimes needed to reach back to the start of recorded history could fit on a rush-hour bus. We rendered the passenger pigeon extinct about 1 L ago.

Look at earth's age another way, word by word. The Stradivarius of encyclopaedias, the eleventh edition of the *Britannica*, contains thirty-two volumes (including supplements) of about 1,000 pages each. It spans a shelf longer than 3 feet in my office. If its contents were equally apportioned to cover the history of the world, the first five volumes would describe a lifeless planet. Leafing

through it, the following not-quite-random items would appear on
the following pages:

Anaerobic bacteria	Volume 6,	page	565
Oxygenated atmosphere	" 19,	"	86
First mollusks	" 28,	"	834
First fishes	" 29,	"	528
Diversified jawed fishes	" 30,	"	292
First amphibians	" 30,	"	570
First reptiles	" 30,	"	917
First mammals	" 31,	"	612
First birds	" 31,	"	939
Last dinosaurs	" 32,	"	549
Neandertal man	" 32,	"	1,000
Birth of Christ	" 32,	"	1,000 last sentence
Invention of gunpowder	" 32,	"	1,000 last line
Atomic Age	The letter *d* in the phrase "The End."		

CHAPTER TWO

Scallops flee the starfish

The Way(s) of the Mollusk

"He was a bold man that first eat an oyster," wrote Jonathan Swift. It would be a very wise man who simply sums up the beast and all its mollusk kin. Collectively, the edible oyster, reclusive octopus, chiton, tusk shell, periwinkle et al. constitute a phylum of 100,000 living species and 20,000 known fossilized ones. Since descending from an archetypal ancestor that vanished without a trace before the Cambrian period, the mollusks have had more than 600 million years to improvise. They've used the time so well and found niches in so many habitats that few statements about them can be made categorically without adding catalogs of exceptions. Most are marine and have shells; many aren't and/or don't. They range in size from some Yucatan snails, which can line up fifty strong before making an inch-long train, to a squid that can grab morsels 48 feet away from its mouth with a tentacle.

Their behavior and characteristics are equally diverse. The chambered nautilus, a biological submarine, rises and sinks in the water by adjusting the volume of gases trapped in its shell's compartments. Scallops swim via jet propulsion and have as many as a hundred eyes to scan their surroundings. Somewhat sedentary, mussels anchor themselves with byssus threads and replace these mooring lines when they break. The semitropical cone shell has a poisonous lance to stab both prey and suspected predators, including humans. A few mollusks can soar through the air, if not actually fly. Coquina clams can jump in the surf. The lavender janthina snail, which is sometimes beached along the Outer Banks, floats its eggs in a midocean raft made of parentally blown bubbles. The New England neptune lays her eggs in columns as big around as herself and somewhat taller.

In sum, the mollusks are a figurative barrel of worms, monkeys, beer, laughs, nails and anything else that comes kegged. As G. Alan Solem writes in his engaging text, *The Shell Makers:* "No two malacologists agree on how many orders and suborders of bivalves should be recognized, exactly how they are related, and what should be the limits assigned to each." He recommends R. Tucker Abbott's field guide as "a best buy . . . packed with facts," even though the two authorities use different names for the chitons' class. Malacologists agree that mollusks are complex but differ on the degree of that complexity and many other matters.

A Victorian ventured the opinion that "In point of intelligence, mollusks must be relegated to a very low position. They give evidence of possessing no more than the most primary instincts, those of self-preservation and reproduction." But they must have been doing something right to have continued multiplying since a time when not much else was around but algae and each other. And how they thrive without a real brain—depending on those instincts alone—certainly denotes an astonishing kind of competence.

When told the size of the bumper grape crop in postwar Champagne, the chronically thirsty Winston Churchill said: "So much to do and so little time." Much of what's being done in malacology today relates to correcting old errors. The first was made by no less a light than Aristotle, who coined the phylum's name from the Greek word *mollis*, meaning "soft." He had the sea hare in mind, not the conch, which pries open its bivalve prey with its own shell. But the name stuck. (And Aristotle was no slouch. He made some observations that systematic scientists wouldn't confirm for 2,000 years.) Some confusions derive from the fact that European sophisticates began collecting shells as curiosities several centuries ago; the casual study of shells as exotic objects proceeded independently of serious biological interest in the creatures that made them. Far earlier than that—30,000 years ago—settlers in central France treasured sea shells as jewelry. Virgil, among other Romans, collected shells for diversion; a collection was found in the ruins of Pompeii.

Regardless of when folks started examining shells for whatever reasons, the objects themselves cooperated very little with the growth of either malacology (the science of mollusks) or conchology (informally the study of shells per se). "Most mollusks are very secretive creatures, often less than 1 inch in size [only one species in twenty exceeds 3 inches] and frequently nocturnal in their activity," Solem writes. "They do not bite like mosquitos, buzz like flies, or scamper through walls like mice. Rarely do mollusks call human attention to themselves."

They must have better things to do. They were here before us; the gastropods alone adapted to more habitats than mammals, the "highest" of which willy-nilly alters habitats to suit himself. Some mollusks don't seem to care. In the hundred years or so since we began polluting the oceans with oil-fueled ships, the common periwinkle has quietly marched all the way south from Labrador to the Chesapeake Bay. Mollusks pay less attention to us than we to them.

In the 1970s, as many papers on their kind were published as had been written before 1890. There are now 100,000 tracts—though there isn't one for every living species, many of which haven't even been named. Alas, the more science knows, the more must be revised.

About twelve dozen mollusks are common along large portions of the beach from the Bay of Fundy to Ocracoke Inlet. Extend the range to Florida and the number doubles. Describing so many species individually would be tedious; reading about that many is worse. (There's much about the mollusks that doesn't bear repeating.) Instead, it seems more worthwhile to concentrate on frequently encountered members of various taxa whose habits are representative or interesting.

Malacologists generally agree that seven classes of mollusks exist. Two taxa comprise small, rare, deepwater groups. The remainder are the chitons (polyplacophores—though there's some disagreement on this); the snails and slugs (gastropods); tusk shells (scaphopods); clams, oysters, mussels and so on (bivalves); and finally the squids, octopi and chambered nautilus (cephalopods). Each class is represented in our shallow coastal waters; many end up dead or dying on the beach—though many more can be seen alive along the littoral by a diligent searcher. One learned malacologist, as soft-spoken as might be expected of a man who spent a career with snails, offered me some valuable caveats about finding these elusive creatures. "Mollusks are very cryptic," said the late Joseph Rosewater at the Smithsonian. Before searching for specific animals, he used to calculate "where they ought to be" and when they were likely to be there. Working the rocks and tide pools mostly at night—which represents its own problems—he encountered "things you never see in daylight." Snorkeling or skindiving also reveals an entirely new molluskan world.

In general, mollusks possess two zoologically unique structures: the mantle and the radula. The fleshy mantle secretes a sea snail's continually growing shell, which emerges somewhat like a stream of newspaper pages off a very slow rotary press. The shell is not molted, as in the crustaceans; instead it grows as its creator grows. Pigment centers on the mantle are responsible for giving the shell color and pattern. A uniformly colored shell is the work of evenly distributed pigment cells in the secreting tissue. Some mantles have pigment cells of several colors, which produce a multicolored shell. When a distinct color center remains in one place on the mantle, it creates a stripe of color in the shell; when it migrates across the mantle, it makes a slanting band on the shell. If a pigment center starts and stops producing (due to changes in diet or water salinity), dots can result on the shell.

The radula is a ribbonlike tongue bearing sufficiently abrasive teeth to rasp rock or, with the help of excreted acids, to bore through the shells of the hardest prey. It goes without saying: many mollusks feed on their zoological cousins. (This is no closer to cannibalism than a man eating another mammal such as a lamb.) Evidently after the first mollusks began thriving on the endless supplies of vegetation and plankton they found in the primeval seas, the next mollusks learned how deliciously easy it was to live off the herbivores. That was the beginning of real diversity among the mollusks. In time the bivalves gave up their radulae as they became addicted to microscopic food strained from the primeval soup. (They gave up their heads too.) The squids modified their radulae and, in addition, developed parrotlike beaks to grasp and kill slippery prey, such as fishes. But overall, every mollusk has some if not all of the following structures: a muscular foot for locomotion; a distinct head; a visceral mass containing organs; a radula; a mantle and the protective shell it makes; and a mantle cavity, which offers a place for excretory and reproductive organs to empty.

As to the mollusk's sex life, it is as varied as the phylum and, in human terms, bizarre. The male squid creates a dense mass of sperm within a chitinous tube. Then he plucks the tube from his body and places it within the female's mantle. Some male snails that lack a penis manufacture two types of sperm cells, the ordinary kind that inseminates and a sort of messenger variety. It piggybacks the other through the water on its conceptive errand, which the absent penis would otherwise perform. Mollusks come male, female, hermaphrodite and all of the above. The sexually agile oyster changes in gender—sometimes repeatedly. But enough of generalities.

The Bivalves

Taxonomically the bivalves are a mess. It isn't their fault; they never asked to play the game of systematics. Nor is it a matter of scientific caprice—contentiousness perhaps. The puzzle of their genealogical relationships is composed of too many pieces that *almost* fit too many ways while fitting perfectly in no way at all that is scientifically satisfactory. Bivalves of two genera that appear closely related in terms of dental work (i.e., the interlocking teeth near the shell's "hinge") may have dissimilar organs or vice versa. Two clams may seem closely related by one anatomical or embryological criterion but only distant kin by another. The results are differences of scientific opinion, which the bivalves themselves do little to resolve. (What is less communicative than a clam?) However, they are astonishingly clever about knowing their own exact kind, and the devil take the in-laws. Witness the female American oyster that spills her eggs minutes after nearby males cloud the water with sperm. Any kind of oyster sperm isn't good enough; she will react only to the seed of her own species.

The confusing and maddening upshot is that three generally

authoritative texts use three different taxonomic systems to describe the higher categories of bivalves. Fortunately they agree on the lower taxa and specific names, which points up the beauty, flexibility and utility of the Linnean system. Taxonomists can wage war on one level while sharing a single arsenal on another. Fighting about principles, they use the same esoteric language—like lawyers. But as it happens, the Latinate nomenclature is almost dispensable here because many of the most conspicuous bivalve families are known by commonly accepted culinary names. So I'll use the happy expedient of kitchen argot and risk the ire of malacologists. But first some more anatomical terms.

Predictably, the garden-variety bivalve has two "valves," or shells. These are hinged by an "elastic ligament," which normally holds them slightly apart. It works against one or two "adductor muscles," which close the shell from the inside. (The only part of a scallop usually eaten by Americans is the single adductor muscle, though the rest of the animal is used in European recipes. In a quahog, bits of its paired adductor muscles are what cling to the shell.) The typical bivalve has a muscular foot, an ordinary set of visceral organs, and a mantle that secretes the shell. In addition the mantle forms two siphons; one brings in water that the other expels after the gills have removed its dissolved oxygen and microscopic food particles. Since a bivalve strains its food from the water, it has no need for a radula, which it lacks along with a head.

Consider the oyster, one of the more familiar, best-studied and familiar bivalves. A quarter century ago—a lifetime in terms of some scientific knowledge—U.S. Fish and Wildlife Service biologist Paul S. Galtsoff wrote *The American Oyster*. Weighing in at 480 pages, this tome is the unabridged *Oxford English Dictionary* so far as oysters are concerned; an apotheosis of detail that's not likely to be surpassed despite its sometimes turgid prose. It covers everything from the structure of gill cilia (which are "indistinguishable from that of the cilia of vertebrates, protozoa, or the tails of spermatozoa") to characteristics of a good oyster habitat. Galtsoff writes:

In several respects the anatomy of the oyster is simpler than that of other bivalves. . . . Only the posterior adductor muscle is present and there are no specialized organs of sight, although the animal is sensitive to changes of illumination. On the other hand, the edge of the mantle is fringed with highly sensitive tentacles abundantly supplied with nerves leading to the ganglia. As in other bivalves, the nervous system is not centralized . . . a condition which undoubtedly results in a high degree of coordination among the various parts of the organism. In addition to performing their principal functions, several organs of the oyster also participate in other activities. The gills, for instance, are not only the organ for respiration but collect and sort food as well. The mantle is used extensively in control of the flow of water through the body; the coordinated action of the adductor muscle, gills and gonad is necessary for the effective discharge of eggs by the female oyster. In other animals such functions are performed by special organs, but in the evolution of the oysters the high degree of coordination developed among different parts of the body eliminates the special structures, and new and complex functions are successfully performed by synchronizing the work of the existing parts.

Yet there remains great variety in oysters. The family Ostreidae now contains more than a dozen living genera. The genus *Ostrea*—the name translates into "oyster"—once comprised all edible species that were considered dues-paying members of the group. Then some important anatomical and reproductive differences raised their metaphoric heads. The genus *Crassostrea* ("thick oyster") was named in 1897 and validated in the International Commission on Zoological Nomenclature's own sweet time fifty-eight years later. Why? For one thing, members of the genus *Ostrea* are typically hermaphrodites: Each individual functions simultaneously as both male and female. *Crassostrea* are normally male or female— given the proviso that an individual changes back and forth.

Several species are found along the Atlantic coast. But who's kidding whom? The one that most people care about is *Crassostrea virginica*, the Eastern or American oyster that ranges from Canada to the Gulf of Mexico. Epicures may call their favorites "Chincoteagues" or "Blue Points," but these names only indicate the place where they were harvested. Most oysters eaten in America are *C. virginica*. It is a very fine species and one worthy of Galtsoff's considerable attention.

To begin with, this oyster's sex life involves a degree of togetherness that borders on mass hysteria. An oyster bed is a den of simultaneous iniquity, and for good reason. Lacking external equip-

1. American oyster (*Crassostrea virginica*); 2. Blue mussel (*Mytilus edulis*)

ment, the males (pro tem) release abundant sperm into the water when they sense the presence of other sperm. When one male ejaculates—normally in response to a rise in water temperature— every male within chemosensory reach follows suit within seconds. Minutes later the females get into the act by releasing enormous batches of eggs. The best Galtsoff could do was to estimate in his laboratory that one 5-inch female laid 114.8 million eggs without exhausting her supply. While she might produce ova in such quantities two or three times during a six-week summer breeding season, biostatisticians suggest that only a dozen eggs in a batch reach maturity. The rest fail to find a suitable place to spend their adulthood, succumb to various infections, become food for other marine animals or simply fall by the aquatic wayside.

One practical reason for the massive, simultaneous mating activity by both genders is that the females, however prolific, never developed much of a muzzle velocity. The eggs they exude (with little, coordinated spasms of muscle and shell) don't travel far. Since these eggs sink only inches away from their spawning dam, their best chance for a vital future depends on being released when the surrounding water is rich with sperm so that catch-as-catch-can fertilization occurs before they touch bottom.

If all oyster eggs were fertilized and survived to breed, according to one theoretical estimate, we'd be buried in a pile of living oysters eight times as large as earth itself within four oyster gen erations. George L. Clark, solon of the Woods Hole Oceanographic Institution, wrote, "The prodigious fertility of nature is a measure of the destructive action that is received from the environment." But that "destructive action" keeps the environment's other inhabitants alive. A simple rule holds that the greater the number of potential young a species naturally produces, the more "destructive" is its particular habitat and the more unsure the future of any one ovum. The corollary: Animals with the riskiest reproductive methods spend the greatest effort on them.

So let it be with the oyster, whose largest internal organ at maturity is the versatile gonad. Furthermore, the sexual health of a local oyster population is a fair indicator of environmental purity. Galtsoff writes, "Oysters living in waters highly polluted by various trade wastes have, as a rule, poorly developed gonads." This is ecological bad business, of course, and something close to culinary catastrophe as well; an oyster with enlarged sex organs is a fat, delicious one.

The reasons oysters change their sex remain unclear. Suffice it that "the sexes are . . . unstable and once a year a certain percentage of oysters change their sex. . . . This change takes place after spawning during the indifferent phase of gonad development." Indifferent indeed. "Spawning may last from a few minutes to nearly one hour, depending on the amount of mature eggs in the ovary. . . . The spawning reaction is always followed by a refractory period of two to several days during which the female is not responsive to stimulation." In other words, after parturition she retires and frequently gives up on maternity by becoming male for the following season.

After fertilization the oyster egg—like all mollusks—develops into a trochophore larva. This stage may last no more than twenty-four hours. The next stage, or veliger, is an increasingly complex organism that develops eyespots, a protective shell and a velum (hence its name). The velum is composed of two semicircular folds with large cilia along their edges. It enables the organism to swim freely, yet the structure is also retractile and after the shell develops can be quickly withdrawn inside.

When the oyster veliger's foot develops, it possesses a byssus gland, like the organ that mussels use to spin the replaceable mooring threads that anchor them to rocks. As the future oyster grows heavier it sinks and with its developing foot begins to crawl over hard surfaces until it finds a suitable spot to settle down for life— typically on another oyster shell.

The foot extends beyond the edge of the shell and the animal reclines on its left side (usually), becoming permanently attached in minutes with a cement secreted by the byssus gland. Then the veliger, which measures about 1/100 of an inch, hastily changes into a minute oyster. Within a few days it reorganizes its permanent organs. The ones not needed for a sedentary life disintegrate or are absorbed: the eyespots, byssus gland, foot, and velum. The minute animal, called a spat, fundamentally has nothing left to do but grow and multiply. In fact, the animal becomes anatomically and neurologically simpler. Galtsoff explains:

> The high degree of specialization of larval organs may be regarded as an adaptive organization of a free-swimming organism to its environment. . . . The pelagic larva of a bivalve has a double task: to distribute the species and grow into an adult. . . . When the larva attaches the substrate, the velum and the foot are no longer needed.

I find it intriguing to think how differently adult humans might behave if we could shuck more of the traits required and acquired in infancy. (Unleavened Freudian theory suggests that we pack every one of them throughout life.) If an oyster didn't give up the velum of its youth, it could never settle down to the immobile but otherwise constructive business of being an adult oyster. It can't move or relocate; the only thing it can change thereafter is its gender.

Crassostrea virginica contorts the shape of its rough, usually oblong shell to grow as best it can in the crowded space of a natural oyster bed. The off-center scar of its adductor muscle and the edge of its shell lining are tinged with purple. In the wild, its varied shape can lead to misidentification; growing in a spacious bed, the individuals may be rather thinshelled and almost circular. The tidiest shapes are found among oysters raised on controlled conditions. At the University of Delaware, experimenters predict that "domesticated" oysters can be raised to market size in nine months instead of the three years they need in the wild. Predictably the secret is an artificial habitat with lots of food, no predators and ideal water. Mariculture can do for oysters and clams in the near future what agriculture did for grain crops at the dawn of recorded history; says one academician, "We are just now crossing the frontier from hunting and collecting marine species for man's use to properly managing and husbanding them." But it can't happen a moment too soon, given the catastrophic decline of oysters in Chesapeake Bay.

Ostrea equestris, called the horse or crested oyster, lives in saltier water than the American oyster. Found from Virginia to Texas, it is a smaller animal than its more famous kin and has a pale muscle scar at the center of its nearly round shell.

Pursuing the other bivalves by culinary category, the clams constitute the informal group of the next greatest importance. The name *Mercenaria mercenaria*, chosen by Linnaeus for the northern quahog, comes from the Indians' use of its shell to make wampum beads, which were used like money after European traders arrived. Those made from the white portions of the shell were small change compared with those made from the small purple parts near the adductor muscle attachments. *M. mercenaria*, which ranges along the entire East Coast, is more oval than round and grows 4 inches in length. Outside of scientific circles, it's called littleneck clam, cherrystone, round clam or quahog.

The larger southern quahog (*Mercenaria campechiensis*) grows up to 6 inches, lacks the interior purple stains and has more definite concentric growth ridges on the outside of the shell. At extreme low tides I've found these sitting on sandbars near the mouth of Chesapeake Bay, high and dry until the tide returns. One explanation is that a spring tide falls so fast that the surface sands dry out before the clam can dig itself in. While it is then somewhat vulnerable to mammal or bird predators, the stoutness of an adult's shell offers real protection from almost anything short of a clam knife. One

1. Southern quahog (*Mercenaria campechiensis*); 2. Northern quahog (*M. mercenaria*); 3. Jackknife clam (*Ensis directus*); 4. Surf clam (*Spisula solidissima*); 5. Ocean quahog (*Artica islandica*); 6. Softshell clam (*Mya arenaria*); and 7. Coquina clam (*Donax variabilis* or *fosser*)

zoologist says it represents "the highest type of shell development among the bivalves." It is exceptionally hard and strong without being ponderously heavy and it contains ample space inside.

The quahogs belong to the Venus family (Veneridae). Several other clams have clans of their own. The Atlantic surf clam (*Spisula solidissima*) is a larger, shallower, more triangular clam dredged from the continental shelf at depths as low as 100 feet. Its thinner shell is fairly smooth despite the growth rings and is cream-colored or brown depending on the color of the sea bottom where it lives. Before this animal is considered edible it must be cleaned of its very sandy viscera, a process that involves separating muscles from internal organs. The flesh is then chopped or shredded to find its way into millions of trademarked clam rolls.

Clams of the family Solenidae are the slender bivalves that many epicures believe to be the tastiest. The largest member of the family is the Atlantic jackknife clam (*Ensis directus*), which grows 6 inches in length. Quick and delicious, it is hard to capture since it burrows straight down with surprising speed. (When digging these be careful how you grab them because their shells seem as sharp as the name implies.) Its shell is covered with a thin, dark brown layer, the periostracum. For inexplicable reasons, the jackknife clam looks like a horn-colored antique straight razor. The razor clams are shorter animals closer in size and shape to pocketknives.

Softshell clams (*Mya arenaria*) often surface under various aliases such as steamer (which might also be a crab), littleneck (which might be *Mercenaria*) or, unmistakably, pissclam. This precise if vulgar designation derives from the animal's habit of betraying its presence in a mud flat at low tide by shooting a stream of water into the air as it digs itself deeper in the face of danger. When walking a New England tide flat, look 10 yards or so ahead of these telltale fountains, which come from a sheathed siphon, the animal's uppermost extremity. The thin, fragile shell is white inside and pale or stained outside (sometimes nearly black), depending on the local bottom.

A Massachusetts shellfish officer on the town dock in Duxbury offered some behavior insights about various clams one quiet day to explain the temporary closing of local shellfish beds. A moratorium had been declared, not because of pollution, but to give *Mya arenaria* time to repopulate. The clam flats had been raked nearly clean and Maine clams were brought in. But they didn't cotton to Massachusetts waters and died. Hence the decision was made to simply let the decimated population reproduce in peace since there was no hope that new stock would spontaneously migrate in from nearby waters. *Mya* doesn't migrate worth a damn, the clam cop said. Once a pissclam larva settles, it hardly moves—except up and down a little. Quahogs, on the other hand, move about a fair amount, while the razor clams are veritable gypsies. Not long ago they were numerous in a certain mud flat in Duxbury harbor, said the officer, and "almost overnight spread along a beach 2 to 3 miles away."

Donax clams inhabit the surf zone along open beaches, migrating up and down the wet sand to stay within the highest reach of spent waves. Tiny and rather triangular, they come in a rainbow of colors that seems to grow brighter and fade as multitudes dig themselves in and out of the sand as the waves come and go. Found south of Virginia, the Florida coquina (*Donax variabilis*) grows to almost an inch or more in length. *Donax fossor*, which ranges from Virginia to New York, is half that size and not quite as colorful. "Some species jump out of the sand as soon as they feel the acoustic shock of a breaking wave," according to Abbott, who notes that 1,500 of the tiny creatures may be found on a square foot of beach. The *American Museum of Natural History Guide to Shells* reports some experts believe *D. fossor* is just *D. variabilis* stunted by a poorer environment. "However, this point has not finally been settled; it has met with vigorous opposition by some malacologists."

Scallops are the least sedentary of the bivalves. The first time I saw them in the wild, while snorkeling in a Chappaquiddick Island bay, I was mesmerized by their antics. Equipped with bright iridescent eyes around the edge of the mantle just inside the shell, they bounce about in the waterlike silent castanets clapping their valves. Though their jerking jumps seem random, they can control direction by changing the shape of the mantle within the shell and forming distinct directional nozzles. A water jet fired straight from the front of the shell forces the animal backward; two jets pointing obliquely aft from either side of the hinge propel the animal forward. It can also turn acrobatically in the water and swim upward from a standing start. When a starfish, one of the scallop's natural enemies, comes near, the would-be prey gets agitated and tries to escape. Left to their own devices, scallops sit on the bottom, dining on a puree of microorganisms at their leisure and peering all around like tourists.

The scallops I first saw were Atlantic bay scallops, (*Argopecten* or *Aequipecten irradians*), which, with their subspecies *concentricus*, range along the coast as far south as Florida. They grow to 3 inches and have many-ribbed shells with undulating edges. The smooth-shelled Atlantic deep-sea scallop (*Placopecten magellanicus*) grows as large as 8 inches and ranges in deep water from Labrador to the Outer Banks.

The mussels, another family of edible bivalves, are notable for their anchors. While a juvenile oyster's byssus gland atrophies after its cementing work is done, the mussel's gland remains active throughout life. It secrets threads which the foot secures to rocks or pilings like a boat's mooring lines. Set in divergent directions, these threads anchor the animal in any current as the bivalve twists to present its narrowest edge against the current. If the threads break in a storm sea the mussel secretes more to replace them. Cast

1. Atlantic sea scallop (*Placopecten magellanicus*); 2. Atlantic bay scallop (*Argopecten irradians*)

completely adrift, it can find another place to anchor itself and spin a complete new set of byssal threads.

The common blue mussel (*Mytilus edulis*) ranges in coastal waters from the Arctic to South Carolina. Its shiny exterior, marked by oval growth lines, is a deep blue-black. Individuals may live seven years and grow to 3 inches in height. The females can lay twelve million eggs a season, and 6,000 bushels of adults may grow in an acre of healthy bay, which hints at the enormous amount of microscopic nutrients found in sea water. The ribbed mussel (*Modiolus* or *Guekensia demissa*) frequents brackish water, sometimes in salt marsh mud flats, and has radiating ribs on its exterior.

Jingle shells are a family of common bivalves with a hole near the apex of the lower shell. The byssus extends through this hole to attach the animal to a rock or to another shell. The heaviest concentrations of the Atlantic jingle (*Anomia simplex*) are found in beach houses where people string them together through the byssal holes and hang them up as wind chimes. They tend towards translucent pastel colors, though some shiny black dead shells wash ashore.

The Chitons

Most scientists agree that chitons are among the most primitive mollusks still around. Built low to the rocks, they are oval-to-oblong and rather flat—like a coolie's hat—with a foot that occupies most of the underside. Uniquely, a chiton's shell is composed of eight overlapping plates. These valves, running in a row down the back, are held in place by the surrounding muscular girdle, the margin of the mantle. The mouth is in front and the anus aft (which isn't always the case among mollusks). Gills run along the chiton's underside, between the girdle and the foot. The animal can lift any part of the girdle to admit oxygen- and food-bearing water. Some species have microscopic eyes and scattered tactile organs in the plates of their shells. These animals must be seen alive or not at all since the valves scatter soon after an individual dies.

Three fastidious species inhabit rocky sections of the Atlantic coast. The mottled red chiton (*Tonicella marmorea*), which roams as far south as Massachusetts, has a smooth girdle and sharply arched valves. The northern red chiton (*Ischnochiton ruber*), which ranges south to Connecticut, has wrinkled valves and a girdle that looks granular. Both are about an inch long. The common eastern chiton, little more than half the size of its cousins, is found in protected places between Florida and Massachusetts. Also known as the gray or hairy chiton, *Chaetopleura apiculata* has some hairs on its narrow girdle.

Sea Snails & Company—Gastropods

By one count, the phylum's largest and most varied class contains 3,000 freshwater species, 24,000 terrestrial types and 40,000 marine inhabitants. The gastropods include unshelled slugs, shelled snails, everything that looks remotely like them and some things that don't. Their distinguishing characteristic is that when a shell exists the gastropod has only one; it is a univalve. The limy shell is made of calcium carbonate removed from the blood by the process of osmosis and concentrated. Glands in the mantle then excrete this material in layers of crystals. As a gastropod grows, the mantle continues to excrete material and the

1. Northern red chiton (*Ischnochiton ruber*); 2. Jingle shell (*Anomia simplex*); 3. Keyhole limpet (*Diodora cayenensis*); and 4. Common Atlantic slipper (*Crepidula fornicata*)

shell grows apace, unrolling and spiraling larger to accommodate its occupant/creator.

Over the course of evolutionary time, gastropods experienced "torsion," so that their gills, waste vents and sexual outlets moved toward the head. In addition the typical shell was skewed to one side; instead of becoming a regular jellyroll affair, it twisted as it grew, like a magazine rolled up on a bit of a bias. The little end of the growing, rolling shell, where the whorls are smallest (since the animal was youngest when it made them), was typically on the right side. The obvious imbalance this caused would naturally tend to twist the shell to the right. Whatever the sequential reasons—and theories differ—these changes had very practical results: The vertical height of a whole animal was minimized without loss of shell capacity or body size. Space appeared in the front of the shell for the head to hide in when danger threatened. The gills on the right side typically atrophied or changed while gills on the left side grew larger to shoulder the whole respiratory burden. Then, a single stream of water could enter the shell from the front left, aerate the gills, make one easy hairpin turn past the anus and sexual vents and exit from the front side of the shell. In addition, most species developed a horny operculum, the trapdoor that seals the shell's aperture after the head and foot retreat inside to safety.

Some of these changes found in the higher gastropods are absent in the lower families. Primitive Pacific Ocean abalones have an arc of holes near the edge of the shell through which water and wastes pass. On our coast the adult keyhole limpets each have a single hole near the middle of the shell. It too is an exit hole for water. This aperture is all that remains of an anal slit that is still found among some gastropods that are more symmetrical, hence considered more primitive.

The keyhole limpets are vegetarians that scrape algae from tide-zone rocks and in the process erode the rocks themselves with their rasping radulae. Two rather flat, oval species are reported along Atlantic beaches. Linne's puncturella (*Puncturella noachina*), a ½-inch-long, gray-brown shell, ranges from the Arctic as far south as Massachusetts. The Cayenne keyhole limpet (*Diodora cayenensis*), which lives from New Jersey to Brazil, is dark gray and has bumpy ridges radiating from the apex of its shell.

The true limpets represent a certain amount of biological advancement and morphological backsliding. One Atlantic limpet, showing its relative sophistication, has a single set of gills. But its shell, shaped much like a coolie's hat, represents a case of secondary evolution. The animal's ancestors first developed a coiled shell, which later evolved into its flatter, simpler shape as the limpet found its niche along exposed rocky shores. In that turbulent environment a coiled shell could be a fatal impediment; the new shape that evolved uses wave action to the creature's advantage. Waves breaking on it simply press the limpet closer to the rock on which it feeds; its external shape disperses their force.

Limpets rummage around feeding on algae at night, then typically return to the same spot on the rock by day. The sexes are separate and these animals mate from April to September, laying tiny mucus-protected eggs on the rocks. By October the young attain one-third of their growth. An inch long at maturity, they'll mate the next spring.

The Atlantic plate limpet, or tortoise-shell limpet (*Acmaea testudinalis*), long considered the only one to inhabit cold waters as far south as New York, is tan streaked with brown. Found on open coasts, its shape is clearly oval. Those more squarish forms that live among eelgrass were long considered individuals of the same species whose environment caused a modified shape. But it now seems possible that they are a distinct species, *A. alveus*.

Between the old and new gastropods (Archaeogastropoda v. Neogastropoda) lies the order Mesogastropoda. The periwinkle is easily the most familiar member of the middle group. Four closely related species are common along the Atlantic coast. The family Littorinidae, named from the same Latin word that gave us "littoral," is versatile, prolific and collectively insatiable. A square mile of shoreline may have as many as 860 million periwinkles busily moving about by working one side of the foot forward and then the other. Together they'll eat fifty-seven tons of vegetation while scraping up another 2,100 tons of rock and debris.

The periwinkle's well-developed head has two tentacles, an eye at the base of each and a stout proboscis between them. The male boasts a prominent penis jutting from the body behind the right tentacle. Needless to say, copulation occurs and fertilization is internal in the female, who releases egg capsules less than ¼ inch in size. Some species' eggs are free-floating; others are laid among the algae on which the winkles feed. Another species, the Northern

1. Common European periwinkle (*Littorina littorea*); 2. Marsh periwinkle (*L. irrorata*); 3. Northern rough periwinkle (*L. saxatilis*); and 4. Northern yellow periwinkle (*L. obtusata*)

rough periwinkle, gives birth to fully formed young, which develop in a special uteruslike portion of the mantle.

The radula, which coils up like a watch spring, is well developed. In one warm-water species with a ¾-inch shell, it unrolls to a length of more than 6 inches. Depending on species, the periwinkle's tongue may have as many as 300 rows of teeth that wear out at the rate of five or six rows a day. If they were not replaced, the animal would soon starve; instead the radula grows continually from its base to replace the business end.

The common European periwinkle (*Littorina littorea*), found as far south as Maryland, is grayish brown to black with many fine spiral bands. It browses in the lower half of the tide zone. The marsh periwinkle (*L. irrorata*), as its common name suggests, lives in tidal marshes from New Jersey to the Gulf of Mexico. Its shell is a creamy gray with brownish streaks on the spiral bands. Both of these animals are about an inch long. The northern yellow or round periwinkle (*L. obtusata*), ranging from Labrador to New Jersey, is only ⅓ inch in size. Smooth and often uniformly colored—an orange or brownish yellow—it sometimes has bands. It inhabits the lower tidal zone and feeds on algae that are rarely exposed by low tides. The northern rough periwinkle (*L. saxatilis*) shares the same geographical range but stays above midtide, often browsing above the high-water mark. A similarly small creature, its shell may be gray, brown or almost black with spiral ridges.

The slipper shells are hermaphrodites of the protandric variety. This is to say that male and female equipment operate in a single individual at different times of life, which effectively prohibits self-fertilization. All younger slippers are functionally male and more active than their larger sedentary sisters (?), which anchor themselves to other mollusks (especially other slippers) and arthropods. Frequently these gastropods pile up in small towers of several individuals, with females on the bottom and males on top, until they grow large enough to change. Rather than rummage about for food, they trap microscopic particles from the water in the mantles, much as the bivalves do. The arched oval shells are notable for the interior shelf that supports the viscera.

Three species commonly occur from New England to Texas. The eastern white slipper (*Crepidula plana*), often found within dead moon-snail shells, is white inside and out. The inside of the common Atlantic slipper (*C. fornicata*) is darker and spotted, though the shelf appears very white in contrast. The reddish brown convex slipper (*C. convexa*) has a hooked apex or tip that may look in profile like an elf's cap.

Moon snails, from the inch-long common baby's ear (*Sinum perspectivum*) to the 4-inch common northern moon snail (*Lunatia* or *Polinices heros*) and the 3-inch Atlantic moon snail (*Polinices duplicatus*), are common inhabitants of shallow coastal waters, where they are uncommonly voracious. Eight species wash up along the eastern seaboard north of Hatteras. These carnivores burrow in sand, hunting bivalves—notably clams. They grasp their prey with the foot and bore a tidy hole in its shell with the radula, softening it with an acidic excretion. Some may eat four clams a day. In turn the moon snails are eaten by a variety of bottom-feeding fish, by oyster drills and starfish. Touch a live starfish arm to a moon snail's shell and the mollusk will spread its foot almost entirely over its round shell. Evidently this leaves the predator without enough hard surface to grasp with its suction-cup feet.

Between meals, moon snails fossick about on the surface of the sand, leaving meandering furrows. Since the foot spreads out when extended, these tracks are half again as wide as the shell, which is generally quite smooth and almost semispherical. The fragile "sand collar," often found on tidal beaches, contains moon snail eggs. (For those who have never seen a Victorian gentleman's detachable collar, this is a thin, round structure that looks somewhat like a gasket from an odd engine.)

The Neogastropods, or members of the latest snail order, include two carnivorous groups of particular importance and perplexing interest respectively. These are the oyster drills and dogwinkles, which are sometimes included in a single family, sometimes separated into two.

As their name implies, the oyster drills demonstrate a dietary dedication that oystermen and gourmets abhor. Boring through the shells of large bivalves with their acid-lubricated radulae, they specialize in eating oysters in the whole shell, as it were. The most common is the Atlantic oyster drill (*Urosalpinx cinera*), a snail that grows to 1 inch in height and boasts a moderately sculptured shell with as many as twelve axial ribs running between the whorls. Found from Nova Scotia to Florida, they may be gray, white, brown or orange.

The dogwinkles are sometimes hard to identify. According to the American Museum of Natural History's encyclopedic paperback, in the northern or Atlantic dogwinkle (*Nucella lapillus*), "variations in color, shape and surface sculpture are bewildering." Exploring a low-tide shore of Mount Desert Island, Maine, I once found large numbers of snails up to 1½ inches that defied identification at first. Some looked like periwinkles with low, indistinct spires, others had sharper whorls—but they all appeared to be of the same ilk. Gathering some diverse specimens, I noticed that most of the individuals feeding on barnacle beds were white dogwinkles. The bright orange ones had probably been living on mussels, whose pigmented meat was responsible for the distinct shell color.

The Whelks

Two families of whelks also belong to the order of Neogastropods. They are notably carnivorous, eating both live prey and carrion. True whelks of the family Buccinidae number some 2,000 species worldwide. The family name comes from the Latin word for trumpet, possibly because these shells make distinguished signal horns as do the true conchs of tropical waters. A Nantucket man who kept a few daysailers for charter got tired of not being able to keep store-bought horns aboard. Following the practice of native islanders in many parts of the world, he substituted large snail shells, the spires of which he cut off neatly with a hacksaw to expose the internal cavity. Blow into this with pursed lips and it makes a marvelous sound.

1. Lightning whelk (*Busycon contrarium*); 2. Knobbed whelk (*B. carica*); and
3. Channeled whelk (*B. canaliculatum*)

The 3-inch common northern, or waved, whelk (*Buccinum undatum*) is a drab inhabitant of offshore waters from the Arctic to New Jersey. It has between nine and eighteen ribs per whorl and a dull white to brown surface. Its egg masses are clumps of tough little sacks containing embryonic shells. Often washed ashore, these were traditionally called "sailors' wash balls" because coastal folks used them for soap.

The genus *Busycon* belongs to a family that includes the Florida crown conch of southern waters. From Florida to New Jersey the clan is represented by the lightning whelk (*Busycon contrarium*) which, as its specific name implies, is perverse. Put another way, it is left-handed or sinistral; its shell spirals the "wrong" way. To tell the difference, hold any large shell with its aperture toward you and its spire on top. Put it on like a mitten (after checking for occupants). If the left hand fits, it's sinistral; if the right hand fits, it's dextral. If you get bitten, there's a hermit crab inside. Most shells of all kinds are dextral, but mirror images may appear. Some experts classify these as separate species; others say a mutation is involved, perhaps caused by a typographical error in the DNA.

The 8-inch long dextral knobbed whelk (*B. carica*) found from Cape Cod to Georgia commonly has a distinctly orange aperture lining and knobs along the shoulder of the spiral. The slightly smaller channeled whelk (*B. canaliculatum*) has a rounder aperture and a distinct channel or groove running along the spiral between the whorls.

Whelks feast on clams, although not by drilling through the meal's shell. Instead, *Busycon* forces open a bivalve's shell using the lip of its own shell as a wedge. Then it pokes its proboscis inside and eats with the radula. Whelks themselves are considered delicacies by many coastal people, as my wife and I discovered a dozen years ago when honeymooning in Mexico; seviche became Mary's favorite lunch. In recent years the market price of these false "conchs" has risen in New England in response to culinary demand.

Whelk egg cases are found on the beach as often as the mollusks themselves. These are the spiraling chains of leathery hollow discs that hang from a tough strand like a necklace. Each capsule, about the size of a nickel but with edges that differ from species to species, contains as many as one hundred eggs. Not all of them hatch; many so-called "nursery" eggs are eaten by their hardier embryonic siblings. This is their only source of food.

Driftwords: Bang

In the beginning—long before the first mollusk appeared—was the
Logos (the word/deed/act), was the "big bang," was the Creation.
Take your pick; you name it. Something happened and nothing's
been the same since. The Bible allows, too vaguely for us moderns,
that "God created the heaven and the earth." The scientific con
sensus holds that a massive explosion occurred on the order of
fifteen billion years ago, a burst that is still rending the universe
apart. (Science doesn't explain what exploded or how the raw material got there in the first place, wherever "there" was.) Some
theorists suggest that the rate of universal expansion is slowing
down; that in time it will stop growing and its component parts
must pull together again; that the universe's matter will coalesce
into another single mass, which will become so dense and hot as it
compresses into itself that it must expand again through another
enormous explosion in the unspeakably distant future. To accept
these things, add equal parts of poetic insight and scientific intuition to the conceptual plot.

W. B. Yeats: "Things fall apart; the center cannot hold; mere
anarchy is loosed upon the world."

Einstein: "The most beautiful thing we can experience is the
mysterious. It is the source of all true art and science."

Render unto science what science can justly claim; namely
some detailed descriptions of finite things, some hard-won theories
about other things and some massive shrugs of shoulders. Whether
or not the "big bang" that created our universe was the first or the
Nth, accept that it happened in the instant we might as well call the
initial one. After the explosion and the first dispersal through space,
huge aggregations of matter were mutually attracted to one another
by gravity, proximity and happenstance. These pieces eventually
formed discrete bodies, which fell into dynamic equilibrium as
solar systems, galaxies and the bestiaries of our constellations. The
sphere that became earth—whatever its origin—found its place in
a localized scheme of things orbiting around a rather ordinary star.
Molten and spinning through space, it must have been like a drop
of mercury on a table, an orb of undulating water before an astro-
naut's face or a blob of the stuff one sees in photographs of blast
furnace crucibles pouring out their liquid load. As it circled (or

ellipsed) the sun, it all responded to physical forces as the oceans respond today, its surface rising and falling hundreds of feet in molten tides.

In time things began to stabilize. Cooling slightly and slowly, the earth began solidifying. In the process volatile gases were released to initiate an atmosphere containing water and to precipitate a cascade of chemical reactions. Rachel Carson writes:

"The gradually cooling earth was enveloped in heavy layers of cloud, which contained much of the water of the new planet. For a long time its surface was so hot that no moisture could fall without immediately being reconverted to steam. . . . As soon as the earth's crust cooled enough, the rains began to fall. Never have there been such rains since that time. They fell continuously, day and night, days passing into months, into years, into centuries. They poured into the waiting ocean basins, or, falling upon the continental masses, drained away to become sea. The primeval ocean, growing in bulk as the rains slowly filled its basins, must have been only faintly salt. But the falling rains were the symbol of [and the tool for] the dissolution of the continents. From the moment the rains began to fall, the lands began to be worn away and carried to the sea. It is an endless, inexorable process that has never stopped—the dissolving of the rocks, the leaching out of their contained minerals, the carrying of the rock fragments and dissolved minerals to the oceans. And over the eons of time, the sea has grown ever more bitter with the salt of the continents."

This is about where the Book of Genesis picks up the natural history. In the comfortable words of the King James Version, "The Spirit of God moved upon the face of the waters." A more exact translation of early scripture evokes "a mighty wind that swept over the face of the waters." Why quarrel with either? The most fertile germ of truth might lie in the synthesis of the two images. Render unto mystery what is mysterious. Since these are matters whose real beginnings elude scientific description, accept them as manifestations of the inexplicable, or manifestations of God, "using that name to comprehend all the great and inexplicable things and the redemptive or destructive powers that lie outside human command and understanding," as Robertson Davies has said. So be it.

As for the prehistoric scribe who wrote Genesis, though he

muddled the sequence of later events, he certainly was inspired—
whether divinely or intuitively doesn't much matter. For though he
couldn't have been there to see it, science confirms there must
have been oceans and wind early on. Earth as we know it couldn't
have become what is is without them.

CHAPTER THREE

Surfcasting below Highland Light, Cape Cod

Fishes of the Beach

The title only looks like an oxymoron; it describes this chapter's scope. The sea is full of fish and the beach itself obviously empty of them, except in various states of morbidity or captivity. While thousands of species depend on beach-protected marshes for their nurseries, few mature fishes have a vital connection with the shore per se; when a connection occurs, it most often involves a mono-filament line with hook attached. Nonetheless, beach people, with or without tackle, encounter these marine vertebrates: the school-ing vegetarians that come ashore to escape predators; the strong swimmers, such as striped bass, which are sometimes seen braving the translucent crests of breakers as they hunt; and the other car-nivorous species commonly caught by even casual fisherman.

The finned swimmers are fascinating in their biological suc-cess, their habits and their diversity. They are also inscrutable in many respects and outrageously complex—unless it's simply that our understanding of them is limited (as could be the case).

In ichthyology, as elsewhere, taxonomists are playing catch-up ball. Successive generations of investigators explained things as best as they could on the basis of available knowledge; successors have then amended or even upset established theses with new tools, theories or discoveries. While new species are described with some frequency, the worst confusions involve the higher taxa as younger taxonomists explain anew how various genera, families, orders and even classes are related.

Consider, for example, the on-again-off-again taxonomic relationship of the striped bass and white perch. The striper was christened *Roccus lineatus*. Then it appeared that another fish already had that name and the striper's was changed to *Roccus saxatilis*. Now it's *Morone saxatilis*. Meanwhile the white perch, formerly *Roccus americanus*, became *Morone americanus*. Years ago Charles L. Wheeler, chief of the National Marine Fisheries Service's intriguing aquarium at Woods Hole, complained to me, "They used to be the same genus. Then someone tore the whole thing apart and switched them out. Now they're in the same genus again. But it's a new one."

In oversimplified terms, one goal of systematics is to determine which primitive chicken came before which egg in the primordial slime. It is a matter of some frustration that there will probably always be more questions than answers, literally for lack of hard evidence—because soft tissues so rarely leave fossil remains. Nonetheless, some fairly certain notions have survived decades of scientific scrutiny. The first vertebrate was a marine creature whose descendants became the earliest known fishes. They, in turn, also sired swimmers that used their fins to crawl out of the sea to become amphibians, whence came reptiles, birds and mammals like us. As one plain-speaking fish man at the Virginia Institute of Marine Science used to tell his students, "You're just Sarcopterygians"—that is, collateral descendants of a creature whose other offspring spawned the famous coelacanths, among other things. (Through a forgotten ancestor, even Darwin himself had a distant cousin in the Dover sole.) To put it more elegantly, the *Encyclopaedia Britannica* states, "In a sense land vertebrates are simply highly modified fishes, for when fishes colonized the land they became tetrapod (four-legged) land vertebrates."

That colonization occurred on the order of 350 million years ago, give or take a few million. While it was in progress and terrestrial life-forms began diversifying to occupy niches in the new environment, marine forms also evolved. But specialization occurred at varying rates on land and in the sea. Taxonomists didn't appear until long after the bony fishes had swum into every aquatic habitat and many of the pioneer species had disappeared. Working with newly uncovered shards of the shattered fossil record, with the old clues of anatomical and embryonic similarities and with increasingly sophisticated tissue analysis (including comparisons of DNA), the scientists are trying to put the puzzle together.

To start making some sense of it, take it on faith that sharks and rays (Elasmobranchs in the class Chondrichthyes) evolved from one early ancestor. Many sharks are relatively modern and certainly successful; some of the 200 species bear living young, which is the height of reproductive sophistication. Yet as a group they seem "primitive" in some important respects, which may simply mean that in some adaptive particulars they decided, "If it ain't broke, don't fix it." Their skeletons are made of cartilage, not bone, and they lack air bladders, organs of interest in the bony fishes. Meanwhile another primitive ancestor sired another group of marine swimmers. The class Osteichthyes comprises all the bony fishes, including separate groups of fleshy-finned fishes, ray-finned fishes (e.g. sturgeons and bowfins) and teleosts, today's dominant group.

A large plurality of all modern vertebrates are fishes; their species may even outnumber all the living birds, mammals, reptiles and amphibians combined when (if ever) the natural world is finally catalogued in its entirety. Counts of species are relatively stable for birds (8,600 species worldwide) and mammals (4,500), but untold amphibians and reptiles wait to be counted for the simple reason that their counters have been fewer than the numbers of ornithologists and mammalogists. The best that one expert could do not long ago was to guess that there are about 40,000 species of fish worldwide, while a Canadian zoologist threw quantitative caution to the wind and enumerated 18,818 living species of fish. Rising above the fray, a senior British scientist suggested with comfortable, even lyrical poise that "fishes are almost ubiquitous and virtually numberless. In the ocean they live at all levels from boisterous well-lit intertidal regions down to the cold, sunless waters that flow over the sediments of the abyssal plains." Another expert, not wishing to grind anything from axes to hatchetfish, suggested 20,000 as a reasonable round figure for bony fish species ranging in size from the Philippine goby, which measures ⅖ of an inch overall, to the 60-foot whale shark.

Life began in the sea, but ocean water is not the perfect environment for complex organisms. Witness the salinity problem. The salinity of a fish's body fluids is midway between the salt levels of fresh water and seawater. Hence fluid moves in or out by osmosis, the phenomenon that tends to equalize the salt content of two liquids separated by a permeable membrane. The animal's epidermis surrounding its scales provides mucus, which serves as a kind of waterproofing as well as a lubricant to reduce external friction and a protective barrier against microorganisms. But osmosis still persists between the fish's body fluid and the external seawater medium. A marine fish loses internal water to the sea this way; it makes up for the loss by drinking as much as 40 percent of its body weight a day. Since the beverage is salty, its salt content must be separated from the pure fluid; excess salt is excreted through the gills and intestine while fresh water osmoses out through the skin. Freshwater fishes, on the other hand, absorb water by osmosis from their surroundings and eliminate it through their kidneys. Some species must do both at various times in their lives. These are the anadromous and catadromous species (from the Greek words for up- or down-wandering). Herring and bass, which swim up inland streams from the sea to spawn, simply switch waterbudget mechanisms, as do the catadromous eels that mature in fresh water before traveling to the mid-Atlantic Sargasso Sea, where they mate once and die.

Sharks and rays solve the problem differently. They recycle a metabolic waste product to their advantage. While most vertebrates expel urea, sharks and rays retain it in the bloodstream. This keeps the internal salt content about as high as the surrounding seawater. Since osmotic pressure doesn't distinguish between salts, a shark doesn't waste energy passing fluid through the skin into the sea. But the high urea content is the reason that shark bound for the table must be well bled soon after capture; otherwise it is unpalatable.

Gills are structures of wonderful design that enable their possessors to extract ample amounts of free oxygen from water. (Fish don't breathe any oxygen that is bound up in H_2O, but only the O_2 that's dissolved in the fluid at a maximum level of about ten parts per million.) Gills work better than our lungs; fishes typically use 80 percent of the oxygen available to them while people do well to absorb 25 percent of the vital gas in the air we breathe. Two elements are responsible for the gill's efficiency: its surface design and the arrangement of its hematological plumbing.

Water entering the fish's open mouth flows over the gills and exits beneath the gill covers. The gill membranes are so intricately folded that a high-metabolism fish like a herring or mackerel may have 70 square inches of oxygen-absorbing gill surface for each pound of body weight. Next, a "countercurrent" arrangement of blood vessels assures the most complete absorption of vital gas. Water and blood flow in opposite directions across and through the gills respectively. Oxygen-poor blood first reaches the rear gill parts across which water with the least oxygen passes. Partly-oxygenated blood flows through parts of the gills exposed to water increasingly rich in oxygen. Blood about to leave the gills passes through parts receiving water with the most oxygen at the front. This arrangement minimizes the difference in oxygen content between the blood in every gill part and the water flowing across that part, and in the process it maximizes the total absorption of oxygen. Were the plumbing arranged the other way around, the gill would work less effectively, since diffusion pressure would be lower. If blood with the least oxygen were exposed to the most oxygen-rich water, and blood with the most oxygen were exposed to the poorest water, the total transfer of oxygen would be less. By the same token, the fish's blood vessel arrangement allows for the most efficient removal of carbon dioxide from blood in the gills.

If fish breathe the same gas that we do, the question arises: Why doesn't a fish out of water take its oxygen from the air? The answer is that many can and do. The walking catfish, an exotic species now established in the southern United States, migrates across land from pond to pond. Primitive African lungfish, the coelacanth's closet living relatives, estivate (i.e., hibernate in warm weather) during years-long droughts in the hardening mud of dried-up lake beds; they breathe air in a state that nearly resembles suspended animation. Other fishes are "obligate air breathers." The bowfins, for example, must reach the surface and gulp air from time to time. Goldfish in a bowl do the same.

But these exceptions beg the question. Most fishes die out of water even though in air they are surrounded by abundant quantities of the same oxygen they cunningly extract in meager amounts from water. The reason is simple: desiccation. Their gills dry out on land. Those fishes that survive significant periods out of water have mechanisms for keeping their gills moist. One miracle of unrecorded history is that both animals and plants found ways to survive out of water in the first place, since every living cell is a wet micro-environment. The statement is not as outlandish as it seems. The bark of a living tree is composed of dead cells; so is human skin. Thick or thin, these dead layers protect wet environments where tissues live. Every land animal spends a great deal of physiological effort keeping its lung linings wet since these living cells must encounter quantities of air to absorb oxygen for the rest of the organism. The ghost crab left the sea to live in the dry sand, but it must return regularly to the water and wet its gills. Most fishes never dealt with this problem; since the medium they breath is wet, they gave little adaptive energy to the matter of preventing gill dryness. But beached by a wave or landed by a fishing line, they face a condition imposed by the alien environment. Then their gills dry out and cease to function.

Like its breathing apparatus, a fish's eye differs from a mammal's. In man's eye, muscles change the shape of the lens to alter the focal length in order to focus on objects at different distances. The fish's lens is of a constant shape and curvature; muscles move the whole lens back and forth (like a telescope) to focus on distant or near objects. Sight is an important sense for both predator and prey species living in oceanic shallows. Because the eyes are at the side of the head—and the lenses usually protrude—most fishes can see aft along the length of the body while they also have a region of binocular vision in front.

Since visibility is limited in even the clearest seas, fishes depend on highly developed senses of hearing, scent and touch as well. A number of icthyological families make audible sounds, evidently to communicate with others of their kind, at spawning time in particular. Most fishes sense water movement through a biologically unique organ, the lateral line. Curved in a way that is characteristic of each species, it runs along the body on each side of the fish. Composed of individual sensory hairs set in flexible swivel joints, the lateral line monitors minute changes in water pressure. Toss a pebble into a pond of minnows or snap your fingers underwater when snorkeling among schooling fish and each individual will turn away from the disturbance almost simulta-

neously. The minute shock wave reaches each fish's side almost at
the same time. The lateral line is constantly useful; at night or in
murky water it warns a swimming fish of unseen objects, since
the water near a rock or another fish responds differently than
unobstructed water.

So much for generalities. Consider in turn some of the fishes
encountered by people along the beach.

Crab-eating Sharks

Although three sharks commonly appear on the beach, none is
a candidate for movie stardom. (And the less said the better about
voracious people-eaters, at least along the coast from Maine to the
Carolinas. *Jaws* is fiction. More Americans die from bee stings than
shark attacks.)

The smooth dogfish (*Mustelus canis*), which often takes a hook
to most fishermen's disgust, occasionally grows to 5 feet in length,
though 2-footers are much more common. "One of the most common sharks in the United States," according to A. J. McLane's
nicely illustrated and straightforward *Field Guide to Salt Water
Fishes of North America*, "this species is well known to anglers who
catch large numbers during the summer months."

Gray or brown to blend with local bottoms, the smooth dog has
long pectoral fins and two large dorsals of about equal size. Armed
with keen eyes and low, flat, grinding teeth set in abutting rows like
cobblestones, "it is perhaps the most relentless enemy of the lobster," write Henry B. Bigelow and William C. Schroeder in the
definitive *Fishes of the Gulf of Maine*. It eats large crabs and small
fish as well. But curiously, according to that Interior Department
publication, this shark doesn't attack healthy menhaden in
aquaria—only sickly ones.

Like all sharks, the dogfish lacks gill covers. Instead it has gill
slits rather like straightened chevrons on a policeman's collar. The
shape and number are characteristic for each species. Its skin is
rough due to pointed triangular scales that look like microscopic
teeth and are composed of similar material. As in the other cartilaginous fishes, fertilization is internal. Male sharks use grooved
"claspers" that is, modified ventral fins—to inseminate the females.
The smooth dog is truly viviparous. Gestation takes ten months; ten

to twenty young are nourished through a placental connection with the mother until they're born live and immediately start fending for themselves.

Despite its common name, the spiny dogfish (*Squalus acanthias*) belongs to a separate family from the smooth dogfish. It has no anal fin, but both its dorsals bear sharp spines in front. The animal uses these defensively. Curling its body when captured, it snaps back and forth and can do considerable damage with the spines.

Aristotle was the first to describe the live birth of this fish whose eighteen-to-twenty-two-month gestation period is the longest among all fishes. As long as 13 inches at birth, it normally grows to only 3 feet, though some may reach 4 feet. Gray- or brown-skinned, spiny dogfish have small, flat teeth with sharp corners that form an almost continuous cutting edge the width of their mouths.

Bigelow and Schroeder note: "Much has been written about the habits of the spiny dogfish, but nothing to recommend it from the standpoint either of the fishermen or its fellow creatures in the sea." Cruising in schools, they prey on everything: worms, crabs, mackerel, cod, haddock. Spiny dogs attack rapaciously, leaving behind much of what they kill and

> have not been of sufficient value . . . to compensate for a hundredth part of the damage they do. . . . [S]o erratic are their appearances and disappearances that when one has had good fishing today he may catch only dogfish tomorrow and nothing at all the day after, the better fish having fled these sea wolves and the latter departing as a result.

Here, as elsewhere, these authorities on fishermen's fish display an unhappy bias as they favor species that "benefit" people,

Smooth dogish (*Mustelus canis*)

usually in raw commercial terms. This egocentricity is short-sighted, at the very least—a prejudice as damaging to its practition-ers in the long run as any form of bigotry. In fact even the ugliest and most commercially useless critter in the sea plays its role in the ecological fabric. The spiny dog, like many predators, may not eat everything it kills; yet in ecological terms it is not wasteful, because its leftovers serve other species. In fact, the more we learn about the natural world, the more it appears that *Homo sapiens* is the unique wastrel. We lose entire sinks of organic materials to the ecosystem as we burn fossil fuels and vent their constituent parts to the atmosphere. But that's another matter.

The sand tiger (*Odontaspis taurus*), formerly known as the sand shark, cruises the length of the Atlantic coast but is most often met between Delaware Bay and Cape Cod. It grows up to 10 feet, though the vast majority are under 6 feet. Its first dorsal fin and anal fin are about the same size; its second dorsal fin is larger. The teeth are slender, pointed and sharp. Despite its formidable appearance, this is a rather sluggish, largely nocturnal shark that eats small fishes, squid and a few crustaceans.

The sand tiger's reproductive pattern represents a compromise between more common forms. Normally two fertilized eggs hatch within the mother and, since there is no placenta, the embryonic sharks get nourishment by eating unfertilized eggs.

Flap-winged Fish

Bizarre-looking, flattish fish belonging to the same class as sharks, the skates are harmless to man despite their appearance and associations. Under water they flap their odd, winglike pectoral fins to swim gracefully like circular or diamond-shaped birds.

These are the animals responsible for the black, leathery (or brittle), purselike egg cases that litter many beaches. Their four long, curly corners seem diabolical to some people, but in fact the long pair of "horns" extracts food and oxygen from the water and the short pair expels wastes. Called devil's pocketbooks or sailor's purses ("because they always come ashore empty"), these egg cases are laid with a sticky substance that attaches them to sub-marine plants. Presumably the glue loses its strength after the young hatch out as miniature adults ready to fend for themselves.

Typically they eat crustaceans, mollusks and small fishes. In Europe skates are eaten by gourmets, and in New England, Yankees seem to be acquiring a taste for them too.

The little skate (*Raja erinacea*), the most common along the East Coast, rarely grows longer than 18 inches. It is gray, tan or pinkish above and white below. The female has a "thorny" body while the male has thorns only along the fins and tail. The largest in Atlantic coastal waters is the barndoor skate (*R. laevis*), which occasionally grows to 5 feet in length. It is brown or reddish brown with irregular blotches on top. The smaller winter skate (*R. ocellata*) prefers cold water. It is light brown with round dark spots and grows to about 3 feet.

Among the order Rajiformes the stingrays of the family Dasyatidae have the worst reputation—because people most often become aware of them painfully and have done so since colonial times. (Captain John Smith recorded being stung by one when he explored Chesapeake Bay.) The stingray goes about its business on the marine floor and when encountered too closely lashes out with its tail, which is armed with a barbed and venomous spine or two. These often break off in the flesh of its perceived attacker—whether the leg of an errant human wader or the snout of a hammerhead shark, a frequent predator. One such shark has been found with ninety-four stingray spines. *Dasyatis centroura* grows to dimensions of 12 by 7 feet; *D. sabina*, to 10 feet square. The butterfly ray is smaller.

These animals, which prefer warm water but range as far

Atlantic stingray (*Dasyatis sabina*)

north as Cape Cod, eat mollusks and crustaceans. Consequently they are bottom feeders and frequent shallow waters. A writer who was stung by one suggests scuffling along when wading rather than lifting one's feet since a ray that is nudged will move away without a fuss. A ray that's stepped on fights back. Sometimes hooked by fishermen, they remain dangerous when landed.

An enormous member of a close family is the giant devil ray or manta (*Manta birostris*). These creatures, bearing earlike flaps in front of the lateral eyes, are known to grow to a 22-foot wingspan. Offshore they occasionally leap from the water and soar like giant bats. But they are so docile that scuba divers sometimes hitch rides on their backs. They subsist on small organisms like small shrimps and plankton.

Menhaden

The first time I visited the Outer Banks something seemed wrong: The high-tide line was not marked with seaweed but with silvery fish for a mile in either direction. They hadn't succumbed to chemical pollution or an oil spill; this fish kill had natural causes. Some of the corpses were whole, others were in parts and the majority were just missing a clean-cut chunk of flesh from the back or throat. They were menhaden, driven ashore by voracious blues.

The menhaden has more aliases than the polygamous skipper of a tramp steamer: pogy, mossbunker, hardhead, yellowtail shad, greentail, fatback, chebug, whitefish, silversider, pilcher and bug head (for the little parasitic crabs often found in its mouth). One of the true herrings (family Clupeidae), *Brevoortia tyrannus* has silvery or brassy sides fading to dark blue or brown above and no visible lateral line. The head is about half as long as the body from the spot behind the gill cover to the base of the deeply forked tail.

Theoretically edible, but rarely eaten by any person who could find another fish, the menhaden is the unwitting mainstay of the largest commercial fishery on the East Coast. It is unpalatable due to its high oil content, the same characteristic that makes it so useful as industrial raw material for fertilizer, fish meal, pet food, soaps, lubricants, leather conditioners, paints and other products. Single offshore catches of a million fish have been recorded in the past, and the annual take sometimes numbers a billion fish. But annual harvests vary widely due to dramatic population fluctuations. In 1890 some ninety million pounds were taken and four new processing plans opened in New England; a year later the catch was down by half.

Like its kin the Atlantic herring (*Clupea harengus*), round herring (*Etrumeus teres*), hickory shad (*Alosa mediocris*), true alewife (*Alosa pseudoharengus*) and others, menhaden travel in enormous, dense schools. Unlike some of the others, it spawns at sea, the specific time of summer probably depending on water temperature. About 3 inches long by the first winter, a menhaden doubles its length in the next year and may grow to 15 inches. Some live nine or ten years, a fact proven by microscopic examination of their scales. (Every fish has a set range in the number of its scales. The arrangement is fixed in each species and as an individual grows from fingerling to maturity all its scales grow apace. Because feeding conditions vary with the seasons of the year, fishes grow at irregular rates. Scales grow sporadically too; they become marked with visible rings which, like a tree's, can be read to interpret age.)

Toothless, this member of the clan eats mostly plankton. Swimming close to the ocean surface (sometimes leaping out), it sieves microscopic organisms with highly specialized gillrakers. These internal structures simply protect the gills of some fish; in the menhaden, as in some bivalves, the gills are food collectors as well as respiratory organs. A single menhaden can filter six or seven gallons of seawater a minute and extract a pint of food an hour.

Menhaden (*Brevoortia tyrannus*)

The reasons for abrupt changes in population are unclear. A scarcity of plankton one year may mean fewer menhaden the next, or overfishing by man, disease or overkill by another predator may be the cause. An important link in the food chain from plankton to some sea birds and all larger fish in the Atlantic, the menhaden is preyed upon by whales, porpoises, sharks, cod, swordfish, tuna, bass, squid—nearly everything but its own toothless kind. As one sport-fishing expert has written, "In the wilderness, death is a way of life."

Bluefish

The bluefish "is perhaps the most ferocious and bloodthirsty fish in the sea"—sharks included—according to one authority with a taste for the dramatic. They travel in what are sometimes enormous schools of like-sized individuals because swimming speed is a function of size; thus, fish of different sizes swim at different speeds. Blues are the game fish most noted for "feeding frenzies," and David L. Pawson, a marine biologist whose profession eschews exaggeration, relates the following (blue)fish story: "About ten years ago on our beach at Avon [on the Outer Banks], bluefish chased ashore hundreds of beautiful spotted trout (weakfish). My wife took a bucket and collected a fine haul. At around the same time, on Thanksgiving Day, a huge blitz of bluefish hit Hatteras Island from Cape Point all the way north to Nags Head—50 or 60 miles! What must have been hundreds of millions of bluefish, all of them very large (some weighed upwards of twenty pounds), came in to the shore and ravaged baitfish (mostly menhaden) for around three hours. It was an astonishing scene. Most blitzes seem to last

Bluefish (*Pomatomus saltatrix*)

for just a few minutes. This one was a gigantic feeding orgy. The waves, as they reared up to break, were filled with bluefish. As we stood in knee-deep water, huge bluefish were washing around us, lolling in the shallows. Mixed in with the bluefish were large sand sharks and red drum in the forty to fifty pound range."

The only more ravenous species along the Outer Banks is our own. When "the blues are running," fishermen flock faster than gulls. They crowd fishing piers in such numbers that they threaten each other with their hooked lures when they cast. They'll crowd a beach, working the surf until a school passes, then pile into fleets of buggies, race a few miles ahead to head off their diminished prey, and fish again.

The solitary member of its family, *Pomatomus saltatrix* has few common names beside "blue," though young specimens are called snappers and mid-sized ones are tailors. The generic name means "operculum cutting"—possibly because this fish often goes for its victim's throat in the vicinity of the gill cover (or operculum). It will go for the hands of captors too and frequently bites a fisherman's finger to the bone if he handles it carelessly.

The bluefish is rather blue-green in color above, fading to white below. Very simply designed, it has neither fancy pigmentation nor extraneous external structures. Its forehead slopes in a regular curve down to its slightly undershot jaw. Along the East Coast it grows to 3½ feet; off Africa a forty-five-pound specimen was reportedly caught from a destroyer's fantail during World War II. Its spawning and migration habits are barely understood.

Five-inch snappers appear off New England in August, presumably the year's juveniles. The following year these individuals measure 12 to 15 inches, then they start growing at even faster rates. They may eat twice their weight a day, gorging on menhaden, mullet and other fishes as well as marine worms whenever the latter leave their sea-bottom tubes to propagate.

Puffer

The northern puffer might not be identified by a weekend angler if it ever kept its cool. But disturbed, threatened or hooked, it inflates itself with air or water like a balloon. The smaller individuals distend their bodies so much that the small fins disappear.

This defensive creature, also called swellfish, blowfish, globefish and bellowsfish, is hyperbolically named *Sphoeroides maculatus* in Latin: spotted spheroid.

Regularly found from Florida to Cape Cod, the puffer has the habit of disappearing irregularly from a habitat where it was recently plentiful. At ease it's a reasonably slender specimen, normally less than 10 inches long, with a small mouth and "buck teeth" that aren't teeth at all but modified bones divided by a suture. A bottom feeder, it uses them to assault mollusks and crustaceans, crabs in particular, which it tries to disable by first biting their well-protected nerve centers. Its scaleless skin is rough due to short, stiff prickles.

Spawning occurs in late spring or early summer when a female lays more than 175,000 eggs. As in many fish, the male is typically smaller than its mate.

The northern puffer belongs to the family Tetraodontidae, which includes about sixty species worldwide, including one said to be the planet's most poisonous fish. People who eat it may die within five hours from a toxin that has no known antidote. In the past this South Pacific oddity provided islanders with arrow and spear poisons. Other members of the family may be poisonous in one area but deliciously harmless in another—perhaps due to a different diet. Nonetheless, lethal poisonings are still common in Japan, where puffer is a very expensive winter delicacy.

Once considered a trash fish in America, *Sphoeroides maculatus* is now marketed to epicures under the tony name sea squab. The flesh along the back is said to be boneless and tasty but the viscera can be extremely toxic. The liver, gonads and roe are especially dangerous. *Bon appétit.*

Piscatorial Pancakes

The order Pleuronectiformes comprises fishes of great economic and culinary importance: flounder, halibut, plaice, sole and turbot. By many other names these bottom dwellers lie as flat on the ocean floor as a crepe in a pan of flaming brandy. While a skate lies just as low on its belly, flatfish lie on their sides—right or left as a matter of each species' preference.

Winter flounder (*Pseudopleuronectes americanus*)

In the process of finding their place in the sedimentary scheme of things, flatfish didn't give up using the eye on the side they habitually lie. Emerging from an egg, ⅛-inch-long flounder swims like any other fish at first: dorsal fin up, ventral down, and an eye on each side of its head. As the young flatfish develops, one eye migrates around or through the head to join its partner on the side that will be uppermost throughout later life. The jaw, however, remains oriented through the face, giving the flatfish a rather sinister sneer as it goes its predatory way. The general appearance, in no way helped by the asymmetrical eyes, is that of a two-bit prizefighter who lost a quick decision to a Mack truck. While they spend a good deal of time literally lying in wait with only their eyes exposed above a thin blanket of sand, flatfish actively pursue any likely prey that passes overhead or within darting reach of the bottom. The different species have various food preferences; collectively they eat all manner of finfish, crabs, lobsters, mollusks worms, crustaceans and even sand dollars.

These fish can be described as "right-handed," or dextral, if their eyes appear on the right side of the head (and they lie on the left side of the body). "Left-handed," or sinistral, flatfish have the eyes on the left side and lie on their right. They range in size from the delectable hogchoker or American sole (*Trinectes maculatus*), which rarely grows longer than 8 inches, to the Atlantic halibut, which has been known to exceed 700 pounds.

In brief, the more common East Coast right-handed flatfish are the Greenland halibut or turbot (*Reinhardtius hippoglossoides*); Atlantic halibut (*Hippoglossus hippoglossus*); American plaice or sand dab (*Hippoglossoides platessoides*); yellowtail flounder (*Limanda ferruginea*); winter flounder, black-back or lemon sole (*Pseudopleuronectes americanus*) and hogchoker. The common East Coast left-handers include the summer flounder or fluke (*Paralichthys dentatus*); fourspot flounder (*P. oblongus*) and windowpane or brill (*Scophthalmus aquosus*).

Noisemakers

Cynoscion regalis' generic name comes from the Greek word for dog. In spawning season the male vibrates its air bladder to make a sound like barking. The female, which has a thinner abdominal muscle, is silent. In English this cosmopolitan species is most often called weakfish. That name, perhaps coined by Dutch colonists in their language, persisted because the weakfish's mouth parts are so fragile that hooks often tear out of them. It's also called sea trout or squeteague after an Indian word. Under any moniker *C. regalis* is a slender, bright-looking fish that swims in schools along the coast and into brackish water. In addition to a diet of crustaceans and mollusks, it competes with the bluefish for scaled food.

The weakfish is slender and handsome, lightly mottled (almost like a Seurat sunrise) and highlighted with yellow pectoral fins. Usually under 2 feet long, it may weigh about four pounds, though a thirty-pounder is on record. They spawn near shore from May to September; after forty hours the eggs produce larvae less than 7/100 inch long.

Other members of the family Sciaenidae include the spot (*Leiostomos xanthurus*), banded croaker (*Larimus fasciatus*), Atlantic croaker (*Micropogon undulatus*), various other sea trouts (*Cynoscion* sp.) and the red drum or channel bass (*Sciaenops ocellata*), a most reputable game fish. While some fishermen claim they can smell quarry through the surf, many authorities agree that the drum's drumming noises can be clearly heard from shore. The fishes must have a better purpose than announcing their presence to human predators; odds are that the noise attracts mates.

Candidate for Extinction

The striped bass or rockfish (*Morone saxatilis* pro tem.) is coastal and anadromous; it seeks fresh water to spawn. Traveling deep into Chesapeake Bay's marshy tributaries and as far as 160 miles up the Hudson River, a large female may produce ten million eggs to be fertilized by a score of small males. The young stay in fresh or sheltered brackish water until their second year when they join schools—enormous congregations—that migrate up and down East Coast waters.

The early colonists valued this fish, which appeared in such numbers that John Smith saw shoaling schools "as will load a ship of 100 tonnes." In 1634 a New England apologist wrote of the "basse. . . . It is a fine fat fast fish having a bone in his head which contains a saucerful of marrow sweet and good, pleasant to the pallat and wholesome to the stomach." Before that decade was out, the Massachusetts Bay Colony banned the use of both this noble fish and the adulated cod for fertilizer. They were too good for such a base purpose, which alewives served well enough.

The striper is olive gray above with silvery sides marked by seven or eight horizontal stripes that fade with age. The largest of these perchlike fishes, which are the females and misnamed "bulls," once ran well over a hundred pounds. Now a thirty-five-pounder is considered big. Very strong swimmers, though not notoriously fast, they can sometimes be seen feeding in the translucent crests of breaking waves. They feed as voraciously as blues on smaller fish and a variety of mollusks and crustaceans, notably lobsters. Bigelow and Schroeder note that these fish will gorge on one kind of prey,

Striped bass (*Morone saxatilis*)

pause to digest, then gorge again in apparent unison. They are most active from sunset to dawn but feed by day also.

Like many species, stripers' numbers fluctuate greatly. In the past they regularly declined for five years running, then in a single frenzied year rebounded nearly to their former numbers. But in *Striper, a Story of Fish and Man*, Maine journalist and former Long Island hand-seiner John N. Cole warned that the cycle may have been broken. The likely reasons, in his view, are freshwater pollution of spawning grounds, offshore dumping of sewage and the sport-fishing craze. Whatever the cause, the results were alarming. The species was disappearing. Bass fishing off Rhode Island was popular enough to support an annual tournament; it was cancelled for lack of fish when one year not a single striper was caught. Waking up to the crisis and to Chesapeake Bay's crucial role as the spawning ground for 90 percent of East Coast stripers, in 1985 the state of Maryland outlawed pro tem the catching of what Free Staters call "rockfish." When the ban was tentatively lifted in the fall of 1990, sport fishermen came out in such numbers—and caught so many stripers—that the embargo went back into effect within days lest whatever recovery had occurred be undone in a single season.

Resourceful or Perverse?

New England fishermen used to predict easterly storms when the goosefish appeared—she's hard to miss when she shows up. This is one of the continental shelf's more grotesque creatures according to human aesthetics. Perhaps as large as fifty pounds, most of that is head, and most of the head is a mouth that gapes to an 8-by-9-inch maw fringed with flaps of flesh that look like tatters. The tapering and camouflaged body is rather squashed in appearance, built low to the ocean floor. Goosefish are so ugly that even their mothers don't love them; they often eat their own.

Lophius americanus belongs to the well-named angler fishes, a breed that fishes for its food. The first dorsal spine is adapted for use as a lure. This slender appendage bears a flap of skin at its tip like a little flag—or more like a carrot on a stick. The goosefish or angler attracts its prey by waving the flag and drawing it down in front of its cavernous mouth. When a smaller fish follows the lure, the angler gulps it down. Some authorities say it bites; others say it simply inhales by opening its gills, which are behind its paddlelike ventral fins, and the prey washes in with the current.

Anglers have been landed under odd circumstances. A Rhode Island fisherman hauling cod felt the line get suddenly heavier and found the cod on his hook. had been swallowed by a goosefish en route to the surface. Small goosefish with several fishes in their mouths have been found swallowed by their own larger kin. A Frenchman of the Renaissance reported finding one on the shore holding a fox by the leg—not a Mexican standoff, but a littoral showdown. The popular name for this resourceful fish derives from stories of its having swallowed geese. Whether or not that occurs, it is reliably reported that a goosefish was found with sea ducks in its stomach. As a food fish, this species has become popular with the cordon bleu crowd in recent years under the alias monkfish.

L. americanus lays her eggs in veils of mucus a foot or two wide and 10 yards long that may contain as many as one-and-a-quarter-million ova in a single layer. The sexual habits of the goosefish's deep-sea relatives are unusual to the point of perversity—though biology makes no value judgments. Bernard Ludwig Gordon de-

Goosefish (*Lophius americanus*)

scribes its ways in *The Secret Lives of Fishes*. In the abyssal darkness

> where courtship could easily prove futile, once the male finds his
> mate, he attaches himself to her, never to let go. The site of the
> attachment appears to be a random choice—sometimes on the
> abdomen, the sides, the head, or even the gill cover. The male
> grips the female with his strong teeth, and his lips and tongue
> grow into her skin. His mouth, jaws, teeth, fins, and gills degen-
> erate. Only his reproductive system remains independently ac-
> tive. The two blood systems become fused, and the male is
> nourished by her blood, literally becoming part of her, his body
> merging into hers. He never grows; if anything, much of the male
> disappears into the female. An angler female taken near Iceland
> was 40 inches long, and the attached male only 4 inches. The
> female was judged to be a thousand times the weight of her mate.

Why is the goosefish a fish of the beach? As Michael J. Ursin's
Guide to Fishes of the Temperate Atlantic Coast reports, "The
goosefish includes seabirds in its diet by capturing them in the
shallows." Beyond that, their peculiar jawbones, armed with one to
three curved rows of pointed teeth, often wash up on the shore.
Some summertime strollers mistake them for the relic of a creature
too grotesque for even this day and age.

Driftwords: Time

The sun set at 7:13:35 tonight by my watch. I'd left the beach below Zack's Cliffs, parked the Jeep and walked back to the berm for a last look at sunset on the rainbow clays of Gay Head. I planned to be early; I was late. Beyond a cloud bank that hovered a pencil's width above the horizon, the sun shone bright orange-red. No doubt geometry has a name for the shape it seemed: a circle with a flat-bottom, as if someone had sliced a slab from a wheel of cheese and set it flat on the horizon's shelf. Then it moved, slowly but percep-tibly in little jerks, as if a galactic rat were pulling it down through the slit between the shelf and the wall. (Of course none of this could be true. The sun doesn't set; the world turns. And not in jerks, but smoothly. When we see the sun set, it is already below whatever horizon happens to confront us, since its light takes several minutes to reach our eyes. It's gone before we see it.) But down it went, or seemed to go beyond the gray horizon beneath the now purple cloud. Then above the apparent flat line of sea there was just a sliver of sun and (blip!) it vanished. Yet for a minute or two it kept reappearing—that is, the thinnest perceptible crescent appeared *below* that 6-mile-distant line, on the water itself, a hairbreadth under the horizon. No doubt the science of optics would explain that the unseen edge of distant cloud beyond the horizon was still struck by direct sunlight and bounced the light off the nearer water toward me. Or a meteorologist might explain that different air lay-ers and masses defract the sun's light at different angles, thereby distorting what we seem to see. But it looked like a specter of the sun trying to return, griping at the feeble Gay Head Light, which had begun its blinking. That's when I looked at my watch, which always runs a few minutes fast.

CHAPTER FOUR

A cascade of terns

Meet the Birds

They are always there . . . like the poor, the rich and the shore itself. Birds haunt ramshackle arcades of the incomparable honky-tonk along Salisbury Beach, Massachusetts, hover above the artificially wide sands of Ocean City, Maryland, and wait out gales on dredge spoil heaps in Ocracoke Inlet. They animate every island, especially those not frequented by man. A beach may be so changed by human use that it lacks even sand crabs and compass grass, but it will still have gulls. Winter may be so cold that spindrift lies in frozen spongy clumps, yet sanderlings still work the swash's edge in comic platoons. Summer's solemn herons patrol the marsh behind a barrier island while on the other side, beyond the surf, gray willets flash bright white chevrons, shy oyster-catchers wield their crimson bills and eager terns dive like darts. Birds are the clowns of the beach, the lions, acrobats, roustabouts, barkers, beggars, pickpockets, cops and constant spectators all. There is a type cast for every role in the littoral circus. Without doubt they are the most varied and visible fauna of the shore.

For all their ubiquity and variety, they lack the stuff of many superlatives. As a biological class, Aves are not as old as fishes nor as multitudinous as bugs. Even in an enormous springtime swarm that smudges a distant sky, then seems to vanish and reappear, the peeps are fewer than periwinkles in an acre of healthy marsh or coquinas in a square yard of wet sand. Birds are less prolific than the crabs and don't become tame as usefully as many mammals. But count them among the most wonderful animals on earth (when they bother to alight).

Because they inhabit air, and perhaps because they're so visible, birds command our wonder and delight. They always have, invading man's darkest mythology and brightening each summer day. A kind of pigeon led Noah to Ararat; eagles gnawed Prometheus' liver as Zeus' revenge for giving our crowd fire. Gulls saved the Mormons from famine to earn Utah's perpetual thanks. Ancient Egypt called birds their gods. I suspect that everything ever written about every flier since Pegasus is at least partly true; nothing is beyond them. Visit Saquish Point off Duxbury, Massachusetts, to see the ruddy turnstone earn its name. On Cape Lookout's 23-mile-long island, which may have more species of birds at one time than human beings, great blue herons stalk the open beach; they haven't read the literature that calls them denizens of the marsh.

Birds do not rank very high in what human psychologists haughtily call "intelligence," but that just points up our myopia and conceit. Could *you* navigate alone in the first autumn of your life all the way from your birthplace to where your folks spend the winter? Could you and your newfound mate build a domicile all by yourselves each spring without so much as a blueprint? Birds do such things and more. For example, no group of animals—not men, spiders, apes or fishes—functions so brilliantly in three dimensions.

Think about it: Birds soar, sink, hunt, flee, swarm and settle in relentless reference to horizontal length, breadth and vertical height. By comparison, other terrestrial vertebrates work only in horizontal planes with an occasional hop through the vertical. A snake crawls on solid ground, opting between right or left and forward or stop. Man and mountain goat do essentially the same thing, functioning more like asps than avocets. Sure, we can climb mountains, one step at a time, so long as there is something to climb on. We can leap from crag to crag like cocktail party conversationalists, but we can barely jump our own height, being slaves of gravity.

Birds command every physical dimension, willing themselves up, down, sideways and through intangible air, free from pedestrian dependence on firm earth. They do all this by using their noodles thoughtlessly, as the kingfisher hovers, dives, spears a minnow, soars up, and settles on a swaying branch. They do it extravagantly too. Albatrosses circle Antarctica aloft, only settling when its time to breed. Mother Carey's chickens take their living from the ocean without ever touching down. Some shore birds migrating from one polar circle to the other cruise at altitudes of 3 miles.

Only a marvelous brain can order and control such physical agility—yet a brain that resembles a modern reptile's more than ours. (This is because the first birds evolved from reptilian stock. Their feathers, the design and functions of which deserve a chapter in another book, derive from scales.) Despite the aspersions often cast on "bird brains," the cerebral centers that control sight and coordinate physical action are relatively huge. Each bird is a virtuoso of instant reaction to every kind of natural physical circumstance. Further, as Nobel Prize-winning behaviorist Niko Tinbergen points out, a bird is not "a mere bundle of immediate response to external stimuli." Each one reacts differently at different times to similar events depending on what's going on inside itself. It's "internal condition causes the bird to go and search for specific situations which can provide the right stimuli" to trigger reactions that the inner bird demands. "In psychological terms: a bird's 'needs vary,' " Tinbergen has learned.

Regrettably, birds' responses to humankind do not vary and many species have been decimated because they could not unlearn programmed behavior patterns that greedy people exploited. In the nineteenth century a breed of men called "market gunners" began augmenting their arsenals in a way that would do Dr.

Strangelove proud, fitting skiffs with ever-larger scatter-guns that one man couldn't lift alone. Setting out decoys in convenient bays and rivers, the hunters lay in wait until water birds approached, then fired away to bring down an entire flock in a single blast. Some species were shotgunned to extinction. William Beebe explained the tragedy in this: "When the last of a race of living things breathes no more, another heaven and another earth must pass before such a one can be again."

Birds' brainpower aside, another awesome aspect is their exquisite design. Take just the element of feathers: What other sort of body covering combines such practicality and beauty in elements from aerodynamic dexterity to species-specific identification? The shore birds' mottled skins provide superb camouflage, yet in breeding season a drab marsh drake flashes half a dozen eye-catching feathers like a battle flag. A common pigeon's broad-spread tail slows its air speed by 60 percent when landing. The wings of gulls are so aptly proportioned for flight that they showed the Wright brothers how to build a machine that flew. A bird's brilliant design is more than superficial. Most birds' bones are hollow to minimize weight and supplement lung capacity with reservoirs of air, but grebes and loons, which hunt fish under water, have solid bones that reduce unwanted bouyancy and allow them to swim submerged fast enough to catch fishes. A peregrine falcon, perhaps the fastest creature that ever lived, has a pinpoint baffle of bone in the center of each round nostril; these enable the birds to breathe at speeds of 175 miles an hour when they stoop for prey over the barrier islands. Since extra weight is literally a drag in flight, most birds' sexual equipment atrophies between breeding seasons and many species empty their bowels when startled from a perch—as much to lose weight instantly as perhaps to blind a predator. . . . The list of brilliant attributes goes on and on, but let's stick with birds of the beach, which constitute a rich enough variety.

The first problem is identifying them, since many look alike. For example, about two dozen basically black-and-white members of a single avian family inhabit or visit the Atlantic coast from Quoddy Head to Cape Lookout. Nearly twice that number of species from closely-related families of the same order also frequent these littoral neighborhoods. Unlike some other fauna, the birds don't hang around while spectators guess their names. You can examine at leisure a clam in the hand, a fish on a line or a crab scrambling in a pail; not so a bird, which can fly away faster than you can riffle the pages of a field guide.

Part of the identification process is simple elimination. For instance, the first step in recognizing an Eskimo curlew is knowing its common relatives well enough to rule them all out before summoning the American Ornithologists' Union to claim a *very* unlikely sighting. To recognize a gull or tern not nearly as invisible as that curlew today requires knowing the Laridae family by more than reputation. And with that, it's taxonomy time again.

For the most part, beach birds belong to a single zoological order. Charadriiformes constitute a large taxon based on similar skeletal structures and feather-distribution patterns. The sandpipers and their numerous kin make up the Scolopacidae family. The plovers and turnstones are Charadriidae, and the gulls and terns are Laridae or (in English) gulls and terns. This breakdown sounds simple enough but—are you ready?—the bird men are tearing up their taxa too. For a time it seemed the gulls' phylogenetic relationships were carved in stone; now some taxonomists are reshuffling things on the basis of behavior! Pardon my tangent, but the value of systematics is at stake. Taxonomy is a subject nontaxonomists love to hate; no sooner do we get the categories straight than they're all reordered. Perplexed by this, novelist and naturalist Peter Matthiessen once complained, "Each bright new nail of information, far from strengthening the taxonomic structure, is now likely to shake and resettle the whole rickety edifice."

I sympathize with the sentiment and share the assumption on which it's based: Taxonomy ought to provide a stable construct. But taxonomists don't see it that way. The purpose of systematics, as it turns out, is not just to serve up all the species in nicely labeled trays. Taxonomic categorization is not simply a matter of Latinate tongue-twisting. The real purpose of it all "is to uncover the evolutionary history of living things," says Richard L. Zusi, a Smithsonian bird man. As that history appears in fragments, episodes and scattered chapters, it illuminates the nature of life itself. Now that is a noble undertaking.

Poring through the scientific literature, it becomes apparent that the people who deal in taxonomics are concerned with matters beyond nomenclature. Yes, they debate classifications, undermining the "splitters" of past generations, who created as many taxa as they could, and adding to the "lumping" trend of contemporary science, in which categories are combined. They reorganize higher taxa, which seems a little like doing Dewey Decimal over again with the goal of reassigning old subjects to newly numbered shelves. But searching through the bound volumes of *The Auk* and *Ibis* and reading file cabinets of little monographs on finely focused subjects, something else comes clear: The taxonomists are exploring specific problems in physiology, behavior, ecological relationships, genetics, anatomy—the subtopics of ornithology. They contribute to taxonomy in passing, as they borrow from it. Most of them use it as a vehicle, not an end in itself. It seems a useful matrix, like a printer's type tray—albeit one in which the partitions are constantly being nudged around.

At times I have been a sailor, and fond of the rule "a place for everything and everything in its place." That implies a system. As a system, Linnean classification is damnably untidy. It seems impossible, just as the flight of a bumblebee is inexplicable according to the rules of aeronautical engineering. As bee wings work for the bee, taxonomy works for taxonomists. Why have I bothered with it all? Because when one writes about something as complex as the biota of the beach, some system of organization is mandatory. One could study and describe all the round animals first, then the black ones, then the soft. One could consider the fauna in alphabetical order, from critters to whiffets. (One series of field guides has its birds arranged by color.) Or the amateur who wants to learn something about the living world of birds can use the organizing system the pros use, knowing it will have strengths and shortcomings.

Biologists, I finally realized, are not so different from the members of my diverse fraternity. Writers, editors, journalists, critics, scholars, poets and linguists consider their work important. We support our favorite dictionaries as avidly as Pittsburgh people back the Steelers. We argue about the serial comma (an obsolete device in my view). We discuss etymology. We use grammar; it is an important if protean tool because our language is a living, evolving thing. Yet very few of us consider grammar an end in itself or consider ourselves grammarians. We're involved in living language, as biologists engage in the living world. But getting back to the birds. . . .

The Linnean relationship between our herring gull (*Larus argentatus*) and the European lesser black-backed (*L. fucus*) points up the difficulties in building the solid structure nontaxonomists might like. Richard L. Pough writes authoritatively that both birds apparently descend from one ancestral group in Siberia.

As this Siberian species pushed out east and west to colonize nearby regions the new populations tended to vary [only] a little from the original stock. These units begat others until finally the two divergent lines met halfway around the world, that represented by the lesser black-back having apparently come from the east, that of the herring gull from the west across North America. Beginning with the present Siberian population (the Vega herring gull) and following each of the lines, one discovers that each group is so similar to its neighbors (often interbreeding with them) that they all appear to be merely races or subspecies of a single species, and yet when the lines meet the end groups breed side by side without interbreeding. This, the surest test of a valid species, poses a problem in nomenclature which some ornithologists have solved by putting all the birds in one superspecies. Why the herrings and the lesser black-backs did not interbreed when they met is hard to determine, but the acquisition by the former of a 2-week-earlier breeding season may have something to do with it.

In behavior and habits the two remain almost identical.

Tinbergen wrote in *Scientific American* some years back, "Even a nodding acquaintance with gulls suggests that their signaling behavior is just as typical of the family as their coloring and physical conformation." A gull demonstrates its gullishness by being web-footed, white-bodied and stout-billed and by sharing behavioral traits with other gulls. Laughing gulls talk to each other and communicate by gesture. To a non-gull such as a behavioral scientist, these vocabularies seem remarkably alike from species to species. (By the same token, the speech and body language of a Cape Breton Celt and a gaucho in the Argentine might seem identical to a migrating Arctic tern.)

Genetic and geographic differences aside, ethologists recognize that seemingly identical physical and vocal displays are distinct enough to keep some closely related birds from getting together. Further, it's apparent that a great deal of gull behavior is latent; cerebral programming changes more slowly than cosmetic plumage. If behavior can be biologically isolating and keep birds of similar feathers apart, behavioral similarities can indicate evolutionary relationships. Hence some taxonomists are now revising the gulls' phylogenetic chart on the basis of behavior. They offer the sensible hypothesis that a species that behaves very much like another but looks quite different may be more closely related than superficial plumage at first suggests. Thus, habitual actions become part of the formula for defining kinship among species.

Only a few scientific generations ago taxonomists compulsively defined species (and genera) according to externals such as feather coloring. They split the birds into as many taxa as possible, it seems. Nineteenth-century ornithology decreed, for example, that our two largest herons, the great blue and the great white, obviously belonged to separate species. Later investigators learned that individuals of both colors regularly interbreed. The great white heron occurs only in Florida (for unexplained reasons), but dark herons summer as far north as Nova Scotia and Alaska; the latter are not "reproductively isolated" in Florida where both appear. Hence they do not belong to separate species. Today the trend is to lump established groups together on the basis of a widening range of subtler characteristics. After all, there is nothing hard and fast about the parameters of a genus or any higher taxon per se. Every taxon higher than the species is an arbitrary category defined by nothing more than scientific consensus, not holy writ.

As in the other zoological chapters, this one will not describe every coastal denizen of its category. It will introduce the birds most commonly seen and offer a short course in instant identification—because an instant is often all one has. But be advised that the first lessons may be the most uncomfortable: Birds are best described in comparison to each other. A great egret is enormous—for a bird. Next to a locomotive it's little. The least sandpiper weighs an ounce, at most, but since the birder can't induce it to sit upon a scale, the species is said to look like a semipalmated sandpiper in miniature. The way to learn birds by sight is to read, watch, remember and compare. First read a bit at leisure. Then simply eyeball individuals of a habitat's most numerous and visible species, like the sanderling and herring gull. Get an idea of each kind's limited variations and fundamental consistencies; then judge every other peep and white-headed gull by comparison in the mind's eye.

Get thyself an illustrated bird guide as soon as possible. Which one? The latest edition of the one you happen to like best. The four "standards" differ more in terms of size and visual style than content. Roger Tory Peterson's *A Field Guide to the Birds* is the fourth generation of the granddaddy of them all. The Golden Field Guide Series' *Birds of North America*, by Chandler S. Robbins, Bertel Bruun and Herbert S. Zim, is the briefest, thus handiest in the field. The *Audubon Society Field Guide to North American Birds* has photographs for illustrations, which is a mixed blessing. The National Geographic Society's *Birds of North America* is very sound and sober (and I'm proud to say I contributed to the text). So pay your money and take your choice; if you get bitten by the birding bug you'll soon own all these and more anyway.

Don't even think about rare species at first. Every bird will seem a rarity to a novice, and there are enough common birds to keep even an experienced newcomer to the beach busy for a weekend or a summer. After that there are enough occasionals, exotic migrants, strays and stragglers to keep a committed birder alert for the balance of a lifetime.

Something else to ignore at the outset: every juvenal. Whether born blind and naked or precocial (active) and downy, a young bird soon takes on adolescent plumage that differs from its adult dress as diapers differ from dinner jackets. For its first winter many a bird acquires new body feathers but retains its juvenal wing and tail plumage. The bald eagle doesn't get its characteristic white head until its fourth year. Most of the many gulls look more like their contemporary cousins than their parents until their third year and are very hard to tell apart. Start with their elders.

The Gulls

From season to season and year to year, these are the most constantly visible coastal birds. (Some wander inland; Franklin's gull is a freshwater bird of the prairies: no matter.) The dominant local species in any habitat from Chekovian drama to Chilmark, Massachusetts, is called, simply, "seagull." Local folk can often tell nothing more about it than a city man can describe nesting habits of *Columba livia*. As common on a beach as those pigeons are in a park, adult gulls have webbed feet, short tails that spread like fans and white plumage except for the mantle and head. (The term "mantle" refers to the top of the wings from tip to tip and the section of back in between.) Not highly specialized, gulls are strong fliers, good walkers and able swimmers. Diving from the air, they catch some food live but find their real bread and butter as scavengers. Without them every beach would be a shambles of dead fish, dead birds and assorted trash—more so than they are today. Gulls eat carrion, garbage, birds' eggs (including their own kin's sometimes), crabs, mollusks, an occasional starfish and their cousins when they can't get anything else.

At times they seem a most cunningly industrious lot. One early November morning on a Virginia barrier island I watched a flock of herring gulls catch Cancer crabs from a falling tide as neatly as embassy wives picking stuffed mushrooms from a chafing dish. Flying into the wind several feet above the water off a point where bay and ocean meet, a gull would stall, belly flop onto the water, stab its head beneath the surface and come up with a little crab. The gulls rarely missed. Each one would come up with a crab almost every time but would often drop it immediately and grab it again. Sometimes a bird would juggle the same crab like a too-hot hors d'oeuvre three or four times before getting it from behind, to avoid the pincers. Then the gull would fly to the beach and prepare the meal. Watching through binoculars and later examining the remains, I saw that the gulls dropped each 2-inch crab on its back on the hard, damp sand and pecked two or three times to kill it. Then the gull would peck the bottom shell away and pick the crab quite clean before flying out again. Gulls came and went for an hour; only about a dozen worked the shoal at any one time, crabbing with deliberate concentration but not haste. Surprisingly, there was little thievery among them.

When gulls go clamming in Maine the spectacle resembles a cross between aerial ballet and fruit-stand robbery. Working the shore at low tide, a gull will pick up a clam, fly above a rock ledge or pavement and drop the quarry to crack its shell. The problem is to fly high enough so that the clam cracks on impact, but low enough to reach the morsel before another gull steals it. For as sure as God let greed govern Wall Street, when one seagull works the shore, two more will try to rob him blind. Some individuals don't seem to hunt their own clams but specialize in soaring around nearby, then darting like pirates amid much screaming and flutter to swipe others' food. Others seem to toss a clam up just as they turn to dive in order to reach the ground barely an instant after the clam. On Nantucket I saw a juvenile cautiously go through a routine while other gulls looked on idly—the young bird was dropping his clam on pebbles, not rock, so it never broke. Evidently sensing something wrong, the gull then moved off a little way to try another surface for its anvil—and dropped the clam onto a wave, which swallowed it. On Nauset Beach I once watched a great black-backed juvenile drop its quarry again and again without the slightest harassment from old gulls; the object wasn't a quahog, but a clam-sized bit of lumber. We all live and learn. (Gulls aren't the only birds that drop hardshelled goods to get the food inside. According to a respected ornithological text, Pliny wrote that Aeschylus departed this life when a buzzard "mistook the poet's bald head for a rock and dropped a turtle on it.")

To distinguish the common gulls, look for the following characteristics:

- The great black-backed gull is biggest. It has a white head, white chest and black mantle.
- The herring gull, almost as big as the black-back, also has a white head and chest. But its mantle is gray. There is a red spot on the bill. The legs are pink.
- The ring-billed gull is slightly smaller than its almost look-alike cousin, the herring gull. It also has a gray mantle, white head and chest. But the spot on its bill is large and black. The legs are yellow.
- The laughing gull, the smallest common gull on this coast, has a black head (in summer) and dark gray mantle. In winter it loses the black cap for slight mottling.

Half a century ago Arthur Cleveland Bent, businessman by trade and ornithological essayist by choice, published a remarkable encyclopedia under the colophon of the Government Printing Office. Now reissued by Dover, the multivolume *Life Histories of North American Birds* is the King James Version of bird books. The nomenclature and some data (such as ranges and migration schedules) are understandably dated, but it remains a useful source seasoned with elegant verbosity. Bent never met a bird he didn't like. Witness the great black-backed gull (*Larus marinus*), which has now extended its range down to the mid-Atlantic coast at the great expense of smaller birds. Quoth Bent:

1. Ring-billed gull; 2. Herring gull; 3. Great black-backed gull

While cruising along the bleak and barren coasts of southern
Labrador I learned to know and admire this magnificent gull, as
we saw it sailing on its powerful wings high above the desolate
crags and rocky inlets of that forbidding shore, its chosen summer home. Its resemblance to the bald eagle was striking, as it
soared aloft and wheeled in great circles, showing its broad
black back and wings in sharp contrast with its snow-white head
and tail, glistening in the sunlight. It surely seemed to be a king
among the gulls, a merciless tyrant over its fellows, the largest
and strongest of its tribe. No weaker gull dared to intrude upon
its feudal domain; the islet it had chosen for its summer home
was deserted and shunned by other less aggressive waterfowl,
for no other nest was safe about the castle of this robber baron,
only the eider duck being strong enough to defend its young.

Perhaps the eider suffered the big gull's presence because it
suited its own purposes. Most gulls are alarmists, the great black-
backed not least of all, and raucously announce the appearance of
possible predators, particularly man. In Labrador people used to
fatten this species for table use, and eggs of all the Laridae were
pirated as breakfast food.

Nesting on remote coasts, *L. marinus* remains a handsome
bird, predatory or haughty depending on its mood. It frequently
permits the company of herring gulls but is much warier of people
than its smaller companions.

The herring gull (*Larus argentatus*) is the popular prototype of
East Coast seagulls, a most vociferous and prolific bird. It is also
remarkably communal. Along the crannied coast of Maine, for example, experiments show that the herring gulls effectively patrol
entire stretches of shore—though only one may be visible from any
single cove. If a particle of food appears, the solitary gull will snatch
it. But discovering a large supply, whether a garbage truck, a school
of herring or an ornithologist testing a hypothesis with a bagful of
fish, the gull never keeps it secret. It flies a telltale pattern and
issues a loud call. Other herring gulls posted out of sight from the
cove but alert to their neighbors' behavior join the feast. In turn,
still more distant gulls see and hear the second wave depart and
also respond.

The two common smaller gulls along our coast are the ring-
billed gull (*L. delawarensis*) and the laughing gull (*L. atricilla*).
The ring-billed looks much like the herring gull but is smaller and

has yellow legs and a spot that seems to circle both the upper and lower bill. A scavenger like nearly all members of the family, it also forages for live food along the wet beach and flies inland to farms, where it follows plows for unearthed worms and grubs.

The laughing gull, which exhibits the most distinctive seasonal change of plumage, wears a black breeding cap in summer but sheds it in fall. This is the bird that follows the ferries between the Outer Banks islands begging for food. A regular vacationer may wonder what's transpired if he returns in winter when these gulls' heads have turned nearly white. It is an agile flier and a successful colonist whose range is expanding.

In his landmark animal-behavior text, *The Herring Gull's World,* ethologist Niko Tinbergen detailed many of the subleties of avian life, as well as some things not so subtle, such as a male gull's nuptial gift. Herring gulls exhibit programmed behavior to a fare-thee-well. One individual's gesture, posture or action—termed a releaser—triggers a specific action by an interacting bird. Consequently a breeding colony of gulls (or terns) is a frenzy of endless counterpoint. Certainly the seasons initiate some internal changes; the lengthening sunlight of spring days stimulates a bird's pituitary gland to secrete hormones that trigger the breeding urge.

The first result is departure for traditional nesting areas—not

Laughing gulls in winter plumage (left) and black summer hood

just latitudes, mind you, but the place where the gull was hatched. Though they winter in loose flocks of individuals—not couples— "herring gulls seem to pair for life," Tinbergen writes, and they reestablish old bonds en route to the nesting grounds again. Once at the rookery, the males establish territories, which they defend from other gulls. Often a ritual display is enough. Threatened on its own ground, a resident strikes a threatening pose, whether the uninvited guest is male or female. Another male usually takes the hint and leaves or else fighting ensues. A female turns her head away in a characteristic, acquiescent posture. Thus the resident male's single act prompts different reactions and those reactions, in turn, provoke different new reactions. Whether the intruder is male or female, a series of point-counterpoint transactions occur before either violent fighting or mating. Some of the exchanges involve only physical posture; others are vocal. Recent investigators have shown that gulls use distinct sounds to communicate various messages—a consistent, cogent vocabulary.

If the newcomer is female, things come to a head when the male walks off a few yards and makes nest-building motions in the sand. She responds with begging signs and sounds. The male seems to try to avoid her solicitations . . . yet he does not walk away. After a while the male's neck swells, the swelling travels upwards, then he opens his beak widely and . . . evidently with some exertion regurgitates an enormous quantity of half-digested food. As soon as the male opens his bill the female frantically pecks into his mouth and begins to swallow the food with incredible greediness. [*Chacun à son goût.*] Copulation is highly choreographed and a little awkward since it requires contact between each bird's cloaca, the alimentary/reproductive vent beneath the tail. To make a long story short, the birds toss their heads and take a few steps around each other. The male utters

a rhythmic, hoarse call. Immediately afterwards he jumps on his mate's back, waving his wings and settling down on his tarsi on her shoulders. His feet rest on the female's upper arm, which the toes are holding in their grip. The female continues and intensifies the head tossing, touching the male's breast every time, and even rubbing her bill against his breast. The male, uttering the copulation call all the while, lowers his tail until it touches her tail, then makes a series of sideways rubbing movements and finally brings his tail down at the side of the raised tail of the female, and, waving his wings to keep his balance, brings his cloaca into contact with hers. This is repeated a number of times. Thereupon the male stops calling, folds his wings and jumps down at the side of the female. There is no postcoition display, but usually the birds begin to preen after a while.

This description of avian coupling seems to pretty well apply to most birds except in matters of detail. The differences between species' behavior in all reproductive matters from early courtship to chick-rearing involve fastidious detail. Some gulls copulate for several minutes on the commodious beach. Great blue herons mate on branches or in their treetop nests and take only seconds to conclude this most important business.

The herring gull's nuptial regurgitation may have evolved because it symbolically anticipates later parental behavior. (By the same token, premature nest-scraping motions evoke the possibility of making a nest together. The convention seems to be: "Look what I can do when the time is ripe.") Gulls feed their young regurgitated food. The parent approaches the nest and leans its bill in reach of the chicks. Experiments have shown that the characteristic spot on the bill serves as a releaser for a hungry chick. The chick pecks at the spot and the pecking prompts the parent to disgorge a meal. A chick that doesn't peck hard enough—an experimentally placed chick of a weaker species, for example—doesn't get fed and starves. A chick presented with the wrong kind of spot may not peck at all, but just thrash and cry feebly until it starves.

The Terns (Sterninae)

Terns are the more graceful black-capped white birds of the summer coast. "Sea swallows," as they're often called because of their darting ways and usually forked tails, are more specialized than their stockier gull cousins. They fish for live prey, often close to the surf line. Flying parallel to the shore, they adjust their altitude so that a plunging dive will carry them as deep as the minnows are swimming. (They don't swim in pursuit like loons.) Head pointing down like a granny wearing half-glasses, a tern hovers, folds its wings and plunges sometimes completely underwater to grab a fish with its sharp bill. Body buoyancy brings it to the surface again. Some terns hunt cooperatively in flocks, each one in turn diving into a minnow school, say, from the left side of the group, then flying up to the right side and waiting its turn again. But ornithologists use the term "cooperation" uncomfortably; it may just be that members of a flock maneuver for the best position, which is downwind of the schooling fish. After a bird has caught a fish, it has little choice but to take an unfavorable upwind position and jockey for a better one.

To distinguish the four terns commonly seen along Atlantic beaches look for these characteristics:

- The Caspian tern, nearly as large as a herring gull, is the biggest of the lot. It has a red bill and a slightly forked tail.
- The royal tern, almost as large as the Caspian, has an orange bill and a noticeably forked tail.
- The common tern, still smaller, has an orange bill with a black tip and a deeply forked tail.
- The least tern, understandably the smallest of them all, has a yellow bill and legs. Its tail is quite broad.

Particularly lively, the common tern (*Sterna hirundo*) has a complicated courtship ritual that begins more than a month before actual nesting. It involves first tentative, then extended, visits to the traditional rookery, and flights in which a male carrying a fish is accompanied by a partner or series of partners, not all of them necessarily female. Finally after several trial runs, a male with fish in his bill settles down on his territory and makes nest-scraping motions with his breast. When a potential partner or hungry male approaches, the territorial male pecks. At that point another male would peck back or retreat; a female keeps approaching and utters a characteristic begging call. Soon the male presents the fish to her; she plays with it and offers it back. They'll pass the fish back and fourth several times until it's in tatters. Then they fly off together. One will fish and feed the other; then they'll exchange roles and fly ritual patterns. Usually these nuptial rites precede actual breeding by more than a week. It's worth noting, however, that these terns will delay the first courtship stages if the weather's wrong or if the nesting area is still wet from spring rains.

In a particularly dense rookery the nests may be only 12 inches apart and territorial disputes are common. There is inevitable fighting and some birds are killed. Yet settled birds may defend an absent neighbor's nest against unknown terns. There are three eggs in the normal clutch, but incubation doesn't start until all are laid. The eggs hatch together, as do the eggs of a number of inland birds whose unhatched young have been shown to peep at each other before pipping and breaking out of their eggs simultaneously.

Common terns prefer sites with some grass, since the young learn to seek its shade when the parents are away fishing. The precocial chicks quickly learn to recognize their parents and, as soon as the chicks can fly, they watch for the parents to return with food and fly up to meet them. Later the chicks accompany the adults and watch while they fish, waiting on a nearby rock or piling to be fed.

When predators approach a nesting ground, the adult terns attack in concert, defecating and striking intruders on the head in flights of two or three at a time. There are old accounts of ornithologists repeatedly having their pith helmets pierced or, more recently, their baseball caps torn.

The largest of the lot, the Caspian tern (*Sterna caspia*) is also the least communal and the most predatory. It fishes alone, nests in small groups or with ring-billed gulls and often robs the nests of other birds. This tern breeds in Canada and winters only as far north as the Carolinas, but it frequents the coasts between its summer and winter homes when migrating.

The crested tern with the orange bill is the royal (*Sterna maxina*), which nests in colonies so dense that the brooding birds are within pecking distance of each other. Very choosy, they seem to have several inflexible requirements for a breeding ground: complete absence of mammalian predators (including man, as usual); general inaccessibility and good visibility; extensive shallows nearby and proximity to an ocean inlet. Hence they colonize remote islands, including new dredge-spoil banks. They habitually nest so close to the high-tide mark that entire colonies are sometimes inundated by storm tides. Unlike some terns, they regularly defecate on their nests until the uniformly dense, round colony takes on a "whitewashed" appearance. This waste material hardens the nests' rims so that they withstand some minor flooding.

Rarely does a pair of royals lay more than one egg in a clutch. If it is destroyed or stolen, they'll lay again later in the season. Throughout the incubation period and during early brooding, roy-

als will abandon their nests at the sight of a predator. They'll flee
from gulls, which then invade the colony and break eggs at leisure,
returning to eat the contents later. After the chicks are a few days
old, however, the adults will attack intruders en masse and "dive-
bomb." The precocial chicks assemble in a "crèche" almost as soon
as they can walk and they stay together. When threatened by man
or dog, raccoon or other predator, the group scurries away, usually
into the water until the danger passes.

The littlest tern, formally called the least (*Sterna albifrons*),
has also flown under the alias of killing peter, little striker and
kill-em polly. It has a yellow bill, gray wings and a white forehead
patch beneath its black cap. Less fastidious than its cousins, it nests
on less remote beaches where it is far more accessible to people.
Before the turn of the century, when least terns sold for a dime
apiece to the millinery trade, this bravado nearly resulted in the
species' extinction. The bird then made a strong comeback, but it
now seems on the decline again.

Among its notable habits, the least tern will dive in the ocean,
return wet to the nest and sprinkle the eggs with water on particularly hot summer days. When a young bird is fledged it accompanies a parent to the feeding grounds and gets fed there by the
solicitous adult. Bent's *Life Histories* includes this almost unspeakably charming report from a contemporary, Edward H. Forbush:

> Near me were two little young, just hatched and their down
> hardly dry, yet they were able to run about a little. Nearby were
> several other youngsters. As I lay there propped up on my el-
> bows, awaiting the return of the mother bird, several of them
> flitted back and forth. . . . Soon the mother of the two nearest little
> ones alighted, and, running to her charges, settled easily upon
> them, shading them from the hot sun's rays. Then she turned her
> gaze upward and called softly in reply to the tender notes of the
> male, which circled overhead. Soon he alighted and took the
> mother's place in shading the young, while she flew away, per-
> haps to fish and bathe. Soon she returned with a little sand eel,
> which she gave to one of the tiny ones, who ran to her for it. Then
> she flew again, descended into the sea and returned to her charges
> which the male relinquished to her care. She stood over them
> with ruffled feathers, and seemed to shake off some drops of water
> on their little panting forms, then raised her wings a trifle to
> shade them from the hot sun. . . . Again the gentle twittering,

and the father came down on the sand with a tiny, bright, silvery fish. A little one stuck its head out between the mother's wing and her body, the father courteously passed the fish to the mother, and she fed the chick, which begged for it with open mouth. Again the breadwinner winged his way over the sunny sea and returned with another fish. Now the little ones were asleep under the mother's breast. He offered her the fish. She refused it. He flew away, but soon alighted and proffered it again, only to be refused again. At last, having full assurance that his family did not need food, he swallowed it himself. Where shall we look to find a lovelier picture of happy, harmonious family relations than that shown here on this desolate beach, beside the roaring surf?"

The account is useful for the actual observations of actions and behavior. Take the anthropomorphic assumptions with a grain of salt, however. How did Mr. Forbush tell the adult male from the female? Nobody else can, except during courtship and breeding.

The *"Shorebirds"*

Laridae aside, several other closely related families populate the beach; the taxonomy becomes too esoteric to be generally interesting. There are the Charadriidae (plovers and turnstones), the Scolopacidae (sandpipers and their allies), then separate families respectively for the oyster catchers and the skimmers. The following selection includes just a handful of the scores of birds that casual beach visitors see and serious birders recognize at a glance. The list includes the obvious birds—the ones that stand out clearly—as well as some other very common ones that mass in perplexingly mixed flocks.

Black-bellied Plover (*Pluvialis squatarola*)

An arctic breeder like many shorebirds, this black-and-white-mottled bird migrates spring and fall along the coast and often winters as far north as Virginia. About as large as a quail, in summer plumage it has a black front and face topped with white, which hangs to the shoulders like an English judge's wig. The back and wings are mottled in the standing bird. In flight a black patch

1. Common terns standing and flying; 2. Least tern standing; 3. Royal tern standing; and 4. Caspian tern calling

appears under the wing. The rump is white. These latter field signs are good all year round. In winter the bird is mottled brown-and-white above and all white below.

The wary black-belly eats quantities of berries, insects and aquatic animals including mollusks, crustaceans, fishes and small lizards. It nests in scratched-out hollows on the tundra where both adults incubate a normal clutch of four eggs. In our latitudes it's most often seen with willets, curlews and its close relative the golden plover. (*P. dominica*, a smaller bird, has nearly the same profile but its mottling is brown and black.) "The black-belly is a strong flier," writes Bent. "In time of storm it sometimes seems to be the only bird aloft." With the great skua and arctic tern it's said to be "one of the most far-flung birds on earth."

Ruddy Turnstone (*Arenaria interpres*)

One of the best-named shorebirds, the ruddy turnstone eats by turning stones and shells over with its bill and snapping up whatever's beneath: worms, mollusks, crabs. (In case it's escaped anyone's attention, our feathered friends of the littoral are ferocious carnivores.) If it encounters a likely obstacle too big to handle alone, it may cooperate with another of its kind and the two will work together. Also, the turnstone will occasionally dig a hole deeper than itself in pursuit of burrowing food.

Like a majority of the look-alike sandpipers, *A. interpres* is about half the size of the clan's largest cousin, the willet. But the turnstone has a most distinctive look. White-bellied in all seasons, it has an irregular white wig in summer and a splotchy reddish-and-black back. (In winter its folded wings take on a more regularly mottled look and its head darkens.) Roger Tory Peterson describes its in-flight breeding plumage as a "harlequin pattern," a striking design of russet, black, and white. One immutable field mark is the "calico bird's" unusual bill, which is thick at the base and tapers like an asymmetrical wedge, turning up slightly toward the tip.

The turnstone arrives at its Arctic breeding grounds in late May. It will nest in exposed tundra or under bushes, lining a shallow hollow with dry leaves and grass. If its four-egg clutch is destroyed, a breeding pair will not replace it. Both parents brood the eggs. When they hatch, the female departs toward the wintering grounds beyond Virginia. The males leave a fortnight later and the juveniles last of all. The following spring yearlings migrate northward but stop in groups far short of the nesting grounds. I've seen them along the Massachusetts coast in midsummer.

Aside from turning stones on the beach, this bird explores seaweeds for small animals, probes into rock crevices, robs gull and tern nests, and feasts on flies and maggots found on sea mammal corpses that wash ashore. This latter habit can be dangerous; these birds have been known to get serious food poisoning from carrion bacteria as a result.

Semipalmated Plover (*Charadrius semipalmatus*)

More colorfully called the ringnecked plover, this bird has several look-alikes. The most famous, which prefers dry lands to the seashore, is the larger killdeer. (*C. vociferus* is notable for feigning a broken wing and limping in helpless frenzy when an enemy approaches its nest.) The ringneck, as its name implies, has a single dark-colored band like a collar. The killdeer has a double collar; the rarer Wilson's plover has a very broad collar and dark bill, while the smaller piping plover (called the "feeble") has a very narrow collar. Now to ice the cake of cogeneric complications: The ringed plover, which breeds no closer than Baffin Island and winters in the Old World, matches the ringnecked plover except for its unwebbed feet. "Semipalmated" means possessing partly webbed toes.

This busy bird flies fast in large flocks that twist and turn in unison. Breeding on beaches in the Maritimes and in Canadian tundra, it winters along the coast below Connecticut. Like many of its relatives, the ringnecked plover works the swash in spurts, running several steps, stopping, and bobbing its entire body as it probes the wet sand for worms, small mollusks and tiny crustaceans.

Willet (*Catoptrophorus semipalmatus*)

There is something of Cinderella—or the Frog Prince—in this lanky sandpiper. Pacing the swash and bobbing its head, probing for worms and snatching little fish, it is decidedly drab—a pauper in an old brown tweed coat who used to be called "humility." But when it flies, this wary vocalist flashes beautiful wings, each one bearing a broad white chevron. The marks seem to combine to form the bird's initial, a W, across its 30-inch wingspan.

In flight, the willet frequently sings one of the brightest one-note songs in the avian repertory. The *Audubon Field Guide* describes it as "will-will-willet"; the *Golden Field Guide* as "pill-will-willet"; the same syllables are used by Peterson, who writes its alternate call as "kip-kip-kip." But the Audubon book notes this latter call as "kuk-kuk-kuk-kuk-kuk." A. C. Bent jots the music down as "wek, wek, wek, or kerwek, kerwek, kerwek, varied to piuk, piuk, piuk. . . . Less frequently another note is heard which sounds like beat it, beat it." All this simply suggests the absurdity of trying to write bird calls in English.

Willet

This handsome, flighty bird nests in open areas along the coast from Chesapeake Bay northward. Parents and brood may abandon the nest on the day the eggs all hatch. One willet has been seen carrying its young one by one across a creek from the nest to hide them in high grass. Seemingly solicitous parents, the adults briefly escort the chicks around to feeding grounds but typically abandon them before they can fly. For a willet this is normal behavior; the species thrives sufficiently that the migrating birds sometimes pass in flocks of thousands.

Sanderling (*Calidris alba*)

Weighing in at between two and three ounces, the sanderling is one of the larger "peeps," a word properly applied to the small sandpipers but widely used for any of the smaller shorebirds. What this character lacks in size it makes up for in numbers and sheer energy. Ralph S. Palmer writes authoritatively in the handsome *Shore Birds of North America:* "In a mixed gathering of peeps, those constantly in a great hurry are sanderlings." The *Audubon Guide* authors say, "Practically every day of the year these birds can be found on any ocean beach." Tireless and cosmopolitan, they earnestly play a kind of tag with the broken waves as they run up and down the foreshore snaring small invertebrates. They're particularly noticeable in winter when they're sometimes the only birds in sight, their reddish and brown upper plumage gone a pale gray above their white breasts and bellies. In flight these little birds flash broad, bright white wing stripes. Their bills and legs are dark, nearly black.

Leaving nonbreeders behind in the lower latitudes, sander-lings nest in the high Arctic where they subsist on buds and berries until the appearance of fly larvae in the ponds. The breeding display begins with the small male vibrating his wings and flying steeply up, then singing on his downward flight. On the ground he puffs out his feathers, lowers his wings and makes nest scrapes in the barren ground. When the eggs are laid, the male rarely takes a turn on the nest during the twenty-three-day incubation period. One parent attends the hatched chicks but both leave before the young fly at the age of two weeks.

This bird looks a great deal like the least and semipalmated sandpipers; its larger size is diagnostic. It's about as big as a starling and was once shot in great numbers by market gunners.

Dunlin (*Calidris alpina*)

A starling-sized sandpiper with a long down-curved bill, the dunlin "gives the appearance of having ballast too far forward," according to one expert. But appearances mislead; this bird has been clocked by a plane at 110 miles an hour.

Dunlins are often seen on beaches as far north as Long Island in winter, when their upper plumage is a dull gray above a pale belly. It is also known as the red-backed sandpiper, a name that is descriptive only in summer (given that any shorebird's red is an earthy tone). Like least sandpipers, these unwary birds don't flee a human until closely approached, though a mob of them will harass intruders on their nesting grounds.

Semipalmated Sandpiper (*Calidris pusilla*)

The most numerous shorebird, the semipalmated sandpiper is a little larger than the least sandpiper, which it closely resembles. When comparison isn't possible, the best field sign is its dark legs. A snatcher and prober, it uses its stubby bill more haphazardly than most peeps, poking into soft sand or mud for insects and larvae. Another Arctic breeder that migrates along the coast, it winters from the southeast United States to Paraguay.

The semipalm nests in the Arctic where one of Bent's correspondents observed:

The parents made no effort to feed the young. It was soon seen, however, that such care was not necessary. The young would stumble about and pick up minute gnats and flies with great dexterity, and the shallow algae-rimmed pools furnished them many a juicy "wriggler." The gait of the young sandpipers was a stumbling toddle, while their large feet and legs were all out of proportion to the rest of their slender bodies. By dropping and extending their wings they were able to use them as crutches, which often kept them from falling.

Bent observed that they were fully fledged about a month after hatching and flew south at the age of five weeks.

Least Sandpiper (*Calidris minutilla*)

The littlest shorebird is the least sandpiper, also known as "ox eyes." It is seen most often along marshy mud flats, though it frequents the beach when fresh water freezes. The least sandpiper's flying weight is less than an ounce. Similar in appearance to other peeps, it stands out by virtue of its yellow legs and lilliputian stature. The size of the literature describing this littoral sparrow approximates its own size.

Preparing to breed in tundra bogs, the male faces a stiff breeze for its territorial nesting display. The male does most of the incubating over the four-egg clutch, but little is known about its brooding habits. It winters along the Outer Banks and southward.

Osprey (*Pandion haliaetus*)

Though rare peregrine falcons hunt the barrier island chains in fall, the raptor most often seen along the shore is the fish hawk or osprey. This bird is a wonder when it cruises the shoreline perhaps 150 feet aloft, its 5-foot wings bent at the "wrist" and held motionless as it glides, eyeing the shallows for food.

Like all the falcon clan, ospreys have exceedingly keen eyes. When an osprey sights prey—it lives on fish exclusively—it folds its wings and dives, then breaks the fall with wings spread and feet forward to grab with its talons. Sometimes submerging, it struggles from the water and flies off carrying the prey torpedo fashion. (Sometimes it is mobbed and robbed by several gulls or a solitary eagle.) The osprey's feet are remarkable. With lumpy, scaled soles, a hind toe that can clasp prey from either side and sharp curled talons, they can grasp the slipperiest fish.

In their way, ospreys are friendly to man. New England farmers used to build nesting platforms in order to attract them. The reason: A mated osprey pair won't tolerate other hawks anywhere near or above their nest but will fly up and defend a large territory, keeping the whole neighborhood free from other raptors. And since the osprey eats only fish, a farmer's chickens were not threatened when a fish hawk nested near the barnyard, while chicken-stealing hawks were kept at bay. Furthermore, ospreys suffer man gladly, given the right sorts of platforms to serve as nests: telephone poles on the Outer Banks, navigation buoys along the Inland Waterway, wagon wheels in trees on Yankee farms or hulks of grounded boats around the Eastern Shore. On Martha's Vineyard their preferred nest sites are poles erected by Augustus Ben David, boss of the Massachusetts Audubon Society's Felix Neck Wildlife Sanctuary. Ben David has been planting these poles for years, and the Vineyard has an exceptionally healthy osprey population as a result, along with generations of summer people whose favorite neighbors are the same osprey family year after year.

These birds exhibit some human virtues, so to speak: After wintering alone, an osprey seeks last year's mate—and the same nest site—as long as both live. If the old nest is gone, they'll build another; if an old mate doesn't return, the survivor seeks another. (If the survivor is the male, he and his new mate get the old nest.) Adolescent ospreys even set up "housekeeping" together by tending a nest and going through all the motions short of laying eggs. When mature birds lay eggs, they may share incubation duties, though brooding the chicks falls to the female exclusively. The male (typically the smaller of the pair) spends much time fishing, often flying an established route morning and evening and bringing his catch back to the nest.

American Oystercatcher (*Haematopus palliatus*)

An oystercatcher on the beach stands out more than a circus clown at a Quaker meeting. This is the bird in the tuxedo with pink feet and a red nose. Its wings are black (with a white chevron in flight). Its shirtfront is white up to the neck. The face and head are black, the eyes have orange pupils and, yes, the feet are pink, sometimes red. But even Cyrano de Bergerac had no nose compared with the oystercatcher's, which is long, straight and bright red. This bird carries itself oddly afoot, as if it were too barrel-chested to stand up straight. Its flight seems surprisingly fast for such an ungainly posture.

Haematopus palliatus is almost well named in English because it eats bivalves, although it doesn't actually catch them. Inspecting a mudflat at an odd pace between a strut and a toddle, the oystercatcher searches for shellfish with their valves ajar in a falling tide. Finding one, it stabs inside with a sharp stroke of the chisel bill. The most popular explanation is that the bird instantly snips an adductor muscle, leaving its prey powerless to clam up. But the bill's end is blunt; it may be that the bird simply stuns the animal.

Audubon said oystercatchers nested as far north as Labrador in his day. Gunners nearly wiped them out along much of the coast but they've recovered as far north as Massachusetts today. They stay far from human settlements—even from individual walkers—and are only seen in quite wild coastal places. Though they winter in large groups (as far north as North Carolina), they scatter in breeding season, each pair preferring a certain solitude. The nests are simple scrapes on a stone ledge, pebble slope or sandy rise with good visibility in all directions. I've rarely seen an oystercatcher alone in summer. Usually they travel in pairs, sometimes quartets. Spot one and you'll soon see another.

Aside from bivalves, oystercatchers also eat small snails and oddities like the purple sea urchin, which they turn upside-down and devour without breaking its fragile shell.

Black Skimmer (*Rynchops niger*)

"You are what you eat," the saying goes. But the black skimmer is what it is because of *how* it eats. *Rynchops niger* is the bird with the enormous underbite. The lower bill grows faster than the upper and is longer by about one-third in the adult bird. Further, the lower bill has compressed sides; it's as thin as a knife blade and has a straight, rather sharp upper edge. This fits into a slight groove in the upper bill.

Towards dusk the black skimmer flies low across calm waters

with the tip of its lower bill cutting through the water. Then it
loops back and flies the opposite course. Scientists guessed that the
skimmer stabbed the surface of the water as it passed, then returned along the line of bubbles snatching up whatever small fish
had been drawn to the disturbance. While it sometimes feeds like
this, another technique is constantly involved. The black skimmer
often catches fish on its first pass even in muddy water, and evidently it fishes at night as well. In fact, it fishes blind. Leading
with its chin, it cuts through the water until it strikes
something—a log, a minnow or anything else. Without missing a
wing beat the bird snaps its head down and pointing aft, it lets go
of a stick or grabs living prey; then it brings its head forward
again. Hence this bird has found a special niche—catching food it
cannot see.

The black skimmer nests in large colonies on open beaches as
far north as Massachusetts. It winters along the Outer Banks and
further south. This is a black-winged and black-capped bird with
white face and underparts and red legs. The base of the unmistakable bill is red, which shades into black towards the tip.

Masters of the Marsh

The way to most beaches crosses marshland and the first remarkable creatures to be seen are the herons—outstanding birds
that look eccentric and deserve mention because of their marvelous
visibility from the Beach Road. They are waders, stalkers and waiters with long stilty legs and, usually, sinuous necks. Notably designed to suit their habitat, they live by catching quick prey from
the shallow waters: fishes, crabs, amphibians, small reptiles and
mammals. Some cunningly shake their toes in the mud to stir dinner out of hiding; the reddish egret spreads its wings in a canopy to
shade the murky water. At rest, with the head nestled between the
shoulders, or alertly standing in wait for a passing meal, or moving
slowly in pursuit, they seem most royally graceful birds. But darting their sharp bills atop those unlikely necks they're invisibly fast.
In size and manner they range from the incomparably shy least
bittern to the ostentatious great blue heron, which is too big to
hide. Standing 4 feet tall, it greets intruders with a loud squawk
and, preferring to be alone, imperiously flies away.

Their common names tend to be self-explanatory, though sometimes so complex that shorter monikers might apply. A sensible kid I know realized that one fisher didn't need a name with four elements that were hard to keep in order. So Jonathan dubbed the black-crowned night heron, unforgettably and suitably, "fat bird." I've heard the cattle egret called "bugger" for its eating habits. (This Old World species, a white bird with tan breast and crown, spread to the shoulder of South America and thence to Florida four decades ago. It has now colonized much of the East, where it's found in lowlands following livestock and eating the insects they stir up.) The snowy egret, a lovely little white bird with black legs and yellow feet, is simply a "snowy," the glossy ibis with its down-curved bill a "glossy." Some eminences, however, never get public nicknames by virtue of their dignity or our respect for them: Oliver Wendell Holmes, Martin Luther King or Great Blue Heron.

Driftwords: Sandy the Bear

Let us now praise Uncle Sam and the seashores he bequeathed to us.

Time was when wild and natural bits of coastline dotted the Atlantic seaboard. I remember walking great lengths of Atlantic shore as a boy without a by-your-leave from anybody. But that was a long time ago. Since then the coast has become increasingly restricted, largely as a result of protective private interests. For one thing, the popularity and relative scarcity of coastal property sent prices through the roof. I've heard locals from the Outer Banks to Maine gossip variously in awe, anger and envy that outsiders have paid cash on the counter when buying waterfront lots for high six-figure sums. Drug money? The fruits of S&L mismanagement? The wages of Wall Street? Who's to say—except that the selling-off and building-up of the beach is variously vulgar, short-sighted, wasteful, ecologically dangerous and fundamentally stupid.

More and more stretches of coast now seem to be inaccessible by virtue of having become built upon, fenced or surrounded by private property. Yet I hate to think how the scene would look if a few heroes had not come along. In this instance—and it's a surprise to see these words roll from my platen—let's hear it for Government! The National Park Service, U.S. Fish and Wildlife Service and various state and local agencies have kept stretches of beach open to all.

Of course their management—especially the Park Service, tends to be bureaucratic to a fare-thee-well with too much red tape by half. Their rules tend to be pecksniffian—aimed at protecting, directing and perhaps restricting the most ignorant and clumsiest folk who happen by. But by and large the people employed by these agencies are hard-working professionals who have a genuine interest in the natural world and some real expertise. Seek them out, you'll learn something. Besides, without these agencies and their personnel, I fear the beach from Canada to Carolina would have all gone to condos.

So next time you're in the neighborhood, stop at one of the national or state beaches that boasts a bit of wilderness. There's not much threat of forest fire along the shore, so you might miss Smokey Bear. Just ask for Sandy, and thank her.

CHAPTER FIVE

Pothead whales—stranded and dying

Snakes and Whales, Among Other Things

No mammal or reptile lives full-time on the Atlantic beach between low tide and the dunes; but many visit there to feed, and some come to die. Tending to be variously shy, solitary or pelagic, the live animals themselves are seen less often than their tracks and remains. An encounter is likely to be tinged with fear, delight, sadness or awe, Nonetheless, there's a wide variety of so-called "higher animals," from the great whales and porpoises playing beyond the surf of Hatteras, to the tiny, timid rodents that ply the Delaware beach grass by night and the family of carnivorous mammals that left a Maine beach when I arrived one summer dawn. (There were three sets of fresh tracks—one adult and two juvenile— along the swash of a rising tide and two Cancer crabs neatly pulled limb from limb. Mink or ermine perhaps?) Rarely there are sea turtles; more commonly that absurd actor, the hognose snake, and the dexterous, resourceful raccoon.

In evolutionary terms all the reptiles, birds and mammals have something in common: an ancestor that branched off from the diversifying fishes to become a primitive amphibian some 350 million years ago. We all spring from the same ancient branch on the tree of life. Phylogeny aside, here's a sampler.

Tidal Reptiles

The hognose snake (*Heterodon platyrhinos*) belongs to the wide-ranging family Colubridae, which includes more than half the 2,700 species of snakes in the world. Neither poisonous nor particularly graceful, this serpent comes in a variety of colors: gray, black or reddish brown. The best field mark is an upturned nose with which it digs for toads, insects, moles and the like. I've seen this snake resting in the swash zone—waiting for little crustaceans, perhaps? Because of a slight similarity to the copperhead, this harmless reptile is often killed by Sunday-afternoon outdoorsmen. A better habit when seeing a snake is to study it from a little distance; the one with the ski-jump snout is a docile hognose. The one with a spade-shaped head and vertical pupils is a pit viper. Leave it alone.

The hognose is one of nature's great fakers—more dedicated to histrionics than even the possum, whose famous game of playing dead may be a kind of catatonic state that occurs when the slow-witted marsupial is frightened out of its wits. Threatened, a hognose snake first puts on an impressive fuss, pretending it's a fearsome creature. Hissing and rearing back, this bluffer broadens the flesh behind its head into a cobralike hood and feigns repeated strikes—though it lacks both dangerous fangs and venom. If an intruder isn't cowed by the performance, the hognose falls over and plays dead, rolling onto its back. Determined to put on a convincing act, if turned right side up it'll roll over again to strike another moribund pose as an encore.

The adult female lays from six to more than forty thin-skinned eggs in soft earth and may coil around them, like a cold-blooded reptilian incubator. Laid in early summer, the eggs hatch six to eight weeks later. Hognose snakes live in open woods, fields and sandy regions. They're the most commonly seen snake on the outer beach, but by no means an everyday visitor.

The cottonmouth moccasin, found no farther north than Back Bay in southernmost Virginia, is the most dangerous of the lot. Related to the rattlesnakes and copperheads, water moccasins are pit vipers, so named for the visible pits behind the nostrils, which are diagnostic of the family Crotalidae. Wildlife authority Roger Caras calls the cottonmouth the third most lethal snake in the United States after the eastern and western diamondback rattlers. But keep in mind that many more Americans die of bee stings than snakebites. Cape Hatteras National Seashore, the most popular area boasting cottonmouth, hasn't had a fatal biting in recent years.

The cottonmouth (*Agkistrodon piscivorus*) may grow 6 feet long, though the average is about half that size. It is brown with indistinct black bands; its yellow belly may have dark markings as well, and a dark band runs from the eye to the corner of the mouth. It is distinguished from nonpoisonous water snakes by its deep, spade-shaped head, light lips and white mouth. A good swimmer, the cottonmouth lives beside marshes on the bay sides of southern barrier islands. Its diet includes frogs, other amphibians and fishes. The young are brightly marked with reddish brown. Between five and fifteen are born live after a year-long gestation.

The Loggerhead's Lesson

A rarity worth looking for despite the odds, the loggerhead sea turtle is born on the beach, leaves as soon as possible, and returns only to breed. Pelagic and wide-ranging, *Caretta caretta* wanders the Atlantic at a speed of about a mile an hour, feeding on mollusks, crustaceans, a few plants and quantities of jellyfish—including the Portuguese man-of-war. Though this dietary staple is 99 percent water, the loggerhead can grow to a length of 9 feet and a weight of 850 pounds. Once numerous, along with four relatives, the loggerhead owes its declining numbers to man—not only man the predator but man the accidental and continuing intruder. The phenomenon has some important implications that deserve attention.

When a pregnant female clambers ashore, she seems quite finicky about choosing a place above the high-tide line to lay her eggs. Finding a suitable spot, she digs a shallow depression in the dry sand, then claws out a hole within the hole with her hind flippers and drops as many as 150 round, leathery eggs into it. To complete her ninety-minute task, she covers the whole nest with sand and beats a hasty retreat to the water. She may mate again immediately in shallow water, then go her largely solitary way.

In one to three months the eggs hatch en masse and the young all leave the nest simultaneously. Emerging through the sand, they head straight for the water—even if their view is blocked by a dune or ridge of sand. Their sea-seeking technique remained a mystery for millennia; people just assumed they smelled the water or heard the surf. These seemed the most likely explanations, but modern research proved an unexpected factor plays a key role. Newly hatched loggerheads seek an unbroken horizon and distinguish the brighter sky over the ocean from the darker sky above land. This cunning device sufficed admirably under natural circumstances, and the species survived without its young developing real defenses against larger carnivores. The large number of hatchlings gave a few in each lot a fair chance to successfully run the gantlet across the beach. Despite land crabs on the shore, carnivorous fish waiting in the water and the macabre spectacle of feasting birds described by Tennessee Williams in *Suddenly Last Summer*, the turtles carried on. Instinct made scores of newly hatched siblings scurry from the hidden nest as fast as their legs could carry them; a highly evolved and subtle sense showed them the direction to flee across exposed sands to the safer water. But man changed the odds, both intentionally and by accident.

For centuries, buried turtle eggs were gathered as human food. Adult turtles were taken by hungry men for their meat as well. The hawksbill turtle, a member of the loggerhead's biological family, was hunted for the scales that were seared from its back to make tortoiseshell ornaments. In time, fortunately for the turtles, American landsmen found easier ways to feed themselves and rim their spectacles. But while our habits changed, our accidental influence did not. First, human settlement drove the puma away from the Atlantic coast. With the demise of this big cat, raccoons multiplied in a wild environment free from natural enemies and became major thieves of turtle eggs. Then the belated discovery of how young loggerheads find their way to sea revealed another of man's unintended intrusions into the natural scheme of things.

Hatchlings head for the brightest light; the subtle difference between the sky over land and the sky over reflective water is eclipsed by electric power. The halo of a city beyond a landward horizon attracts young turtles at night, which would naturally be the safest time for them to emerge. So does a stream of headlights along a coastal highway, or a few beach walkers carrying flashlights. Quite simply, any human development or presence can lengthen the odds against a few hatchlings reaching the relative safety of the sea. The lights we need lead them astray. As a result, the once-thousand-mile range of breeding beaches along the Atlantic coast has shrunk drastically. A few southern islands are all that remain. The northernmost place they still breed spontaneously with regularity is Cape Hatteras, where hatchings have increased in recent years.

Even the short-term loss of a specific beach can permanently affect an entire species because turtles don't gather indiscriminately off any coast. Adults return to the beach where they were hatched. Authorities have tried to induce loggerheads to return to Assateague Island, which straddles the Virginia-Maryland border, but the results are not encouraging. Eggs were imported from farther south and allowed to mature in raccoon-proof containers. Some hatched successfully, but few females have returned to nest in succeeding years. In decades of beach browsing I've only encountered four sea turtles: a 300-pounder on a lower Chesapeake Bay beach, another about the same size on Assateague and a hatchling behind a barrier dune a few miles north. All were dead. The fourth—possibly a sea turtle and most likely a loggerhead—was certainly alive when I saw it far out at sea. Sailing from Bermuda to the West Indies, I was at the sloop's helm late one calm night when something appeared in the water. It was only a glowing shape, bigger than a medicine ball but not as round, that rose to hover a foot below the surface of the ocean, then sank out of sight as we passed. If it was a loggerhead covered with phosphorescent growth, it would have had a pronounced beak, at least five scales along each side of its shell and an inability to completely retract its head. (Perhaps because it can't retreat entirely inside its shell, the reddish-brown loggerhead is vicious if molested.)

The other members of the family Chelonidae tend to be smaller than this one seemed. The green turtle (*Chelonia mydas*), which is brown, takes its common name from the color of its fat. It grows to 4 feet and has been known to range as far north as Massachusetts.

The female of this species evidently mates only every three years but makes up for the hiatus by laying as many as six clutches of eggs in her breeding year. The hawksbill (*Eretmochelys imbricata*) grows to 3 feet and has overlappig scales. The gray-shelled ridley (*Lepidochelys kempi*) grows to 2½ feet and has five scales along each side of its shell like the loggerhead. (The other two have four.) The leatherback (*Dermochelys coriacea*) belongs to another family and is the only sea turtle with an unplated leathery shell. The sole surviving member of a distinct biological suborder—and a giant that grows to 1,200 pounds—it is rarely seen.

However inevitable it may seem, the continued decline of these ancient creatures is deplorable. If we need a simple reason to hope for their return, just remember that they eat the Portuguese man-of-war. The larger reasons are ineffable.

A Promiscuous Pest

In 1613 John Smith noted: "There is a beast they [the Indians] call Aroughcun, much like a badger but useth to live in trees." A century later, a Tidewater Virginia colonist wrote home to England about the same animal: "If taken young [it] is easily made tame but is the drunkenest creature living if he can get any liquor that is sweet and strong." This gentleman said his wild drinking buddy caught crabs cleverly, though whether drunk or sober isn't clear (and, truth to tell, I've never seen this behavior hinted at elsewhere, though it makes a nice story). The animal reportedly backed up to a tidal creek and dipped its luxuriant tail in the brackish water. When a crab bit, the crabber leapt inland, grabbed it with quick hands, tore off the claws and ate at leisure.

Now alarmingly familiar, the raccoon has prehensile digits, with which it eats. This is only one of its anthropomorphic traits. *Procyon lotor* is one of North America's great opportunists. It has taken great advantage of the recent absence of natural predators like the puma. With its own numbers largely unchecked, it has become a pest that does more serious damage than raiding campsites and robbing garbage cans. The recent decline in coon hunting as a sport has also undoubtedly contributed to the increase of this cunning animal, whose intelligence rivals that of many monkeys.

Inquisitive, adaptable and omnivorous, in recent years the raccoon has invaded many cities to feast on any kind of leftovers it can steal from people, except onions. Wildlife biologists say the only real remaining check on its numbers is a form of distemper that flares up and thins out the population every few years.

Common throughout the continent (except in the tundra and high mountain regions), the raccoon prefers to nest in hollow trees. It regularly visits every beach within foraging distance of a forest. Largely nocturnal, an adult raccoon unencumbered by young will use several nests and visit several feeding sites each night. Evidently it looks for new sources of food while making regular rounds of a wild (or settled) neighborhood. The notion that the raccoon always washes his food is a myth; many live in deserts. Given a choice, however, it seems to prefer aquatic animals and actively hunts crayfish, minnows, mollusks and crabs. A few raccoons have reportedly been found trapped by large oysters after an unmovable bivalve closed its shell on a coon's paw and the hunter couldn't escape an incoming tide.

Raccoons use their hands in surprising ways—even to block out unpleasant reality. (If the use of the term "hand" seems inappropriate, examine a coon's tracks.) Driving along a wild October beach at dusk with a skilled naturalist, I spotted a small raccoon poking around the swash. We cornered the animal in the dunes and he put up a game fight, even lying on his back to bring his hind feet into the clawing action. The naturalist tossed a hat at him and caught the varmint with bare hands to examine him. When the little coon realized he was captured, he surrendered abruptly, issued a few piteous mews, closed his eyes and covered them with his paws in a parody of melodramatic human fright. Released again, he ran swiftly inland. (A full-grown raccoon may weigh thirty pounds. Despite my naturalist friend's example, even a little one shouldn't be trifled with. Armed with sharp claws and fierce teeth, this wild animal is a ferocious fighter that can disembowel a hound.)

Promiscuous and fecund, raccoons first mate in late winter and bear litters averaging four cubs after a two-month gestation period. The mother, who may mate three times a season and live a dozen years, might produce a gross of offspring, which she raises and trains alone. The boars are solitary.

Whales & Company

The truly marine mammals are animals to wonder at. Intelligent, even apparently articulate, these warm-blooded creatures live in an environment man can only visit. Some wag once remarked that their ancestors must have had better foresight than ours: Having gone to all the evolutionary trouble of colonizing the land, they looked around and returned to the sustaining sea, while our antecedents stayed ashore that we might delight in things like war, gasoline engines and the Big Mac.

We've been acquainted with whales, inside and out, since Jonah's time, but we never got to know them intimately. One of the ironies lies in the fact that, while the study of marine mammals has mushroomed along with the other natural sciences, we've been hard-pressed to learn substantially more about them, in part because there are fewer whales to study. Of ninety-two species, a dozen are on the verge of extinction or worse. The cause of their demise and the extent of our knowledge combine in another irony: For centuries man observed whales in order to kill them. Some of the best de facto treatises on their biology and behavior were written in the cabins of whaling ships during the nineteenth century.

Nonetheless, many of the marine mammals' habits have been studied for their own sake—as opposed to the whalers'—in recent years. A few have been explained. Some will never be because their possessors have been exterminated so that people could continue to have cheap sources of things like mink-farm food, watchmaker's oil, bicycle saddles and brushless shaving cream! Americans no longer participate in the slaughter, though other nations continue. Was it excusable a century ago when folks "didn't know any better?" In his still useful treatise "On Cetology" in *Moby Dick*, Herman Melville noted c. 1851 that the right whale was hunted as a source of "the oil specifically known as 'whale oil,' an inferior article in commerce." Farley Mowat, author of the extraordinary lyrical tragedy *A Whale for the Killing*, summed up the modern obscenity: "As I became older the whale became a symbol of the ultimate secrets which have not yet been revealed to us by the other animals. Whenever anything came to hand about whales I read it avidly; but the only thing which seemed to emerge . . . was that the whales appeared to be doomed by human greed to disappear and carry those secrets with them into oblivion."

People like James G. Mead, curator of marine mammals at the Smithsonian, are doing what they can to stem this tide and to learn what can still be learned. Knowledge is where one finds it; in the case of whales, dolphins and porpoises the place is often a beach where these animals become stranded and die. Anyone who encounters such an unhappy spectacle can help science get some good from it by doing a couple of things. First, says Mead, take photographs while the animal is still in reasonably good condition. Include something of known length in each frame like a yardstick or more likely a fishing rod, to establish an ascertainable scale. Second, send word to some appropriate authority: the National Park Service (if they hold sway at that beach), the Fish and Wildlife Service or Mead's Marine Mammal Event Network at the National Museum of Natural History in Washington, D.C. (202-357-1923).

Given our limited and slowly expanding knowledge, what is a whale (for the time being)? By biological definition, it is a member of the order Cetacea, a cetacean. One suborder (Odontoceti) comprises the toothed whales, including the sperm whale (*Physeter catodon*, e.g. Moby Dick), the narwhal (*Monodon monoceros*) whose single tusk in the male perhaps inspired myths of the fabulous unicorn and the true dolphins and porpoises. A second suborder (Mysticeti) includes the baleen whales, those enormous filter feeders whose curious mouth parts strain tons of plankton, small crustaceans and fish from ocean water.

The earliest sea mammals returned to the oceans from land on the order of fifty to sixty-five million years B.P., long enough ago to have found ways to use the density of the aquatic medium to their advantage. For one thing, they telecommunicate, speaking across— or rather through—hundreds of miles of water in some cases. For another, they evolved into the largest animals to ever live, since the water itself would support living bulk too ponderous to carry on land. The largest dinosaur, a swamp inhabitant and vegetarian, approached 70 feet in length. Three whale species just about match or exceed that dimension alone. The 100-foot blue whale weighs about four times as much as any brontosaurus ever did. (The largest on record was a female measuring 106 feet and weighing 150 tons.) But it may be that the blue, one of the baleen whales, is about to become as extinct as the dinosaur. Reduced from perhaps 300,000 to an estimated population of 9,000 and largely confined to the Antarctic, this once cosmopolitan species' numbers may have diminished beyond the point of no return.

If living in water had advantages, it also presented severe problems which these air-breathers solved with remarkable evolutionary inventiveness. The nostrils moved to the top of the head so a whale could respire without standing on its tail. The bronchial tree developed cartilaginous arches (like the human windpipe) down to the smallest branches to facilitate fast breathing. A whale can empty its lungs and inhale 500 gallons of fresh air in two seconds. These speeds and quantities are responsible for the larger whales' visible spouts, which differ from species to species. Air compressed in the lungs expands and its moisture content condenses when released.

At first the ancestral whales must have been content to inhabit surface waters. But over time they contrived ways to plumb the depths and reap the benefits of vast new food supplies. The sperm whale, which feeds almost exclusively on giant squid, can dive at least 3,000 feet. (Some have tangled with transoceanic telephone cables at that depth and drowned.) The physiological engineering needed to enable such dives is extraordinary. Blood supplies to muscle tissues are reduced in deep water in order to conserve oxygen for the brain and vital organs. In addition, something had to be done to prevent "the bends." If a large-lunged animal like a human diver rises too fast from oceanic depths, changes in pressure cause formation of nitrogen bubbles in the blood with crippling or fatal results. The diving whales got around the problem by reducing the relative size of their lungs by 90 percent and storing oxygen in muscle tissues. Their flesh contains the same oxygen-binding component as our red blood cells. To increase hydrodynamic efficiency, they shed their body hair. To cope with cold they grew layers of insulating blubber, which also provides a reserve supply of metabolic food. Their circulatory systems became arranged so that cold blood returns to the heart in vessels surrounding and being warmed by the arteries. To conserve a whale mother's internal water supply, whale milk came to have the consistency of cottage cheese. This milk, which is pumped out by muscle contractions, has four times the fat content of primate milk. Thus the infant has a high-calorie diet, but not a very moist one. How do the young avoid dehydration? Metabolic breakdown of fats creates large amounts of water as a byproduct.

The physiological marvels go on and on. Yet one of the most startling facts is that these mammals exhibit some of man's best traits: affection, loyalty and humor. They direct these emotions not only to others of their own kind but to us as well, despite what our species has done to them. Since it is understandably difficult to observe these animals closely in the wild, much of the most carefully documented behavioral data has been collected in aquaria and marine parks where several of the smaller whales thrive. But whales' charity to man has been seen at sea as well. There are reliable accounts of dolphins driving away sharks (their own natural enemies) from human swimmers, even of helping a floundering person stay afloat and reach shore. In controlled environments analogous behavior is clearly seen in the way common and bottlenosed dolphins treat their young. All cetaceans are born tailfirst and a newborn dolphin that doesn't spontaneously thrash to the surface to breathe is helped—nudged up—by the mother or an accompanying "midwife." The companion female will swim with the new mother for as long as three months, frequently in formation, with one adult protecting the young calf on either side. Active assistance of another individual is not simply maternal behavior; dolphins will also surround an injured adult and physically help it reach the surface to breathe.

These animals talk back and forth in high-pitched whistles that clearly communicate information. They can also mimic human speech, which must seem to them a slow and monotonous language since they can make and hear sounds from 150 to 150,000 cycles per second, well beyond human hearing, indeed beyond the aural ken of everything but bats. It addition, they navigate with another kind of sound, a form of biological sonar, emitting as many as 400 curious, highly directional clicks a second and reading the echoes for precise information about what's ahead—food fish in particular.

It goes without saying that of the many cetaceans, only a few are seen from the Atlantic beach. The following are the most common.

Porpoise v. Dolphin

Generally speaking, porpoises have blunt noses and stubby bodies, while dolphins have long noses and slender bodies.

The harbor, or common, porpoise is no exception. *Phocoena phocoena* reaches 6 feet in length and a weight of 120 pounds. Not one of the notably playful cetaceans, it doesn't often jump or gambol around boats, although it does enter rivers and come close to the New England shore in summer, searching for bottom fishes and schools of herring, menhaden and mackerel. Generally dark gray or greenish brown, this porpoise has an almost triangular dorsal fin with a sloping rear edge rather than a deep curve.

These porpoises travel in pairs or groups of up to 150 and mate in late spring. The young, born eleven months later, are half their mothers' length.

In contrast, the common dolphin (*Delphinus delphis*) often leaps from the water and plays in the bow waves of boats. Its taller dorsal fin has a curved trailing edge. Also called the saddleback, Delphinus has a black back, white belly and distinctive crisscross pattern along the sides. The snout is slender. A wide-ranging animal, it is the topic of some taxonomic controversy that revolves around a simple question: Do slightly different characteristics represent distinct species, subspecies or races of the same species? At the moment the consensus leans toward including them all in one species, but of course this division is subject to taxonomic change.

Along the East Coast the common dolphin is most often seen not far from the Gulf Stream, which in some years meanders quite close to the Outer Banks and Massachusetts' outer islands. The adult may measure more than 8 feet from the tip of its nose to the cleft of its flukes.

The closely related bottlenose dolphin (*Tursiops truncatus*) is lighter colored and larger, growing to 12 feet. Blue-gray above and lighter below, it shows no distinct pattern along the flanks. "Flipper" of television fame was one of this breed. In captivity juvenile males engage in rather lively masturbatory activity. They direct their affections at "almost anything that moves, from fish to turtles to other dolphins,"—even to qualified mammalogists swimming in the same tank.

The pothead, blackfish, or pilot whale was hunted unmercifully for meat and blubber. Thoreau saw them stampeded by fishermen into the shallows along Cape Cod in the 1840s. The question remains why they came near shore in the first place, since these are deepwater denizens. Today their occasional mass strandings are still unexplained. For a while it was suspected that ear parasites damaged their sonar so that they failed to pick up the changing echoes of a gently sloping mud bottom. But later research disproved this notion. In *Globicephala melaena* ear mites are "common as fleas on a dog." Even the healthiest animals have them, or so it now appears. Since they've rarely encountered a stable physical obstacle in water, Dr. Mead believes "they're unaware the ocean has sides." The reasons a bull leads his herd ashore remains known only to him.

Solid black except for a white belly mark between the flippers, the pothead or pilot whale has a globular forehead as round as an antique iron kettle. The sloping dorsal fin, much wider at its base than at the top, has a deeply curved trailing edge. At birth the pilot whale is 5 feet long. Females mature at about six years, males at about twelve. They grow to 28 feet on a diet of squid, small fish and invertebrates. Some authorities believe they live twenty-five years; others estimate a life-span twice that long.

Call Me Orca

The killer whale does not deserve its wretched reputation. Were it a car, a toothpaste or a movie star, someone would simply announce a rechristening and it would soar in popular esteem. *Orcinus orca* grows to a robust 30 feet of hydrodynamic power; it may be the fastest animal in the sea. Sheathed in an ebony-black skin highlighted by a dashing patch of white behind each eye and a white belly, this noble wolf of the oceans boasts the tallest dorsal fin of all the proud cetaceans. (Get the idea?)

Certainly orca is a killer, but so's a kitty cat when it gets the chance. Like wolves, African lions and primitive men, these whales hunt strategically in packs to bring down prey that a single individual couldn't handle. A group will even vanquish the largest baleen whales. Unlike sharks and the highly regarded blue-fish, they are not known for wanton killing. Nor is there any documented account of their having attacked a human swimmer. In captivity (where they're well fed), they accept training and peaceably share a tank with dolphins which they'd hunt in the wild.

Killer whales hunt other warm-blooded creatures—not only other cetaceans, but seals and birds. In the higher altitudes, orca will rear out of the water to snatch prey from an ice floe. This takes not only what we consider ferocity, but great agility and sophisticated sight as well. Consider one example: From a whale's underwater viewpoint, the apparent position of a penguin on a ledge is skewed by the water's refraction, yet this carnivore compensates for the distortion to grasp its quarry.

Killer whales are often seen in large groups, notably at the northern and southern extremes of the Atlantic coast. The sharp, straight-edged dorsal fin, almost the shape of a dunce cap in profile, is unmistakable.

Little is known about orca's reproductive cycle. Recent investigations suggest that these whales engage in episodic homosexual activity. Young males are escorted away from the rest of the herd and apparently "raped" by older bulls. This zoologically rare behavior may be a form of training or a way to establish dominance within a social group.

Great Whales

The fin, or finback, whale (*Balaenoptera physalus*), also called the common rorqual, is sometimes seen off our coast. "Rorqual," used to describe all whales with throat grooves, comes from a Scandinavian word for tube; when finbacks were butchered, the throat skin looked like a sliced row of hollow cylinders. Grooved or tubed, the throat skin functions like an accordion's folds. Swimming through great swarms of small fish such as herring or shrimplike crustaceans called krill, the whale takes hundreds of gallons of water in its mouth, expanding its throat in the process. With the mouth closed, its two-ton tongue squeezes the water out through the baleen plates that hang in thick fringes inside the lips. The krill are trapped inside the baleen and swallowed. When not expanded for feeding, the throat skin returns to its pleated appearance.

The fin whale's lips are not symmetrically colored. The lower left jaw is gray, the lower right white. The left side of the tongue is not pigmented, the right is. This whale may be 70 feet long. On a calm day its spout may rise 20 feet straight into the air.

The humpback (*Megaptera novaeangliae*) is another rorqual that sometimes appears off the beach. Averaging less than 50 feet, it has very long white flippers and many irregular lumps on its head, snout and flippers. The most acrobatic of the great whales, it often jumps out of the water and rolls on the surface. Its spout is described as "low and bushy."

The 50-foot right whale is another filter feeder but not a rorqual since it lacks the pleated throat. It has a very bulbous lower jaw. While its near relatives have small dorsal fins, *Eubalaena glacialis* has none. This was once one of the very common cetaceans, but now only a few hundred remain in the Atlantic because it was "the right whale to hunt" for its blubber—hence its common name. Those that survive migrate close to shore early each year, appearing off Florida in January or February, arriving off Cape Cod in April and summering north of the Gulf of Maine. Evidently they return south farther from shore, for they are seldom seen making fall migrations.

Often the right whale's spout is almost invisible, because when this whale swims along the surface it breathes every minute or two; thus it doesn't compress vast quantities of air in the lungs to form condensation clouds when released.

Gregarious Seasonals

The most common mammal of the coast is a ubiquitous seasonal migrant found in huge numbers, sometimes hundreds of thousands, crowding a few miles of sand from dune line to surf zone. Growing as long as 2 meters, it exhibits a range of coloring from pale pink or whelk-foot beige to a brown as dark as the nut clam. Sexual dimorphism is the rule, the larger males tending toward hirsute bodies with glabrous heads, while the reverse is found among females. Individuals of either gender may have rich, hairy growths on the head and lesser pelage on the four extremities. The female possesses two mammary glands above the abdomen for suckling her young like a cetacean. External genitalia may not be apparent due to the coverings the species acquires, much as the spider crab camouflages its carapace with algae. Whether this trait is of defensive or predatory origin has not been determined. It may have a sexual function.

Behavior is as erratic as individual morphology, which ranges from acutely slender to the rotundity of sea lions. Terrestrial air breathers, many of these creatures gambol in shallow waters, apparently in forms of play, like otters. Others are lethargic for entire diurnal periods, though they wake to feed more frequently than the walrus. Sexual and pseudosexual behavior patterns have yet to be satisfactorily explained. Breeding habits are so complex as to defy simple categorization. For example, some pairs seem monogamous, while coupling among others appears almost random after brief courtship rituals. There is no correlation between copulation and seasonal, meteorological or temporal conditions, though mating commonly occurs at night. Despite their enormous numbers and reportedly frequent coupling, actual monozygous reproduction rates suggest high sterility. Sexual activity among individuals of the same gender occurs in highly localized sites. As many as 4,000 males have been observed massing on summer nights along one mile-long stretch of inner dune on Fire Island and engaging in inevitably fruitless behavior. (There is no satisfactory biological explanation for this activity, which is rare elsewhere in the natural world except among a few marine mammals such as orca and dolphins.)

Their senses are not acute. Being poor swimmers and lacking swift mobility even on land, they seem to survive by virtue of their large numbers, omnivorous habits and dominating presence. As architects, the species exhibits a degree of activity surpassed only by some ants and African termites. Outside our range, some of their structures last for millennia, though nests and habitations along the Atlantic coast rarely survive more than a few decades and often less than a year. The detritus of their building activity—and of their seasonal appearance—is enormous. In small numbers their affects on the habitat are negligible. When they mass locally, however, they must be regarded as highly pestiferous. In large numbers they totally dominate a locality, decimating vegetation and driving away other animal species much as the great black-backed will exclude other gulls from a New England cove. They also extirpate prey species—birds, crustaceans, fishes, even other large mammals. While some scattered individuals may be seen along the beach in winter, most appear during warm weather. *Homo sapiens* is an evolutionary oddity, the only extant member of its genus.

Driftwords: A Most Instructive Fish

Tomorrow is the equinox. Tonight will be longer than the day, and I am closer to the end of this writing than the beginning. Worse, I'm drowning in information. Natural systems become imponderable in their infinite combinations. Data swarm like schools of fish, finding elusive safety in their very numbers, which is why small prey species swarm—so that individuals can elude predators. Some days I feel like a red-tailed hawk who can't zero in on a single sparrow in the flock. So he rests a while and is mobbed by passerines. One at a time I might capture every concept, but they're flying at me in flocks: Pheromones. Hypothalamus functions. Ecdysis. Rhizome regeneration. Decapod population dynamics. Percolation rates of sand. Elegant questions like "Are There Any Obligate Halophytes?" Crude ones like "Which taxonomist is right about the mollusks?"

The work becomes mesmerizing in its distractions; the information so diverse there can be no order. I search for similes to describe why I surrender more often every week—then every day—to the notion that there can be no simple explanations, but the metaphors themselves fail. I want something as elegant as the cycle E. B. White perceived on his Maine farm: "The worm fattens on the apple, the young goose fattens on the wormy fruit, the man fattens on the young goose, the worm awaits the man." But life along the littoral isn't that tidy.

The interactions of marine systems are insensibly complex. Consider the unspeakably extended food chains. They work this way: Microscopic plants (phytoplankton) make living matter out of inorganic material. (That's the textbook definition of a plant, after all, and the inherent talent that distinguishes plant from animal. Plants make food; animals must eat organic stuff to live.) Little fishes eat the plankton, a slightly larger fish eats the fry and is eaten by a bigger fish in turn, which becomes dinner for a tuna or an osprey. When that predator dies, it is eaten by maggots and carrion birds that defecate into the sea, returning a few wet particles to the water. They sink, decompose, break down into inorganic components at last, then well up with a current of cold water to be absorbed by phytoplankton again. And so it goes. Cyclical? Not really. There are cycles, of course, but the system depends more on vegetative manufacture of new organic matter from inorganic minerals—a form of creativity fueled by the sun's energy. Yet this all requires so many intermediate steps that it becomes vague as it stretches out.

Yesterday, more out of duty than anything else, I read about an incomparably drab fish. Everybody's heard of the menhaden; nobody cares. Too oily to eat and too numerous to have any more heroic appeal than lemmings, menhaden are like dust motes on the Yellow Brick Road of marine science. They seem like something to be washed away by tank trucks filled from fire hydrants while a city sleeps. Beneath contempt, too common to spark interest. Sure, because they are so numerous that a hundred drab industries depend on them for everything from paint to pet food. I couldn't have cared less as I took *Fishes of the Gulf of Maine* from the shelf. The book is one of those exhaustive catalogs that tells absolutely everything known (pro tem) about something. Information for the record. Boring facts aligned like cobblestones. Tedious data laid brick upon brick in a Chinese wall of information. Has a scientist said "Eureka!" since Archimedes' day? I yawned and read till the library closed. The epiphany came after dinner; a jot of knowledge emerged like a scarlet butterfly from the cocoon built by a brown worm, like an iridescent scarab out of the dung (a critter the ancients considered holy because it seemed to spontaneously create itself out of manure).

Bigelow and Schroeder noted that no other local fish

has a filtering apparatus comparable to that of the pogy, nor has it any rival in the Gulf in its utilization of the planktonic vegetable pasture. Menhaden feed . . . by swimming with the mouth open and the gill openings spread. We have often seen specimens in the aquarium at Woods Hole doing this. And we have watched small ones in Chesapeake Bay, swimming downward as they feed, then turning upward to break the surface with their snouts, still with open mouths. The mouth and pharyngeal sieve act exactly as a tow net, retaining whatever is large enough to enmesh, with no voluntary selection of particular plankton units. The prey thus captured (as appears from the stomach contents) includes small annelid worms, various minute Crustacea, schizopod and decapod larvae, and rotifers, but these are greatly outnumbered as a rule by the sundry unicellular plants, particularly diatoms. . . . And the food eaten at a general locality parallels the general plankton content of the water, except that none of the larger animals appear in the stomachs of the fish on the one hand, nor the very smallest organisms . . . on the other. The menhaden, in short, parallels the whalebone [baleen] whales, the basking shark, and the giant devil rays in its mode of feeding, except that its diet is finer because its filter is closer meshed.

The menhaden filters phytoplankton from six quarts of seawater a minute. This is their only food. Straining the sea with their gills, they live on the most elementary plants. In a year a menhaden grows to 6 inches. It lives and manages to multiply because each school is too enormous to be obliterated by marauding predators, whether other fish or man. In turn the menhaden is fodder for every predator fish in the sea that deigns to snap at it: cod, haddock, tuna. When the rapacious bluefish massacre the menhaden, far more of the little fish are killed wantonly than eaten. They become carrion, food for both "higher" animals and lower ones—gulls, beach fleas, sand crabs—and fertilizer for beach plants staking out temporary turf at the spring tide line.

But their living tissues are only a step away from being inorganic matter! Some of the stuff that is a menhaden today lay at the bottom of the ocean floor last night as particles of sodium, phosphorus, magnesium and the rest. A minute plant absorbed these molecules and used solar energy to convert them into living vegetation. Menhaden ate these plants, metabolically converting them into fat and muscle before they themselves became the food for bigger fishes like the crazy blues, for birds like gulls, terns and ospreys, for foraging mammals like coons along the beach, even for man's stinking factories. Chemicals naturally became meat. (Eureka?) Here was a food chain small enough to grasp. The drab menhaden—a fish numerous enough to feed a multitude without a miracle—is the missing link, the single connector between an alpha and omega.

Doesn't something else eat plankton too? Of course. It's the nutritional wherewithal of every filter feeder, the bivalves in particular: mussels, scallops, and clams, which are eaten by snails, starfish and a thousand fin fishes. Go further. Zooplankton and shrimplike krill eat the tiny plants; baleen whales eat the krill in millions—a blue whale eats four tons a day. Now there's a noble link, a nexus of true grandeur, from inorganic molecule to Mysticeti in three easy steps. I love it. It lets me grasp. With the simple examples in hand I could compound it. Phytoplankton feed zooplankton; krill feed the whale. A larval crab, a barnacle or a sea clam eats a diatom. A moon snail eats the clam, a starfish eats the snail, a lobster eats the starfish and a cod eats the lobster. As a kid I was dosed with cod liver oil and must have needed it because it tasted good. Phytoplankton fed me! And still do. Tomorrow I'll celebrate with a lobster, thanks to plankton and the sun.

PART TWO

The Physical Beach

Before the beach became a fertile habitat for countless birds, clams, crabs, insects, fish, worms, amphibians, reptiles and more (and before it became a place for mammals including man to visit) it had first to become—well, a beach. The geological processes that made it began eons ago and, abetted by evolutionary botany, show no signs of stopping. This place, ancient and perpetual, continues to change. Enchanted, man has tried to arrest the beach, to settle here and alter it for his convenience. Yet it continues to grow and change to suit itself. It always will.

CHAPTER SIX

Glacier's legacy: a New England cove

$E = 41\ H^2T^2$
—Littorally Speaking

Serene as it may seem on a calm day, the physical beach is bewil-
deringly complex. The forces that made it—and constantly remake
it—vary from glacially deliberate to quick as spindrift. Barrier islands may grow and shrink imperceptibly for millennia, then vanish
during a single storm. Sand spits can lengthen for centuries or
appear overnight. The time frame and geographic range of the
dynamic Atlantic coast are enormous, yet all change depends on the
individual movements of infinitesimal sand grains. And therein lies
the secret to understanding the physical aspects of beaches. Things

happen grain by single grain or one wave at a time. Each process is simple—even commonsensical—but the combined results are staggering because waves keep coming ashore endlessly, and each one picks up or deposits infinite numbers of particles. What changes the face of the shore (and what boggles the mind) are the progressions of events, the interactions of diverse forces, the geometrically compounded results of many phenomena. Considered singly they are easy enough to understand.

The bottom line is plain: Every beach changes constantly, even those that appear the same on each visit. Every wave brings sand with it and carries some away. If the amounts are about equal over a day's time, or a decade's, the beach looks no different. In fact it is not the same beach, just, as Buddha said, a river appears the same but is different hour by hour. Composed of a most incohesive material, a beach moves minutely; it grows or shrinks with every ripple and tide. Some accrete and erode in an annual cycle; others build out or recede for decades at a stretch. Some, destroyed in a single hurricane, reappear again by spring or emerge somewhere else.

A reporter for the *Vineyard Gazette* tells this perplexing tale. To the nineteenth-century entrepreneurs who bought it, Skiff's Island, off the southeast corner of Martha's Vineyard, seemed a lovely place for a Victorian resort. They returned with a high-priced architect the following spring for a site inspection, but they couldn't find the place. It was gone. Years later it emerged again and lingered to become a traditional turning point in an annual sailing race that was won year after year by the same yachtsman. When a challenger finished first one year, the cup defender cried foul; the first boat had cut a corner and sailed inside that mark. "What mark?" the newcomer asked. The island had sunk again.

That's the way with things made of sand; they come and go. But left to their own devices, an Ivory-soap percentage of the world's sand beaches take care of themselves quite nicely, thank you, for generation after human generation. They are made, unmade and remade by three things: wind, water and sand.

Since earth's adolescence, wind and rain have eroded the mountains, creating broken rock, boulders, gravel and sand—especially incalculable amounts of the latter. By definition sand is bits of inert material ranging in diameter from .0625 to 2 millimeters, or from the size of a pin point to that of a pencil lead. We think of erosion as a negative process: It makes a coast retreat; it steals a farmer's topsoil; it makes molehills out of mountains. But erosion is also creative; sand is its end product, the raw material of beaches. As the mountains were worn down by wind and rain, the smaller stuff they became was washed downhill. Rivers continue to deliver sand into the oceans today, and the ocean water continues delivering sand to the rims of islands and continents.

The material of most North American beaches is 90 percent quartz, a major component of granite, visibly earth's most plentiful rock. Many trace elements and varying amounts of gemstones, such as garnet and topaz, are found on any beach. There are also heavy minerals, like ilmenite and magnetite, an iron ore especially plentiful on Block Island's Crescent Beach, which was mined in colonial times for material to blot manuscript ink. When strong winds scour a beach, the lighter stuff is blown away and the heavy particles remain. Crescent Beach can turn so black that newcomers suspect an oil spill. Parts of Fire Island turn nearly blood red in winter, when only heavy grains of garnet compose the surface. Broken shell is another common ingredient of littoral sand. Many beaches below the Outer Banks are composed mostly of the crumbled exoskeletons of marine animals. On St. Croix in the Virgin Islands, a short stretch is made entirely of tiny, intact seashells the size of a baby's fingernails.

Since some sand is created in the ocean from shingle or gravel—grist for the ceaseless marine mill—it might seem that all sand is on its way to becoming powder. This is not the case. When each grain becomes a critical small size, it collects a film of water. This wet cushion keeps it from touching other grains and disintegrating more. (The fact that sand grains don't touch uniformly, like a brick wall, has another marvelous result. Spaces between the grains constitute an aquatic habitat for the meiofauna, a multitude of microscopic animals. Too inconspicuous to be included here, they stand on the bottom of a certain zoological pecking order—the predator food chain—since they are the smallest prey animals of the beach.)

In deep water, below the reach of surface wave energy, some sand lies still. But anywhere water moves—whether in terrestrial streams or at sea in response to tides, currents and some waves— sand moves as well. This brings up the matter of "competence," or the inherent ability of water to transport solid stuff. It is one fundamental mechanism responsible for the beach. The amount of transported material depends on the size and density of particles and on the speed of the moving water. Slight currents transport silt, the stuff that by definition is smaller than sand; a two-and-one-half-knot current moves inch-round stones. When a given volume of water moves fast, it picks up more material (and bigger particles); when the same current slows down for any reason, it drops some of its solid burden. Coastal waves carrying sand from an offshore bar lose their competence, when they break upon a beach, they drop the sand that builds up the shore. When stronger storm waves run up a beach, their water swashes back fast enough and in sufficient amounts to carry sand away. Then the shore retreats. (Rocky beaches seem more stable than one made of fine sand. In part this is because it takes more water moving faster to move stones; it's also a function of percolation. More water sinks through the surface of a beach made of big particles. The finer the sand, the slower the percolation rate and the more water runs along the surface slope to carry anything present away.) This, simplistically, is how the edge of a beach comes and goes. (The upper beach responds to another medium, to be covered later.) Entire beaches, one expert writes without fear of contradiction, are "the most dynamic systems of the physical landscape."

The variables of water volume, water speed and particle size account for the way huge boulders remain in place in the surf off Martha's Vineyard and for the way a weeping actress's mascara smudges her cheek. Some objects are just too big to be moved by waves, so Vineyard settlers could use offshore boulders to mark their farm boundaries. Old photographs of Gay Head prove that some rocks have remained in place at least since the last century. It bears remembering, however, that the ocean periodically displays extraordinary force. In *The Sea Around Us* Rachel Carson noted that Scottish engineers were dumbstruck in 1872 when a storm destroyed a huge concrete breakwater that weighed 800 tons and was tied to underwater rocks with iron rods. They replaced it with a stoutly anchored pier that weighed more than 2,600 tons. Five years later another storm carried that away, too.

Glaciers of the last ice age played key roles in creating today's coastline. During cold phases of the weather cycle, more snow fell each year than melted and evaporated. This meant an annual increase in the snow cover of the polar regions. As the snowpack accumulated over Labrador (in particular), its lower levels were compressed into dense ice. The Wisconsin Glacier, the last of the Pleistocene epoch, grew to a thickness of 10,000 feet—2 miles, or about the height of the *tops* of fair-weather cumulus clouds today. Its enormous weight made its lower portions behave in a plastic manner like something between a true solid and a liquid. Acting like viscous, chilled honey, the lower plastic ice squeezed out around the bottom of the thickening glacier as new snow kept accumulating and making the whole mass heavier. In effect, the glacier grew horizontally in all directions and "advanced" down across what would become New England.

As the ice advanced like a frozen flood, it changed the existing mountains drastically, cutting through them in places, wearing them down, breaking, grinding, polishing, creating sand and raw material for more sand through erosion. The glacier moved "downhill" across inland New England, crossing Maine to carve steep valleys and fjords, including the 1,000-foot chasm of Soames Sound on Mount Desert Island, until it finally ran aground miles offshore. The glacier's leading edge swept the land clean, pushing all loose (and newly loosened) material ahead of it. When the ice began to melt and the glacier shrank, this mixed debris remained behind in moraines like rows of sweeping compound left by a colossally careless janitor. The sinuous outermost moraine formed Long Island's backbone to Montauk Point as well as Block Island, Martha's Vineyard and Nantucket. The glacier melted, then advanced again to push up another moraine. This one made Orient Point (the other half of Long Island's swallow-tailed east end), the edge of Rhode Island, the Elizabeth Islands that run northeast to the armpit of Cape Cod and the humerus of the Cape itself. Familiar with the Vineyard, I felt a sense of *déjà vu* the first time I visited Block Island. Some cliffs seemed the same as those on the Vineyard; they are composed of the same clays transported by the same glacier.

The glaciers had other legacies as well. They would surround masses of material, then wrench it along as they advanced and drop it when they stopped. This resulted in isolated pockets of debris or drumlins, such as the three dozen islands in Boston harbor. When the glaciers receded they didn't creep backwards of course. They melted where they were. Their water carried finer material downhill, creating outwash plains broken here and there by distinct streams running to the sea. Melting summer after summer, they distributed material fairly evenly across shallow seaward slopes as far south as Delaware Bay. Melting was not perfectly uniform. Blocks of ice broken off the glacier would be isolated. Sand and gravel would build up in natural dykes around their frozen forms. When these blocks melted, they left depressions in the new land, which became "kettle ponds" if the bottom was impermeable clay. Block Island, only 7 miles long and 3 miles at its widest, has 365 of these freshwater ponds. Cape Cod has dozens more, most of them characteristically rounded from the action of windblown waves on their once ragged shores.

A secondary result of that ice age was the fall of sea level around the globe as eight million cubic miles of the world's water was trapped and stored in the glaciers. During the last glacial period, sea level fell some 300 feet below its present level. Until as little as 12,000 years ago the Atlantic began a few hundred miles east of where it's found today. Elephant teeth 25,000 years old have been dredged from mud 80 miles offshore. With a warming climate and melting glaciers, sea level rose rapidly for millennia—perhaps 8 inches per century. The modern coastline took its shape between 3,000 and 5,000 years ago, not much earlier than Stonehenge. As the glaciers melted, sea level rose. New England coastal valleys flooded. North-south chains of glacier-carved mountains became islands and irregular peninsulas separated by bays and inlets. Maine's labyrinthine coast is the modern legacy of ice-cut chasms that were filled by the encroaching sea.

But the changing relationship between land and sea over the ages is complicated by the fact that while sea level has risen, the land has rebounded too. The incalculable weight of ice depressed even the "'bedrock" of the earth's crust (which actually floats on the planet's fluid mantle). Boston was 600 feet lower 15,000 years ago. Much of the Down East coast is still slowly rising, like the surface of a pillow on an unmade bed after a late sleeper has run off to work. Meanwhile, other coasts seem to be submerging today because sea level continues to rise at the rate of about 4 inches a century. This is particularly important on the mid-Atlantic coast below New England, the stretch composed almost entirely of barrier islands: Fire Island, the New Jersey shore, the Delmarva Peninsula, the Outer Banks, Georgia's Sea Islands and the east coast of Florida. Along this enormous reach the ocean doesn't pound the continent itself as it does from northern Massachusetts to southern Maine or from Oregon to Mexico. Rather, the chain of low sand islands absorbs the impact of the seas and protects the low-lying mainland. Being malleable, the islands move and migrate in response to the sea.

There are several theoretical explanations for barrier islands. Less than a century ago G. K. Gilbert suggested that they resulted from sand spits that formed parallel to the coast from corners of mainland or rocky peninsulas. Here water's competence comes into play again, since an alongshore current moves up or down almost every beach. If a deepwater source supplies sand, the alongshore current (or littoral drift) drops the sand wherever the water slows down—on a shoaling bottom, on a sandbar that impedes the waves or on the downstream side of a point where the current changes direction. Flowing continually, the current brings new sand with it. Shoals rise if they retard the current; spits lengthen. In many places the littoral drift built spits across broad inlets, turning them into landlocked ponds cut off from the sea by a straight, narrow barrier of sand. Look at a map of Martha's Vineyard. The ponds on the island's south side were once open bays until sandspits closed them. Some time ago that coast was ragged and irregular. Now it runs remarkably straight for 15 miles from Chappaquiddick to Chilmark.

If a spit didn't completely cut off ocean access, it created a lagoon between the mainland and the new barrier, a prime place for salt marshes to grow. In time the original spit would be breached at random places by storms. Long, narrow islands resulted, as along the New Jersey coast. Where that coast now lacks islands, as at Sandy Hook, it is because the broken sandspits have slowly migrated all the way to the mainland, pushed by the relentless sea.

In our time V. P. Zenkovich, a Russian geologist, proposed the "drowning hypothesis" to explain other barrier island chains. It apparently applies to the Outer Banks in particular, which may be the remains of a huge ancient river delta. This theory holds that when the Atlantic seaboard was farther east, the coastline inevitably featured some lines of hills and river valleys. As glaciers melted and sea level rose, a rising ocean drowned the river mouths and invaded the valleys behind the outermost hills. The results are easy to imagine. Waves began breaking on the old hills' eastern slopes as sea level continued to rise. In fairly short order, inland plants must have perished from salt spray; soil and silt washed away. The soluble matter disintegrated or dissolved, leaving only inert detritus, or sand. As the old hills shrank, waves and tides brought new sand to them from offshore. During gentle weather, the beach built out from the edge of the old hill; during storms the hills were eroded more and sand was deposited on them. This sand would be distributed by wind. Thus the old line of hills gradually changed into a barrier of sand, which continued to protect the lagoons and marshes that developed. Though superficially the Outer Banks look like pure sand islands, borings between Wimble Shoals and Ocracoke Inlet reveal layers of old red clay that were deposited during the Pleistocene. The overlying sand came after the ice age. (Elsewhere, notably on the land that became the Vineyard's colorful Gay Head, the glaciers pushed around old clay deposits of previous ages.)

One of the earliest barrier island theories, suggested by a French geologist more than a century ago, held that as waves crossed the shoaling continental shelf, they built up ridges of sand that finally broke through the surface of the sea. An attractive but largely discounted idea, it had a weak point as fragile as the sandbars it depended on. Bars do build up off many coasts as ocean currents bring sand from deepwater lodes. But when these bars rise close to the surface of an ocean or active bay, waves and tides usually carry their sand away before the bar can emerge as an island. This is another function of competence and the energy trapped in ocean water. (The emergent theory works most commonly in lakes and calm bays. Skiff's Island is exceptional. That odd island comes and goes due to a rare combination of factors: the convergence of two sand-laden littoral currents; fluctuations in both the weather cycle and the rate of sea level rise; the presence of shoals; and the probability that a glacial island once stood there.)

The rule that undermined the Frenchman's theory brings up a fundamental factor in beach dynamics: waves. They are deceptive things that exert themselves underwater as well as on the surface. Actually each individual wave is part of something larger, a series. An ocean wave is manifested energy. Wind blowing across the water confers energy to the fluid; the water receives energy from the passing air to become kinetic, to have superficial waves. Surprisingly, perhaps, individual particles of wind-driven ocean water do not move major distances as the waves move. Rather, the water particles describe small circular orbits that remain in place while the waves pass. (Certainly water particles move en masse with tides, currents and surf, but those are different circumstances.) If the water isn't moving, what is? Pure energy. The apparent motion of ocean waves is the manifestation of energy borrowed from the wind, which disturbs the visible surface of the water. It is much the same as a sound wave or the energy wave a child in a cowboy suit imparts to a length of clothesline when he jiggles it to make a "snake" along the ground.

An ocean wave is not an independent entity, like a punch in the nose; each visible "wave" is part of the waves before and behind it. Every wave in the ocean is connected to all the other waves that derive energy from the same source. We use the word to mean a single crest; the wave is also the entire stream of energy—the whole series of crests and troughs. The energy imparted by a storm flows through the water until it is released on some shore. Hence, a gale off Tierra del Fuego can be felt by sensitive instruments on the coast of Cornwall 6,000 miles away.

Take it on faith that many energy waves pass through the same bit of ocean simultaneously. Some pass obliquely. Some, going in the same general direction, travel at different speeds. Some nearly identical waves, meeting head-on, almost cancel each other out. In midocean, where waves come from several directions and at different frequencies, the water rises to cone-shaped peaks and then subsides, as the high points of several waves coincide at one place for an instant. In a gale, of course, the wind's energy moves across the water in one direction, creating a surface pattern that dominates all the energy waves coming from other sources. Close to their source, waves tend to be steep and irregular; over long distances, they organize themselves, extending the wave length (the distance between crests) to become gentler, more regular swells. They keep going until something interferes, such as the sheer Dover cliffs, or a breakwater at Atlantic City, or a low, sloping natural sand beach. This is why waves still wash a coast on perfectly windless days.

When the bottom of a wave runs into shallow water, it "feels" the bottom; some of its energy is lost through friction against the sloping sea floor and the wave slows down. Land changes the course and character of every series of waves. Any obstacle—even a sandbar—alters waves that reach it; the ocean and shore interact, each affecting the other. Along a reasonably straight coast, underwater topography organizes the waves so that they approach the land more or less parallel to it. In turn, the sandy bottom and the beach itself respond to the direction of oncoming waves and are shaped by them. If a coast has points and peninsulas, they receive the brunt of the waves' energy; coves are struck more gently as the waves bend around the points and lengthen. Thus less forceful waves reaching into protected water are not as steep. They bring in sand grain by grain and leave it on the shore, creating a pocket beach.

When waves approach a sheer cliff they bounce back, returning seaward and directing their energy elsewhere. But some of their energy is lost in the collision. In time the repetitive action of the water breaks off pieces of the rock face, which is weakened by chemical action. Rocky outcrops succumb to air pressure as well as to the force of the water. As a wave curls, it traps air beneath it. Breaking directly against a cliff, the wave can force a large amount of air into the rocks' crevices where it is compressed even more. Given enough compression, the air pressure bursts the rock apart from time to time. Another cause of cliff erosion is the crumbled pieces of rock that have broken off before. Later waves toss these back at the vertical shore like missiles.

Though water particles don't move far as a result of waves, the effects are dramatic when water itself is transported, rather than just disturbed by energy passing through it. This happens when currents or tides occur or when waves break. Surface tension holds a wave together as it rises—up to a point. But when wave length (the distance from crest to crest) becomes less than seven times the wave height (the vertical distance between trough and crest), surface tension is no longer strong enough to hold the wave together. Then it falls down upon itself, whether at sea or along a coast.

When a wave enters shoal water and feels the bottom, the lower part of the wave slows down while the top of the wave continues moving at the original speed. The average wavelength shortens as the waves pile up against the coast; the crests move ahead of their supporting foundations and the waves break as surf. The energy that created the wave carries water physically up the beach face. Since the energy is spent on the beach, the only force drawing the water back down to the ocean is gravity. Because the returning water has less energy, and because there is less volume when some of the water sinks into the sand, the dying wave is weaker.

Consider the matter of water's competence again. Moving briskly up the beach, a wave carries sand with it from the offshore bar; moving more lethargically back to the ocean, it hasn't the strength to carry as much sand away, and the sand remains. This phenomenon means that waves breaking on a beach on calm days leave more small material than they take away. Thus the beach builds up as new material is dropped. Come stormy weather or a tempestuous winter, stronger waves disturb the swash zone and attack the beach. They bring in larger sand grains; more important, they can carry away smaller stuff because their larger water volumes and higher velocities translate into greater seaward competence. (The steepness of both the waves and beach face complicate these phenomena—but that is an esoteric matter.) Storm waves big enough to carry away more sand than they bring steeply erode the beach face and the berm—the part of the beach between the normal high-tide line and the dunes. If the storm waves persist, they may carry the whole old berm away, then attack the dunes themselves.

When waves break across the full width of a barrier beach in severe storms, they entirely remake the place. They remove natural obstructions and push the sand around and level the outermost dunes to create a very shallow, usually quite broad slope. This is the shape of a natural ocean beach, one that hasn't been artificially altered by dunes that build up around man-made fences. Beach grass or sea oats grow from the dunes toward the water and build new dunes, which retard and withstand some storms. But stronger surges of water wash them away, rearranging their material. "Permanent" dunes, built by sand collecting around native plants, rise only beyond the reach of normal storms and tides. Yet nothing is actually permanent on the beach; every dune may be touched sooner or later by an extraordinary storm. Undermined, it crumbles; the sea collects its sand and carries it away or bears it inland with the following wave. In sum, the beach is shaped by the ocean and continually responds to its changing forces. Severe winter weather normally robs Atlantic beaches of sand deposited there during summer idylls. Typically, a winter beach is narrower; in summer the same beach will be broader and composed of finer sand grains.

Whether a beach erodes or grows depends in part on the energy of the waves. The energy in foot-pounds per foot of wave crest can be computed several ways. The basic formula is

$$E = \frac{W\ L\ H^2}{8}.$$ (E is energy; W is the weight of 1 cubic foot of sea

water, or sixty-four pounds; L is wave length; and H is wave height.)
This formula uses the *square* of wave height—not a single power of
height—because the height of the wave has a multiplying effect. A
2-foot wave has more than twice the energy of a 1-foot wave and can
do more than twice the work—whether constructive or destructive
depends largely on its steepness. A variation of the formula em-
ploys wave frequency (or T for "time period" in seconds) instead of
wave length: $E - 41\ H^2T^2$. This is easier to use on the beach since
it's easier to count seconds than to accurately estimate wave lengths.
Regardless of formulas, a storm wave can pack six tons of power to
a linear foot of shore.

Pacific Coast beaches change dramatically between winter and
summer. Winter storms bringing stronger waves in a "fetch" thousands of miles long come from the same direction as summer zeph-
yrs. Where the alongshore current is negligible, sand removed in
winter settles in underwater bars facing the beach it came from.
When summer returns, the weaker waves pick up this sand and put
it back on the beach. So the beach builds until autumn.

On the Atlantic coast it's a little different. Prevailing winds
are westerly, while storm winds notoriously come from the northeast. Hence seasonal change occurs, but it is not as distinct as the
results of bad weather. Storms at any time of year can make astonishing changes. Early one fall I was at Assateague Island observing a peregrine falcon migration study. Driving up and down
this 32-mile island twice a day, we passed through a simple gate
nestled against the man-made dune above normal high tide. A
modest barrier, it was a single cable hooked to a post at about
ankle height. No doubt it had originally been much higher before
sand slowly collected along that stretch of beach over several
years of gentle weather. That fall a northeaster struck and made
the beach a different place. Dunes that had built up around snow
fences lost their steep faces where waves reached them. Now
there was a ragged line of gentle hummocks instead of the artificial barrier dune. At the south end of the island a growing sandbar, exposed at low tide, hooked for half a mile around Fishing
Point. And near the island's north end I was nearly garroted by
the clearest index of change—that gate. The cable now hung from
a hook higher than my head. The gatepost's apparent growth
proved that nearly 6 vertical feet of sand had been removed from
the place by a single storm. No doubt much of that sand became

the new hook at the south end of the island where it had been carried by the alongshore current and the storm. As the current changed direction to enter the protected bay behind the island, it slowed down and dropped sand stolen from further north.

Year in and year out littoral currents have remarkable effects. Fishing Point has grown 4 miles since the Chincoteague Lighthouse was built more than a century ago. The west end of Fire Island has grown a similar distance. The Cape Hatteras Lighthouse, built 1,000 yards west of the beach in 1852, is now in danger of being undermined by storm tides. The swash now laps less than 50 yards away. (The Lighthouse would have toppled some years ago but for the steel barrier built to protect it.) But the point to the south of that tower, once a mile and a half away, has grown another mile. Given a steady littoral drift, sic transit sand.

The Delmarva Peninsula is growing outward at both ends, toward Chesapeake Bay to the south and into Delaware Bay at the north. Offshore somewhere in the vicinity of the Maryland-Virginia border an underwater "nodal point" causes the prevailing wave pattern to diverge. North of this topographical feature the littoral current usually moves northward. At Ocean City, Maryland and along Assateague Island it usually moves south. It might seem to a first-time visitor traveling the entire peninsula that inshore currents are as fickle as the inscrutable beach, which seems to broaden and shrink twice a day. Except under a storm's influence, the currents are quite constant. As for the tides, which rise to cover a foreshore and fall to expose it, they are as certain as death and taxes.

Everyone has heard that tides are controlled by the moon. Pliny observed the phenomenon 2,000 years ago. Newton's theory explained it in 1687. Gravitational force does the work, just as it dumped the apple on Sir Isaac's noggin. (Theoretically, gravity is responsible for every raindrop's attraction to the farthest star. But don't expect any practical results from that, nor from the barely measurable "earth tides," as bedrock rises and falls in response to the orbiting moon's gravity.) Imagine the face of an antique clock representing an ideal "earth" covered with water and orbited by a perfect moon. When the moon is at the top of the diagram it draws earth's water toward it, creating a high tide at 12 o'clock; the water is deepest there. At the bottom of this perfect planet, at 6 o'clock, where the moon's gravity is not felt strongly, another high tide results from the force of the planet's rotation. The water for both these high tides comes from adjacent areas; the water at 3 and 9 o'clock has become shallower and low tides occur there. (Next diagram, please.) When the moon moves to the right of the clock-faced planet it continues to attract the earth's watery blanket and creates a high tide at 3 o'clock. Rotational forces—consider them centrifugal—create another corresponding high tide at 9 o'clock, and low tides appear at 12 and 6.

On our imperfect earth the same phenomena occur, though things are vastly more complicated because irregular landmasses funnel the flow of water between the interconnected oceans. None-theless, the moon constantly circles earth, drawing the closest water toward it as it passes; earth constantly rotates on its axis, creating another force most strongly manifested where the moon's gravity is barely felt at the moment. The two high tides that result are fed by water from adjacent seas. Since earth's rotation and moon's orbiting are both continual, ocean waters move up, sideways and down in a constant motion that peaks and ebbs at every point on every tidal coast with predictable regularity. Because the dominant tidal insti-gator, the moon, circles earth in about twenty-four hours, fifty-two minutes, the cycle takes a little longer than a day to complete. High tide and moonrise occur about an hour later every day.

A number of other forces also operate to make the tides vary from place to place and from day to day. The sun plays a particularly important role in counterpoint to the moon, again because its grav-ity attracts the earth's fluid blanket. The force of gravity increases in direct proportion to the mass of the objects but decreases with the square of the distance between them. Our familiar sun, with a mass 333,400 times that of earth, has less than half the effect on ocean tides as the smaller but much closer moon. Yet when sun, moon and earth are in a straight line, tides range higher and lower than normal because the sun's gravity augments the moon's. The highest and lowest tides of the month, called spring tides, occur when the sun, moon and earth are most nearly aligned; then the moon appears full or as a crescent. Neap tides, when the rise and fall are smallest, occur when the sun and moon form a right angle with the earth. In effect the sun is then at odds with the moon, gravitationally speaking, and cancels part of its tidal power.

Since distance is such an important factor, tide ranges also change as the earth travels in its eliptical orbit around the sun and the moon follows its oval course around earth. Higher and lower tides occur when earth is closest to the sun and/or moon. Add to these variables the fact that earth, like the moon, rotates on a tilted axis, and you have a notion of why some tides are higher than others in a given place even under similar weather conditions and phases of the moon.

In addition, there is the less understood and independent function of distinct ocean basins. A basin holds water like brandy in a snifter. When the liquid moves back and forth in a swirled glass, it rises and falls greater distances around the sides of the glass; the level near the center remains more constant. Liquid in any restricted space, whether ocean basin or brandy glass, has a given period of time in which the liquid naturally takes to move back and forth from one end to the other. This is the container's "resonance." The Bay of Fundy's resonance happens to be about the same as the moon's orbiting time, according to one expert; these two independent factors reinforce each other to cause higher and lower tides. For reasons that aren't fully understood, the difference between spring and neap tides in the Bay of Fundy isn't as great as elsewhere. Nonetheless, tides there range 60 feet; waters rise and fall the height of a six-story building twice a day. Of course that's the worldwide extreme. Some coasts have tides of almost no consequence, largely because of their relationship to the oceanic basin. The Mediterranean Sea has virtually no tides at all.

Regular cycles aside, tides can vary greatly in a single place in response to several irregular factors that affect the play or torture of surf upon a beach. Onshore wind has an obvious influence as it piles water up along a coast. Atmospheric pressure is another factor. During large storms the ocean is not pressed downward as hard by the air as during fair-weather highs. Warmer water in summer is yet another; higher temperature expands the volume of water in the oceans minutely. Freshwater runoff from the land in springtime is yet another factor as it adds to the volume because it is less dense than salt water.

Variations in tides have been so constant for so long that government agencies publish annual tables and TV weathermen predict them. But before the vacuum tube or even government was invented, the natural world depended on regular tides. Many beach animals rely on periodic immersion though they live on land. Marsh plants that would be defeated by hardy inland vegetation have adapted to saltwater flooding twice a day and would perish without it.

The shore itself must cope with all the variables. It has coped with them; it has survived. The extraordinary thing about it all is that shores persist with their repertoire of self-effacing actions in response to the bludgeoning sea. It would be silly to attribute intelligence here, as if a coast had a choice to do anything but persist, even though the practicalities are so ingenious. Suffice it that the physical beach is a creative thing and its creativity is helped along by its biota. If that idea sounds outlandish, consider two examples: Beach grass collects sand around its stems to build the dunes; the sand in turn stimulates the grass, which grows more and collects more sand. Many mollusks live in or on sand along the littoral; after death their pulverized shells become part of sand-poor southern beaches. In any event, there is a nearly organic tenacity in the aggregation of sterile, organic and inorganic elements that make a beach.

Driftwords: On the Rise

Various Cassandras (including me?) bemoan abuse of the coastline in the name of demographics, politics, economics or selfish pleasures and at the expense of ecology, biology, aesthetics or other highminded causes. Alas all of these issues ignore a major element in the future of coastal affairs. This culprit is relatively hidden and absolutely implacable: the rise of sea level. In fact we are losing ground along the littoral quite literally. Make no mistake about it: The water is rising relative to the land. There are several known reasons, most of them primeval, all complex. Here are a few:

- Undersea volcanism. Ridges along the ocean floors—submarine mountain chains really—mark regions where molten material wells up from beneath Earth's crust. As this hot lava encounters cold water, it solidifies as rock, raising the sea floor and the surface of the sea as well.
- Subsidence of coastal lands. In areas where much groundwater is removed by wells and such, the water table falls, causing the land to sink and, relatively speaking, sea level to rise.
- Local weather. Sea level rises locally in response to atmospheric lows; for each millibar change in atmospheric pressure, sea level moves 10 millimeters. Ordinary low pressure systems can raise sea level by a foot. Storm surges from major hurricanes typically and alarmingly raise tides 15 feet or more above normal.
- Global warming. This much-heralded but imperfectly understood phenomenon results from a constellation of factors—some of them natural and others almost certainly accelerated by man's prodigal use of fossil fuels since the dawn of the industrial age. The planet has been warming slowly since the last ice age 18,000 years ago; whatever the many causes, inundation of the coastline has gone on that long and will continue. (For each degree of mean temperature rise, sea level rises 100 millimeters, according to an expert calculation.)
- One result of global warming is the melting of polar caps and of glaciers. This turns ice into water, which perforce must drain to the sea, adding more water and raising its level worldwide.
- Another result of global warming is swelling of the oceans through thermal expansion; warmer water fills a greater volume of space. The mass of the ocean increases and this raises its level.

In sum, the National Academy of Science's National Research Council reports that sea level was 100 meters lower when the latest ice age ended. The Council predicts that in the next half century, sea level worldwide will rise at least half a meter and perhaps as much as a meter—if recent trends continue. Such an elevation of the seas will have important consequences for many island nations and for virtually all coastlines. Yet an even more alarming possibility is that recent trends may accelerate, thanks to any number of factors. Should this occur, the results will be disastrous to the status quo.

Some causes of sea level rise will always be beyond human control, such as the rising of sea floor ridges from volcanism. Earth's innards will keep swelling up until we honor the words of the wry bumper sticker and "stop continental drift." And that absurd statement simply raises an intriguing fact: There is an unknown in every prognosis, and that X factor is the effect of human actions. Will we stay the present course? Will we make matters worse? Will we use our unpredictable ingenuity to improve matters? Might mankind reduce human impact, say by going "solar" or by achieving zero population growth, whether by dint of the pill, apocalypse or a pandemic?

Certainly our prodigal burning of fossil fuels is a contributing factor to global warming. This raises such questions as whether civilizations worldwide will exercise restraint on a titanic order in order to reduce the release of "greenhouse gases." The paramount remaining question that remains is not, "Can we do anything about that?" The key question is, "Will we?"

If yes, then what? If no, what then?

CHAPTER SEVEN

Inner dune: beside beach grass, a swatch of wild rose, round patches of poverty grass, spires of seaside goldenrod, wide-leafed beach pea

The Starring Roles of Vegetables

A barrier beach without plants is like a ship without a sail, a boat without a rudder, an egg without salt, dinner without wine, a politician without an issue, or a rebel without a cause. But a plantless beach has even less future. Once sand comes ashore, the pawn of waves and currents, it becomes the slave of a new medium— dynamic air. A breeze as slow as nine miles an hour blows sand away. Even wind that gentle picks up dry grains and moves them significant distances to start the process of saltation: As each wind-blown grain falls to the surface of the beach, it jars others up into the wind. The net result is leeward dispersal of the beach. Hypothetically a gale can carry a naked barrier island away as fast as it builds up and dries out. The fact that beaches and barrier islands don't all blow away inland every year is largely due to plants. Even heaps of dredge spoil, the byproduct of deepening a ship channel, become stabilized in the course of a summer as airborne seeds colonize them and take root. Islands survive because of plants. Viva vegetation.

Certainly a beach is a constantly dynamic, moving thing. But there are degrees of dynamism. Islands move and migrate—slowly, thanks to plants. Normally the sum of undramatic vegetable growth is almost equal to the sporadic forces of meteorological events that do most of the dramatic work in a natural scheme of things. The relationship between vegetation and beaches is like some good marriages: slowly productive, fundamentally stable through small accommodations by each party and occasionally but not fatally tumultuous. To overstate for the example's sake: An established island fails when things get too rough for the ever accepting plants or when the vegetation doesn't hold up its end of the bargain and lets things fall apart.

To outline one more overall observation, muddle the marriage metaphor and consider a *ménage à trois* of sea, shore and salt marsh. The material of the beach itself—grains of quartz—is sterile. But it snuggles between two of the most botanically fertile swingers on earth: the oceanic shallows and the marsh. The party to windward, the ocean, is largely responsible for the beach's ability to support life at all. Having carried the sand there in the first place, the ocean provides a variety of nutrients, from drab minerals in its spray to bouquets of organic debris and armies of voracious bacteria. In turn, the vital barrier beach cradles the leeward marsh, the nursery and garden upon which most higher marine life relies. (By one expert estimate, 95 percent of Virginia's commercial and sportfish species depend exclusively on marshes and bays for shelter or for food during at least one phase of their lives.) Marine vitality demands healthy marshes, which rely on protective barrier island beaches, which need the strapping ocean. Of course it didn't start out that way. These responsibilities were not ordained in any contract, and opposing forces also operate continually. The surf erodes and salt spray kills many plants. But this threesome settled in and carries on. The fabulously creative (if metaphorically bizarre) cohabitation of sea, shore and marsh depends on the constant support and contribution of vegetables.

First and fundamentally, what is a plant? It is an autotrophe as opposed to a heterotrophe (an animal); that is, a plant is an organism that makes its own food. Most plants—and there are 350,000 species of them—produce their own sustenance from inorganic materials. Everything else must consume food that's already organic, whether vegetable or animal. Scratch a carnivore and you'll find that its food supply originally derives from plants. Peregrine falcons thrive on flickers, which eat insects, which live in grass. The cod eats sea snails, which eat algae. Man eats potatoes and steaks from steers fattened on corn. But whether the original food source was a diatom or an ear of Silver Queen, the vegetable survived on a diet of water and "essential elements": carbon, hydrogen, oxygen, phosphorus, potassium, nitrogen, sulfur, calcium, iron, magnesium, copper, zinc, boron, manganese and molybdenum. With these it created its own organic sustenance through photosynthesis, a process of Gordian entanglements. Oversimplified, the formula reads

$$CO_2 + H_2O \xrightarrow[\text{Chlorophyll}]{\text{Light}} CH_2O + H_2O + O_2.$$ (Translation: Carbon dioxide and water, in the presence of light that's "fixed" by chlorophyll, become carbohydrate, i.e., starch or sugar, plus water and oxygen.) But like all other things biochemical, the process turns out to be more complicated, so much so that even the biochemists haven't sorted it all out to their satisfaction. For one thing, water goes in and water comes out—but not the same water. The plant breaks down the original fluid, uses its constituent elements to make carbohydrates for its own use and, fortunately for our entire biological world, releases oxygen as a byproduct. New water, reconstituted from leftover hydrogen and oxygen, is another byproduct. Chlorophyll, the visible green pigment found in plants, is the agent responsible for perhaps the most important aspect of the entire proceedings. This substance absorbs energy from sunlight to bind the inorganic raw materials into new, more complex organic materials. Vegetative things developed differently, and much more slowly, before the evolutionary advent of chlorophyll. The bottom line now, according to expert testimony, is simply this: "Photosynthesis is the source of all living matter on earth and of all biological activity." It provides the nutritional wherewithal for all life here; lowly plants are the repository for that awesome process.

Though beaches and their environs support a vast variety of vegetation, these places are hostile habitats at best. Sand is sterile, inhospitably dry and too porous to hold water well. The sea is far too salty for most plants and fraught with motion so constant that it would make a mighty oak cry "uncle." Guarded by the barrier, the marsh is frequently calm, but it experiences daily tides that drown its flora's roots, then leave them drying in the sun. Further, brackish marsh water is too salty for most vegetation. Yet the plants are there, thanks to some remarkable evolutionary adaptations. These are the halophytes, plants that can survive salty environments, usually by absorbing extra water or by expelling salt molecules.

Begin with the plants of the beach itself and American beach grass in particular, a well-named plant as energetic as Manifest Destiny. It occupies the beach as aggressively as nineteenth-century Americans claimed the West and clutches its territories just as tenaciously. First, it keeps the beach from being blown away by stopping saltation in its tracks. Though a healthy stand of *Ammophila breviligulata* covers less than 8 percent of the surface area, its simple presence inhibits the wind, greatly reducing its speed at the surface to reserve the sand already there and collect newly dropped grains. A gale may whip spray from the surf and blow sharp sand in someone's face until walking into the wind along an open beach becomes painfully impossible. But the wind at ground level among the dune grass is a zephyr or less. Collectively the blades of grass create a barrier that dissipates the wind, which drops its sand on a surface that is less disturbed. The stems trap grains that would otherwise roll past. Called "compass grass" for the circles its bending leaves make in sand on a windy day, it inhibits sand movement in any direction and gathers grains around its shoots. Obviously any roots anchor both the plant and the material it grows in—even sand—but this plant's above-ground stems also collect sand, to the advantage of both the beach and the grass.

Beach grass's major stems run horizontally beneath the sand. These rhizomes have characteristic nodes every few inches. The nodes have roots, which are thus distributed widely beneath the beach surface to absorb as much rainwater as possible, even though the green plants above seem sparse. A fraction of the underground nodes grow vertically as well and produce short, sharp stems, which develop more roots. Tall, slender leaves grow up around each stem, and in dry, bright weather they curl around the vertical stem like corn husks around the ear. While the convex outer surface of a curled leaf is smooth, the inner surface is composed of ridges and grooves that run the length of the leaf. (These features are barely visible to the naked eye but can be seen through a hand lens.) The plant's pores lie along the bottoms of the grooves, which close when the leaf curls around the stem in dry weather. Working like the squeezed side of an accordion bellows, the ridges effectively seal the grooves shut to conserve vital moisture within the plant and, as botanists say, retard desiccation. Furthermore, the grooves are so narrow that particles of salt cannot invade them but instead adhere to the higher ridges when the leaf is not curled. This prevents the killing salt in seawater spray from entering the plant's pores.

Where do salt particles come from? Salt spray, of course. When air bubbles in the ocean (or surf) burst, tiny droplets of sea water explode from the surface to be carried by the wind. Whether they evaporate en route or happen to land, they transport particles of sea water's dissolved components. These include some botanically essential substances, notably magnesium and potassium. Dissolved by rain and washed down through the porous sand, they're absorbed by the grass roots. Others of these airborne particles— common salt (sodium chloride) in particular—kill or retard most vascular plants. But they don't harm beach grass because of its leaf design. Hence beach grass benefits below-ground from growing close to the spray-giving sea but protects itself from the spray above the sand's surface by the same ingenious device that keeps it from drying out in this often arid place.

A. breviligulata thrives in sand; nay, it depends on it. For reasons that remain unclear, sand grains collecting around its stems actually stimulate the plant's growth. It may be that these roots are short-lived and that the only way the plant stays vigorous is by sending out new rhizomes and growing new roots with them. Beach grass bears seeds, but a classic American study revealed that it spreads most actively through rhizomes. Indeed it regenerates at its fastest rate from dormant rhizomes in springtime. Its phenomenal reproductive methods are crucial to a beach's persistence. Its talent "for potentially unlimited horizontal and vertical rhizome growth" is extraordinary, according to a Dutch authority. (*Ammophila arenaria*, a plant of the same genus, grows along European beaches and stabilizes them.) One *Ammophila* or the other is responsible for the birth of impressive beach dunes wherever they appear around the world. As sand collects around these plants, the grasses grow up through it. They can be buried deeper than one yard and still emerge. The Dutch botanist writes, "The stabilization of sand surface by vegetation differs from other forms of stabilization [i.e., man-made ones] in that the plant cover can keep pace with the accreting surface." And if sand fails to collect, *Ammophila* becomes less vigorous. Where *Ammophila* remains healthy, dunes continue to rise. "There are two major phenomena that enable maritime dune formation to proceed. The first and most important is a supply of sand together with wind to move it." Sand washed up into low-tide flats or onto the beach face is enough. "The second is plant colonization"—by plants that can survive burial under new layers of sand.

Beach grass typically covers the inland side of a dune and may run down the face of a gently sloped dune to colonize the foreshore to the point where spring tides or storm surges drown it. When storm waves attack and erode a vertical scarp in a low dune, the tangled web of subsurface rhizomes is strikingly visible—as on the point of Plum Island on Massachusetts' northern coast. But even then the tangled rhizomes hold the sand far longer than would otherwise be the case. Scarps in grassless sand tumble as fast as sand castle walls. When plants along the ridge of a coastal dune are trampled by thoughtless walkers (or wildlife), the dune doesn't regenerate—because beach grass won't take hold if sand is removed. A little path through the edge of a grassy dune soon becomes a "blowout."

Here the particulars of aerodynamics come into play. Wind blows sand away from the slope wherever it's not held in place by grass. (I've stood on a 200-foot Cape Cod cliff with an eroding face and been blinded by beach sand riding a strong onshore wind up the bare slope.) Gravity adds to the loss and a mobile dune takes the shape of an airfoil. The greatest wind pressure is felt near the top of the dune; sand loss is greatest there. Since sand is lost from this area, this is precisely where beach grass won't regenerate to repair the break. Instead, as wind continues to sweep sand up the dune face, the little blowout becomes a major breach in the barrier.

South of Chesapeake Bay, beach grass gives way to sea oats, a very long-stemmed grass that bears plumes of flat-cased seeds like little flags. A hardy plant that can survive both sand burial and exposure from erosion, it has a slender grace that belies its toughness. At Shackleford Banks below Ocracoke, North Carolina, 90 percent of the vegetated dunes support *Uniola paniculata*. In turn, the sea oats support the dunes. This grass stabilizes enormous stretches of southern barrier dunes because of its extensive root systems. Though it also sends out rhizomes, they are not as robust as *Ammophila*'s.

The spikelets of the sea oats' plumes fall in autumn and early winter. Many animals feast on them: mice, rabbits, song sparrows and redwing blackbirds. Only the seeds that are swiftly buried in new sand survive to germinate the following spring. Slender new stalks appear annually for several years, frequently growing 6 feet tall and arcing away from the wind with their heads of tattered-flag seeds.

Both beach grass and sea oats, which are perennials, survive uprooting by storm surges and fragmentation. In fact this is one way they disperse. Broken up by waves, the pieces wash up on another beach and take root where they land, frequently along the high-tide, which is fertilized by decaying vegetation that didn't survive the passage.

The beach pea (*Lathyrus japonicus*), which grows as far south as New Jersey, approaches dominance in some locations. Resistant to salt spray and desiccation, it fixes nitrogen in the soil and helps fertilize the dunes. Its stems creep along at ground level, supporting slender branches with pointed heart-shaped leaves, curly tendrils and blue flowers. Settlers in Newfoundland are said to have staved off starvation with beach peas, and some nineteenth-century Cape Codders preferred them to garden peas, which their pods resemble. (Lee Peterson's *A Field Guide to Edible Wild Plants* recommends boiling beach peas at least fifteen minutes, then serving them hot with butter and pepper. But this useful and careful book warns that other members of the same genus are poisonous.)

Dusty miller (*Artemisia stelleriana*), a perennial, also grows on exposed growing dunes. A complex-looking plant found in low clumps punctuated with flowering stalks in autumn, it survives fragmentation particularly well. Hence an area reached by last winter's storm surges is likely to have a few clumps almost as soon as the first shoots of beach grass appear through the new sand. Dusty miller's name derives from its appearance; the leaves are covered with a pale, blue-gray cuticle that looks dusty and keeps the plant from drying out.

Sea rocket (*Cakile edentula*), a fast-growing annual, grows on the berm and disperses easily. Bearing lavender flowers from mid-summer to early fall, it has rocket-shaped seed capsules. Particularly well suited to dispersing seaside progeny, these capsules fall off and roll down the beach to the swash. Surviving saltwater immersion for long periods, the seeds germinate when washed up on another beach. Or, when an original site is inundated by a storm tide, this succulent's capsules float inland and colonize the inner dunes.

Behind a barrier dune, low beach heather and bearberry take over. Throughout the swale on Fire Island these two plants grow in great profusion, preferring, as they do, eroding sites where beach grass can't survive but requiring some protection from salt spray. Vast carpets of these plants are found north of New Jersey. Lilliputian beach heath, "also called 'poverty grass' because it grew where nothing else would," according to Thoreau, goes formally by the name *Hudsonia tomentosa*. Bearberry (*Arctostaphylos uva-ursi*) grows in somewhat bushier stands of small, shiny, dark green leaves and hard red berries. These are said to be edible, but I'm told that no less a forager than Euell Gibbons tried fixing them every way he could think of and found each dish less palatable than the last.

Wild, or salt-spray, rose grows in impressive clumps on Maine's rocky islands and along the rims of Cape Cod cliffs, where its exposed, briary roots clawing the empty air prove the swift pace of erosion. *Rosa rugosa* has ostentatious blossoms with large but delicate petals and hairy, thornlike growths along the stems. The fruits, called rose hips, turn from orange to red as they ripen and grow as large as Ping-Pong balls. In Maine, trapped by the tide on a wild island one hungry day, I found them delicious. But those picked from a plant beside a cement walk in one of Fire Island's towns seemed pulpy and tasteless. Dominating some natural sites, these plants seem as native as poison ivy. But this rose is an exotic introduced as a garden shrub from Japan in 1872, according to a New England account written a century after the fact. A botanist reported that cuttings were carried "aboard the ship *Franklin*, wrecked on Nauset Beach in the spring of 1849, and that this rose was introduced to the Cape" with the flotsam. The substance of that story has spread with the wild rose itself and is repeated just about every place the plant occurs. I don't doubt that there were disastrous and tragic wrecks along every stretch of coast—only that so many of the ships carried rose hips and cuttings.

As for poison ivy (*Rhus radicans*), it too dominates large expanses of high dune, inner dune and bayside uplands, often running down to the tideline of a marsh. I can't think of a place I haven't seen it and thanked my stars for immunity to the stuff that drives some folks mad with itching rash. (Alas, such immunity doesn't last a lifetime.)

The swale behind a barrier dune often has a number of trees, many of them stunted beyond easy recognition. On Assateague Island mature loblolly pines stand no taller than a man but spread out their branches 3 or 4 yards in every direction. On Fire Island runty, half-century-old pitch pines sprawl like the caps of Chinese mushrooms in a chicken dish. These deformities—adaptations really—show the effect of salt spray on species with little tolerance for it. Often the inner dune is stable enough to hold deciduous and evergreen trees. Despite superficial appearances, a barrier island may have ample fresh water floating atop the heavier saltwater table in a convex "lens." Also, a mature swale has sufficient chemical nutrients for trees to grow. At first the nutrients came from salt spray. Then as the first inland plants colonized the place, their leaves or needles (and finally all their remains) decomposed, contributing chemical constituents back to the sand. In this way the living and dead flora of a maritime forest represent a rising organic spiral; the dead nourish the living, as old nutrients are recycled and new ones arrive with the wind. But trees only grow as high as they can reach before sea spray salts their leaves or needles. Unable to exclude salt from their pores, as *Ammophila* does, exposed portions of the tree are constantly pruned by the aerosols. As a result, they take contorted shapes that indicate the sweep of wind over a dune and down its lee.

Back at the beach the seaweeds, algae all, are among the most productive plants on earth—or in the water. Members of an ancient and successful group, some reproduce both sexually and asexually; one grows a few feet long but can muster the anatomical wherewithal for only two layers of cells. Lacking distinct veins, they also lack true roots. Instead they attach themselves to rocks, empty mollusk shells, pilings and almost any other hard surface (including live spider crabs, as noted) with characteristic holdfasts. These organs, shaped like fingers or disks, develop from fully half of the original embryonic material; the other half differentiates into stems, fronds, reproductive organs, bladders and other structures.

Growing from the high-tide line to as deep as sunlight penetrates, these algae are as important to their own habitat as land plants are to barrier islands. In some submarine locations a single species dominates the aquascape as thoroughly as beach grass dominates a dune. To divers and snorkelers in such water, it seems that algae and the rocks that anchor them *are* the habitat—a mesmerizing, undulating marine jungle that sways with the waves to reveal every kind of animal—fishes, mollusks, crustaceans—and then hide them again.

The seaweeds are undeniably plants of the beach. Many of

them, such as the rockweeds along Maine's stony shores, appear as soon as the tide begins to ebb. A walk at low water reveals an entirely different place than the perpetually aloof land. At night especially, many rarely seen creatures forage along a rocky littoral without fear of their traditional predators, the diurnal gulls. But one can also find green crabs, Jonahs, limpets and scores of snails on every boulder during a daylight ebb tide. They hide in the rockweed waiting for the water's return. Seaweeds are also high tide beach plants—albeit dying ones—because so many of them come ashore, their stems or holdfasts broken. With them come multitudes of invertebrates and banquets of nutrients that seep into a sandy beach as the algae decompose, creating a ragged line for some of the hardier vascular plants to colonize. Or, as on the stony south coast of Block Island, seaweeds seem to be a permanent feature, lying along the base of a cove's cliff in dense, mixed carpets 2 or 3 feet deep.

Botanically classified by pigments, the seaweeds are supremely useful plants. Some were traditionally used to pack shellfish for market or even to pack fragile household goods. Some are harvested for food—but far less in America than in Europe and the Orient. Many more are gathered for chemical and industrial processing.

The brown algae include the family Fucaceae, which is well represented along the Atlantic coast. Ten-foot bladder wrack (*Ascophyllum* sp.) is not one of the most diaphanous marine plants. It has fairly thick stems, irregular flexible branches that are round or oval in cross section, and two forms of air bladders. *Ascophyllum* is a source of many substances: iodine (in concentrations more than 200 times that of the surrounding water), soda, potash and half an alphabet of vitamins. The *Fucus* genus comprises the closely related rockweeds, which are flat in cross section and have distinct median ribs. They too branch randomly and have visible air bladders that keep them afloat. Generally only 1 to 3 feet long, depending on species, some can double their weight in a week's time if they are thinned out regularly by harvesting.

Kelp (*Laminaria*) is another genus of brown algae with several species common from Maine to New Jersey. The fronds are not branched. Instead they're like leathery straps that grow in various widths and in lengths from 5 to 10 feet. Their ancient common names outshine the Latinate: oar weed, tangle, devil's apron, sole-leather and ribbon weed. Depending on species, the single flat fronds may be wrinkled (*Laminaria agardhii*), smooth (*L. saccharina*), ragged (*Alaria esculenta*) or perforated (*Agarum cribresum*). Some are annuals and some perennials that live as long as a dozen years.

Despite its common and formal names, sargassum (*Sargassum filipendula*) doesn't come from the fabled mid-Atlantic Sargasso Sea. Rather, this brown alga thrives offshore along the warmer parts of the Atlantic coast. Easy to identify, it has fronds resembling bayberry leaves and berrylike bladders that make it seem like a terrestrial plant that lost its way.

Irish moss (*Chondrus crispus*) contains chlorophyll, although that pigment is often entirely masked by deep purple coloring. Dried, it turns white to look like tattered Kleenex. Growing in dense patches and coming ashore in handfuls, its leaves resemble kale or collard greens. Like the other red algae, it grows in slightly deeper water than the browns, to be exposed only during some low spring tides. Offering a dense, complicated cover, Irish moss shelters as many as fifty species of invertebrates down to depths of 60 feet or so. Traditionally this has been the most marketable seaweed in many parts of the world. Eaten in Europe, it is a common source of agar and gelatin and has been compounded into an anticoagulant drug. Its euphonious common name shows up on supermarket product labels, since it is an ingredient of cosmetics, toothpastes and ice cream (as an ice-crystal inhibitor).

Dulse (*Rhodymenia palmata*), another edible red alga, also grows below the normal low-water line. Dark red, it is flat, broad and ribless. Its dark red frond separates into wide segments that sometimes have distinct leaflets.

Uva lactuca is the bright green undulating stuff known from Florida to Hudson Bay as sea lettuce. Like so many other algae, it's edible, but recipes call for chopping it fine—probably a tedious task because of its unusual toughness. This is all the more surprising since it's only two cells thick. Nibbled on a beach, it seems an unlikely salad green. Slightly irregular, like stretched crepe paper, its inch-wide fronds grow 2 feet long.

Eelgrass (*Zostera marina*) is not an alga but belongs to a family of fifty flowering marine grasses (as opposed to true grasses). On soft bottoms from Cape Lookout to Campobello, it may be the dominant underwater plant down to depths of 150 feet. Its branching rhizomes have nodes as close as every half-inch, from which six or eight 3-foot leaves rise. Ephemeral shoots bear as many as 1,000 seeds—food for innumerable fish and water birds, especially brants. Eelgrass beds shelter many shellfish (especially scallops) and may support 200 species of algae. In 1931 a disease wiped out 95 percent of the eelgrass along the East Coast and caused ecological havoc. Fortunately the species seems to be making a strong comeback at last.

Behind almost every barrier beach there is (or was) a marsh. It may be barely visible, as in parts of New Jersey's asphalt jumble, or it may be extinct, as along the Norfolk docks; but marshland is as much a part of the total beach as dune grass and gulls. In the classic text *Life and Death of the Salt Marsh*, John and Mildred Teal state:

> Two-thirds of the value of the commercial catch of fish and shellfish landed on the East Coast of the United States comes from species that live at least part of their life cycle in marsh-estuaries. . . . It is estimated by fishery experts that 80 to 90 percent of the fish gathered for market throughout the world come from shallow coastal waters. . . . Experiments . . . have shown that marsh ponds can produce 250 to 400 pounds of fish per acre per year, 100 pounds of crabs and from 300 to 400 pounds of shrimp.

Economic and household food budgets aside, it's horrible to think what kind of biological apocalypse might occur if all the marshes were summarily filled and paved. The oceanic biota as we know it would immediately change, like a clock without its small hand. And the world, as we and every other animal know it, would change too.

The vegetative wealth of a salt marsh is proven by an unlikely source: the petroleum industry. A coastal geologist who once worked for an oil company described gathering seismic data in order to map ancient barrier islands. After these islands sank thousands of feet beneath increasingly heavy layers of sedimentary rock, the weight on them became enormous. The pressure turned much of the vegetation into oil. The oilman's problem, then, was to plot the location of the erstwhile marsh, then locate the former barrier island itself. This is because the oil wouldn't stay put as it formed but would be squeezed into the porous sand nearby. Thus, today's living marshes may turn the Outer Banks into rich oil fields—in a million years or so.

Driftwords: Welcome Back!

When my son Tim was four years old, we summered by a beach on an island favored by ospreys. Every morning one appeared—the same one, doubtless—flying along the edge of our bay in a looping course like the series of linked *O*s that penmanship masters used to demand. Doubtless also, it was the male of a pair, fishing to feed his mate and brood. Flying from his inland nest, he'd work the bay from south to north, soaring in not-quite-lazy loops, covering his territory with easy efficiency. Like as not while in our sight he'd break his pattern, hover, shift position, hover again, then suddenly fold his quick wings and plunge beak-first toward the water, rearranging himself in the last instant to strike feet-first, often plunging out of sight with a splash. Then he'd emerge, struggling from the sea, getting airborne and shaking in flight like a wet puppy—but with a silver shape held fore-and-aft in his talons. On some calm days he'd break the pattern and fly along close to the water, then with a swing of the legs neatly pluck a fish from just beneath the glossy surface. Not that he scored every time he wet a foot; I'd say that old bird made good two times out of three.

That autumn, back in Washington, my old friend Dan Crowley had room to spare on his sailboat one brisk Saturday. For some reason Tim didn't want to go until I promised him an osprey; yes, he wanted to see one more fish hawk before winter came. I cannot say what *Pandion* means to him except that it is a warm-weather friend, one of the neighbors in that sandy place where we like to live in summer. For me it is a redemptive bird. Because the osprey, of course, was the bellwether of both the DDT crisis and its reform.

It was the nesting failures of ospreys near Connecticut beaches that first alerted ornithologists, and then the nation, to the awful threat that loomed so dangerously. Like the other raptors, these birds live at the top of the food web: a farmer spread new pesticide, a gnat ate it, a minnow ate the gnat, a fish ate the minnow, an osprey ate the fish—ate a hundred fishes and got a hundred doses of DDT, which built up in the bird's tissues and upset its internal chemistry. In particular, the synthetic chemical reduced the thickness of the shells a female osprey produced, so her eggs broke before the embryos grew into chicks. When this was discovered and explained, we banned DDT from common use—hardly a season too soon—and within a few years osprey populations began to recover. They never vanished altogether from the Chesapeake, though when I first sailed the bay in the early sixties, just to see one was a treat. Now they are commonplace, and I say three cheers for that. To me the osprey is living proof that mankind may correct what he has put awry.

So we sailed out of the broad South River and chased white-caps around and about the Bay until the day turned cold and the sun began to sink. We saw a dozen nests, but not a single fish hawk, and Tim had long since given up looking—even given up asking his dissembling dad when he might see his favorite bird. Dan was steering the last leg of our course for the marina and I was furling sail when a heavy wingbeat caught my eye. "Raptor!" I cried, relieved to make good a small promise to a small boy. It was flying across the wide tidal river from the south bank, a big bird, a strong bird, a fishing bird that scanned the water as it flew. "Look Tim!" I said, jumping to the cockpit, pointing for the boy made clumsy by slicker, life jacket and woolens against the cold. "There's your osprey!"

But the bird proved me a liar a moment later. As it crossed our wake, we could see in the dusk the head and tail gleaming white against the darkened sky. It was no fish hawk; they'd all gone south by that autumn day. It was another recovering raptor come to reclaim part of its ancient range—Tim's first bald eagle.

Maybe next summer we'll see one of those on our island beach.

CHAPTER EIGHT

One man's summer castle—after the storm surge

The Onimod Theory

I have seen the hungry ocean gain Advantage on the kingdom of
the shore.

—Shakespeare

Something there is that doesn't love a beach.

—Anonymous

An idea returns like a forgotten tune: That the inanimate elements
of the beach act in ways that are almost organically creative. Combined, they enable the beach to persist, as if a sterile strip of sand
has an interest in continuing to be, as if inanimate things have
intent and natural systems have the ability to create order out of
chaos. Why not? Nebulous hydrogen and oxygen combine to become palpable water: in the unspeakably distant past inorganic
compounds combined into amino acids, the building blocks of life.
The nature of gravity itself encourages cohesion, often the first step
toward organization. Without gravity the stuff that went bang so
enormously in the first place would have simply dispersed, but

instead parts coalesced as objects with relationships of dynamic equilibrium, namely orbits. So be it with the beach. How so? Very simply, because when left to their own dynamic devices, beaches in general and barrier islands in particular take care of themselves. But they do it with little regard for humankind's "kingdoms of the shore," whether a sovereign state along the Atlantic coast or one man's summer castle in the sand.

The shore is a moving thing, even a vanishing thing, since portions amounting to 90 percent of the East Coast are eroding from purely natural causes at surprising rates. While a beach may look stabile, static, even solid, it is in a kind of perpetual motion— or dynamic equilibrium—as it responds to wind and the constant drumming of ocean waves. While they grow outward at specific seasons and places, most stretches of coast recede by greater amounts at other times of the year, and over the long term they wane more than they wax. In response, beaches move, and it is through this kind of dynamism that barrier islands maintain themselves—to the dismay of landowners, people who are obviously smarter than beaches, citizens bent on exercising an inalienable right to own property. We worship permanence in stable public utilities such as power lines, in rock-solid property boundaries, in extravagant vacation dwellings. To protect our rights (and our properties), we take certain steps aimed at making the beach stay put. But each thing we do requires another step. When a man builds a groin out into the water to halt the erosion of his beach, lo and behold the beach broadens, though at the expense of the shore immediately adjacent; so his neighbor builds another groin . . . and another, and another. If this all resembles a row of dominoes set up for idle play, don't forget that the purpose of setting up the dominoes is to knock one down and see them all fall. Thus the Onimod Theory—"domino" spelled backwards.

Witness Ocean City, Maryland, a resort village until 1933. Then a hurricane carved an inlet where none had been before, and fishermen found it convenient—a shortcut from the bay behind their barrier island out to the open ocean. When the inlet began silting up and threatening to close the following year, the town persuaded the U.S. Army Corps of Engineers to build a rock jetty, which kept it open. The littoral current, moving southward at less than half a knot, slowed down to negotiate the obstacle and, losing competence to carry solids, dropped sand on the north side of the jetty. Soon this broadened the beach above the barrier and created all sorts of room for ferris wheels, french fry stands, penny arcades and assorted honky-tonks. Getting past the jetty, the current picked up new sand; thus the jetty helped to keep the inlet open but had some additional effects farther down the current. One thing leads to another.

Before the inlet-making hurricane of '33, barrier islands stretched more or less smoothly and continually for 70 miles from Virginia across Maryland and all the way to Delaware Bay. Now the part of it below the Ocean City inlet, dubbed Assateague Island, began to experience erosion on its seaward side, while for complex reasons its landward marsh began moving westward into the existing protected bay. There were plans to develop this island; house lots were laid out and some roads built. Fortunately the plans were cancelled by the creation of Assateague Island National Seashore, which with the associated wildlife refuge now occupies this island's 30-odd miles. Since then the north end of the island has moved toward the mainland more than its original width. Viewed from the air, Assateague's outer beach is clearly to the west of Ocean City's bay shore. The house lots platted for Assateague, if measured from a point on the mainland, now lie beneath the open Atlantic. One thing leads to another. Yet barrier island environments being what they are, the north end of Assateague looks pretty much intact, as if it's always been right there. Certainly what appears there today has been part of an island in that general vicinity for a millennium.

North of the inlet and jetty the beach broadened at first, and the growing town of Ocean City gained in human popularity. Swelled by tourism all it could do was offer more to tourists, who came in greater numbers, supporting more hotels, motels, guest houses and summer bungalows. These accommodations pushed the town's apparent edge farther and farther north along the barrier island; then in the 1960s, condominiums arrived to push living spaces higher and higher into ever more bizarre towers. Maryland has 10 miles of ocean front, and virtually every inch of it has been developed into a high-rise spectacle. And all this is on a sandspit, a barrier island, a bit of terra infirma that is intrinsically unstable.

During years of gentle weather, all seemed well enough, though in fact the beach was receding, arguably as the result of natural causes at first. And at first nobody seemed to notice— especially not the local boosters nor the mayor and his political pals, who rode a bandwagon of electoral popularity on the Maximum Growth ticket. Perhaps tourists, tenants, vacationers and second-home folks wanted so badly to be near the sea that they welcomed its coming closer and closer by the year. The natural narrowing of the beach prompted the construction of groins—those low wooden walls built straight out from the shore in shallow water. Each groin performed exactly the same function as the jetty at the south end of the island: As it slowed down the southbound onshore current, it collected new sand on its up-current (northern) side, and it hastened erosion on its down-current side. Thus the city constructed groin fields, so to speak; the serial groins marched out of sight, because a single groin does as much harm on the down-current side as it does good on the up-current side. Another thing leads to another.

When the groin fields failed and the beach kept on coming closer, the powers-that-be decided they'd had quite enough of a good thing, especially after the weather cycle brought a series of stormy winters that carried away the beach front. The beach became so narrow in places that it could no longer accommodate a requisite number of sunbathers. It lapped at the foundations of some buildings. Ludicrously, big bulldozers were dispatched to push sand up from the shallows into steep dunes that would hopefully protect the condos. By the eighties an alarming number of oceanfront buildings were showing their pilings as winter storms sent tides over the beach, threatening these new "improvements." As a last resort (to borrow a phrase), Ocean City is trying replenishment, which comes a good deal costlier than a 'dozer and the man to drive it.

After dune building had failed, after more and more groins had failed, after bulldozing sand from the swash zone had failed, Ocean City embarked on a serious, expensive and essentially endless civil engineering project. Here it involved anchoring a barge over an offshore lode of sand and connecting it to the stricken beach by an umbilical cord of gargantuan pipe. Pumps then force a slurry of sand and seawater through the pipe from offshore onto the highest part of the beach. The pumping goes on night and day. Gravity does the rest; the water drains off the beach and the sand remains.

But the new sand lies at unnaturally high levels and in arbitrary profiles. Thus each high tide carves a vertical scarp in the new sand, so the beach drops suddenly away wherever the highest recent tide occurred. Further, this sand is unstable and lies in uneven densities, often harboring little impoundments of water that look like wading ponds but can behave treacherously like quicksand. And what will happen when a storm surge rises a few meters higher than normal? It must carry a great deal of sand with it—carry it either inland onto roads and parking lots and under stilt-supported buildings or carry it back to sea again. It will all depend on how high a storm surge rises.

Initially Ocean City's replenishment project seems to have served the purpose of broadening the beach and holding back the waves that previously lapped beneath a number of beach-front buildings. On the other hand, the imported offshore sand is darker than the sand that made Ocean City a popular resort in the first place; it absorbs more heat from the sun on a summer day—so much so that a resident tells me people must dash across the now-hot open beach to go swimming. The darker sand has made this beach less of a place to loll away summer. This darker sand also happens to be larger in particle size than the medium-fine white sand that Ocean City boasted before. Looking at the bright side, observers to the south on Assateague say that since the resort's replenishment program began, their "unimproved" beaches have taken on a new and gentler profile and their sand has improved, becoming finer and whiter.

Because one thing leads to another, one can't help asking whether the adjacent state of Delaware followed Maryland's lead out of greed or aversion to originality. A few miles north of Ocean City's forest of condominium towers, Delaware has sprouted several hundred multifamily condos in clusters like mushrooms. Three state parks remain on this recently empty and unimproved coast, but most of its length has now been dedicated to beach- and bay-front homes, with appalling results.

One thing has always led to another. Witness the chronic activity of the U.S. Army Corps of Engineers and the sorry history of the west end of New York's Fire Island. Francis P. Shepard, solon of coastal geology at Scripps Institute of Oceanography, wrote about it in his definitive catalog of America's coastlines some years ago:

> When Army engineers built the Democrat Point Jetty (1939–1941) several changes resulted. The westward growth of the point was temporarily stopped. Sand built the outer beach of Fire Island out to the end of the jetty in a few years; [behind the island]

a new projection grew northward from the point across half of the inlet. [A new bar appeared in the channel between Fire Island and Oak Beach on the island it overlapped.] The strong current in the channel increased as a result of this bar and attacked the western point of Oak Beach, cutting it back variously from 150 to 200 feet . . . Consequently the beach was built out artificially and a new channel was cut by the State of New York at about the middle of the inlet. This channel soon filled, necessitating more dramatic action, so a jetty was built across the north channel. The erosion has stopped; but according to the 1960 chart, no adjacent channel now enters the bay. The future of Fire Island inlet will depend . . . on how much the shore is controlled by man.

Farther out on Long Island, the fabled Hamptoms have long been famous for extravagant summer houses, lavish living and galloping erosion that cannot be arrested even by the expenditure of small private fortunes. It was out here that the chairman of the board of one of the nation's largest corporations built a private groin to protect his private beach—back in the benighted days before environmental laws placed limits on the havoc that individuals could inflict on the natural world. His groin worked beautifully, as a member of the local gentry sniffed aloud: "It built a lovely sandy beach on his property. But the house next door, where one used to play croquet on that gorgeous lawn, is under the waves." The littoral drift inevitably washed it away; the groin made it do it.

One thing leads to another, and people have been "improving" beaches for so long now that in some places the real beach seems to have gone away. The seaside metropolis of Virginia Beach, the Old Dominion's answer to Ocean City, Maryland, is a sandy strand bordered by an elevated concrete promenade. New Jersey's barrier islands run for more than 130 miles, and, save for a few scattered enclaves, most of this distance has been paved from the edge of the marsh to within a frisbee's toss of the high-tide line. The Garden State's penchant for turning beaches into exurban playgrounds is so excessive that it has lent a name to overdevelopment; Oren Pilkey, Jr., a Duke University geologist, coastal Cassandra and leading exponent of shoreside sanity, has been warning for years against "the New Jerseyization" of his beloved Carolinas. The term is as clumsy as the phenomenon itself, which features block after block of two-story, rambler-style houses surrounded by lawns of pebbles instead of grass.

"Each man kills the thing he loves," Oscar Wilde wrote. People who love the shore and insist on living there have been killing it with their buildings and engineering works and then having their structures destroyed in turn. After one winter of devastating storms, a public official charged, "People who built glass houses on exposed beaches violated nature. They bulldozed dunes to see the ocean from their homes, and the ocean wiped them out" because dunes weren't there to protect them from even moderate storm tides. It might be said that would-be beach dwellers violate nature most egregiously by ignoring its ways and by acting on convenient assumptions and old wives' tales. Witness what Smithsonian geologist J. W. Pierce calls "the Singapore scenario." This natural phenomenon is named for the supposedly impregnable British fortress that fell in World War II when Japanese troops simply attacked from its undefended rear. It works this way:

When a hurricane approaches the Eastern Seaboard, its winds are typically felt first coming from eastern points of the compass— from offshore. These winds force water into the bays behind the barrier islands and hold the water there for hours at abnormally high levels, sometimes for an entire tide cycle so that the next high tide packs enormous quantities of water. As the storm center passes northward up the coast, the winds quickly shift 180 degrees and blow with equal strength from western points of the compass. These winds then blow all that water out of the bays, flooding barrier islands from the inland side where natural "defenses" are weakest and man-made ones often nonexistent.

This has happened innumerable times over the ages in many island chains, with understandable results. North Carolina historian David Stick writes that the phenomenon is responsible for most of the "inlets" along the Outer Banks. They're really "outlets" formed when high waters rushed back to the ocean, taking the shortest courses they could find or create. There are eight breaks in that island chain today; in the historical past thirty such gaps have had names and there is physical evidence of another eighteen. They come and go, most of them filling in naturally after a few years. Presently the most famous one, Oregon Inlet, is spanned by a spectacular bridge (that was spectacularly severed when a runaway barge hit it in an autumn storm in 1990). For decades Oregon Inlet has been trying to close—or move away from the bridge site; it stays open thanks only to constant and expensive dredging operations powered by the can-do determination of the Corps of Engineers and the life-or-death lobbying efforts of local fishing interests.

Wondrous natural attractions aside, the fabled Outer Banks has been a natural science laboratory and proving ground for decades and deserves our special attention. This chain of barrier islands bellies out into the Atlantic below Chesapeake Bay and loops back to the North Carolina mainland near Beaufort. Its total length exceeds 200 miles, the average width is perhaps 1,000 yards and the mean elevation is about 20 feet above sea level—depending on the tide and the barometer, of course. More than half this captivating stretch of sand is now in the public domain thanks to a plan authorized by Congress in the 1930s. Cape Hatteras National Seashore began to be realized two decades later when philanthropist Paul Mellon provided funds that enabled the purchase of most of Ocracoke and Hatteras islands and much of Bodie Island. In the 1970s, bicentennial fever fueled the public purchase of the islands below Ocracoke; thus Portsmouth, Core Banks and Shackleford Banks became Cape Lookout National Seashore. Despite their proximity, these two parcels had quite different histories, displayed very different appearances and experienced different effects from passing storms. The "improved" islands sustained costly damage during storms—and only in part because those islands boasted houses and roads that could be washed away. The wilder islands seemed to survive violent storms with fewer long-term changes. They just shrugged off gales and flood tides.

Lightly inhabited for centuries, the islands of the Hatteras seashore had been built-upon and "improved" during the 1930s when well-meaning officials made work for jobless people by having them build dunes in order to "stabilize" the islands and make them safe for more development. This spine of dunes runs along most of the Hatteras Seashore islands, which also boast a dozen full-fledged towns and vacation communities. (Their growth was so excessive in the seventies and eighties that human demand outstripped the fresh water supply, which has been augmented by desalination.)

The island of Cape Lookout Seashore, on the other hand, had never been developed in realtors' terms. Some parcels of land were privately owned, but the most intensive uses were brief and highly seasonal. In particular, a segment of 40-mile-long Core Banks was frequented by sport fishermen who built flimsy shanties and, alas, brought cars generally too dilapidated for mainland roads; these served as beach buggies until they broke down and were abandoned in the sand. In any case, Core Banks was in remarkably good shape; that is, very much in a natural state. The foreshore sloped quite gently and a wide, bare berm reached from the normal high-tide line to an irregular line of low, natural dunes. As the National Park Service began the process of planning Cape Lookout National Seashore, it ordered basic surveys of these islands. One of these, published in 1976, was the landmark study *Barrier Island Ecology* by Paul and Melinda Godfrey. It described the sustaining dynamism of Core Banks and, by extension, revealed the relative competence of man and nature to sustain an island.

In a word, Core Banks coped naturally with the rigors of its native environment. To use belligerent human terms, when it was "attacked" by a storm it surrendered rather than confronted the onslaught. Its very shape encouraged a storm surge to wash over all the way to the landward bay if necessary, dropping new layers of sand as it passed. The Godfreys demonstrated that such an island actually benefits over the long term from passing tempests. Overwash leaves new sand on the berm, and winds later blow this sand into dunes. "As sand is moved into the interior of the island by overwash, and on dunes by wind, the height of the island increases and tends to keep pace with the rising sea," they wrote, referring to the age-old phenomenon of sea-level rise.

Accumulation of new sand stimulated growth of beach grasses—largely sea oats in this case—which in turn contributed to the gently-sloped dunes. "Natural vegetation and new dunes have developed on these terraces during the past decade," they wrote in 1976. "Thus much of the island consists of a series of quite recent overwash terraces. New dunes form on the terraces only to be buried or eroded by overwash in their turn. The sand, however, is carried further back into the island during an overwash instead of being lost to the littoral currents, and so it is conserved." As sea level rises slowly and the waves carry away the seaward side, the island grows slowly upwards and moves slowly toward the mainland. Nutrients provided by periodic overwash enrich the soil, encouraging native vegetation. Occasional overwash and the natural profiles of berm and dunes also assure that only hardy seaside plants will survive for very long, rather than faster-growing inland species that can crowd out salt-resistant vegetation. Thus the island nurtures plants that quickly recover from storms and rebuild natural dunes, while the entire island migrates westward at such a gentle pace that it appears to be permanent. In short, here was an ecosystem in place and in gear.

By contrast, the Godfreys observed, "on the islands of Cape Hatteras National Seashore, these natural processes have been greatly altered by the heavy hand of man." Settled for centuries and heavily developed, Ocracoke, Hatteras and Bodie islands had been "protected" by the line of relatively steep dunes raised along man-made fences. The mechanics were simple enough, even "natural": Build a barrier of brush or wooden slats, and it will check the wind, causing it to drop whatever sand it carries. Grain by grain the sand collects until it buries the fence. Plant another fence along the rising dune and the sand rises even higher, creating an imposing barrier against prevailing winds and common storms, and a sheltered lee that folks find comforting. Dune building "in past years was done in good faith," wrote the Godfreys, looking back as far as the 1930s when the Civilian Conservation Corps fought unemployment on the Outer Banks. Authorities then believed that artificial dunes would help preserve the Hatteras seashore and heal scars of past abuses, such as the wholesale livestock grazing that had destroyed native grasses. The Godfreys confided:

> However, this approach has led to attempts at total stabilization, the desire to hold everything in place, and to prevent the sea from washing over the islands. Such a program has come about to protect roads and buildings and with this development it has become necessary to hold all the sand in place and prevent dune movement, overwash and the opening of inlets. A continuous artificial dune line has been built the length of the Seashore . . . effectively a dyke which stops all ordinary overwash. The beach has become very narrow and irregular . . . Therefore storm waves impinge directly on most of the dune, since they cannot roll over the island, and rebound from the dune faces, eroding beach and dune sand into the littoral drift and out into deep water.

One thing leads to another. As more sand is washed away from an island, and as overwash no longer adds new sand to it, perforce the island shrinks.

University of Virginia geologist Robert Dolan published simi-

lar conclusions in *Science*, the journal of the American Association
for the Advancement of Science:

> Although intuition suggests that by stabilizing the dunes one suc-
> ceeds in stabilizing the entire beach system, the dunes are, un-
> fortunately, a response element of the system, not a forcing
> element. If the dune areas are stabilized, the new system must
> adjust to any changes in the barrier itself. That is, if the sea level
> rises and the beach zones shift landward, the dunes must also
> shift, or the beach sector of the system is reduced in width, the
> energy dissipation process is changed and the entire system is
> forced out of equilibrium. . . . In the early 1930s the barrier
> islands of North Carolina were in what might be called a natural
> or equilibrium state. Changes were [naturally] rapid, but the
> system was well adapted to accommodate powerful natural
> forces.

Just how powerful? Consider the Ash Wednesday Storm of
1962, a so-called hundred-year storm—one that is statistically likely
to occur once a century through a coincidence of extreme natural
conditions. The center of a powerful low-pressure system lingered
700 miles off Cape Hatteras. Hurricane-force winds built up waves
that must have self-destructed at sea as they rose too high to support themselves. Even the wind's energy remained trapped in water that reached the continental shelf. Steep waves built up in ever
shallower water. When they reached the shoals their force was
compressed more and the kinetic confusion became enormous. The
sea battered dunes that had been built with the best intentions.
Waves with crests 20 feet high and 200 to 400 feet apart came
marching ashore at six- to eight-second intervals. Then waves 21
feet high came ashore—and carried away the pier that held the
measuring gauge. As the storm continued, the shore retreated.
Frontal dunes were levelled. Buildings fell or washed off their footings. Roads were buried or broken like peanut brittle and carried
away in pieces. The shape of the coast was reordered, rendering
recent maps and charts obsolete.

A later example of a powerful storm visited New England for
two days in the winter of 1978, remodeling New England shores
and crippling Massachusetts. Boston reported 27 inches of snow
and seventy-nine-mile-an-hour winds. Communities on Cape Cod
were ravaged. In Chatham the wind rose to ninety-two miles an

hour and nearshore breaker heights exceeded 16 feet. The storm
surge at Eastham rose 4 feet above spring tide level. Along the
coast 10,000 residents fled and 12,000 homes were damaged or
destroyed. Geologist Stephen P. Leatherman, then director of a
National Park Service research unit, reported extraordinary
changes along Coast Guard Beach, keystone of Cape Cod National
Seashore. For each meter of beach, 16 cubic meters of sand were
carried away. The dunes receded 30 feet. The parking lot was
destroyed. A few miles south of Nauset Beach, a little hamlet of
fishermen's cottages called Three Cabin Hole implicitly became
Two Cabin Hole. Nearby, a National Literary Landmark was swept
away. This was the dwelling Henry Beston inhabited and remembered in his classic *The Outermost House.* Along the length of the
Cape, cliffs were scarped back. But the beaches reappeared after
the storm passed and the tide fell.

That's not always the case, as the terse remark of Virginia
waterman George West made clear to me years ago when he ferried
me out to the islands of the Virginia Coast Preserve. "I owned a
thousand acres right about here," he said, as porpoises played
around the boat. The area had been an island before the hurricane
of 1933. Indeed, like many of those islands that lie east of the lower
Eastern Shore, it was an inhabited island. "All got in safe except my
grandfather and old Mr. Cobb. We didn't know anything about
hurricanes then—called them northeasters. Nobody could conceive
a tide could come that high."

Building on the sand has made little sense since biblical times,
but it has only been in recent years that the reasons have been so
carefully studied and particularly quantified. Recent surveys, using
newly developed mapping techniques, prove that 90 percent of the
East Coast is receding. The beach is steadily losing land at an
average rate of 2 to 3 feet a year, reports Stephen Leatherman, now
director of the University of Maryland's Laboratory for Coastal Research and a national authority on littoral dynamics. Natural erosion
is making the south coast of Martha's Vineyard move north about 10
feet a year, and Cape Hatteras 12 to 15 feet a year. (Nothing like
Louisiana's 30 to 50 feet a year.)

A case can be made that Ocean City, Maryland, Atlantic City,
New Jersey, the Hamptoms on Long Island and others should never
have been developed so extravagantly; that thousands of homes
should never have been erected on the Outer Banks; and that New

Jersey's coastal resorts should have been located landward of natural bays rather than on the barrier islands. The fact is, each of these absurdities has acquired the status of Everest: It is there, now. In terms of political and economic realities, these places will not be abandoned any time soon—unless, perhaps, a major hurricane comes ashore in such an area and renders it literally uninhabitable. That could happen too. One thing leads to another.

Driftwords: Kopper's Law

For the record if you please, my First Law of the Littoral, articulated a dozen years ago, states that a beach's relative merit—its beauty and overall appeal—increases with its *in*accessability, its remoteness. Conversely, the easier it is to reach a beach, the more generally wretched that strand will be, witness Coney Island. Obviously the working principle here is that inaccessible beaches have fewer people, and fewer people generally mean a better beach.

A contentious statistician might work out an equation built around a mathematical constant to quantify the human enjoyment of a beach. One solitary person at dawn on a stretch of empty beach experiences K amount of pleasure; 1,000 teenagers lolling around one lifeguard station experience K amount, or one one-thousandth each. The example is burlesque, of course, though I insist in all seriousness that the search for restorative solitude is one of the great reasons to go beaching.

Yes, I've gone in the dead of winter. Often I've driven an extra hour to reach a bit beach I could call my own for an hour. I have traveled hundreds of miles for the single purpose of fetching up on an island where I would not see another soul for days. Where was that? I'll tell you exactly. It was here and there, then and earlier, thither and yon, now and anon. I dare not write the names for fear that too many people will beat a path to these places and change empty islands into Coneys; call it the Pamplona Syndrome. But here, nonetheless, are directions: On a map study the islands close-in and offshore. Then locate the places that are hardest to reach, most inconvenient, least accessible or most remote. It is such a place that you must find, for there have come to be too many of us.

PART THREE

The Arts of Beaching

The beach "is there"—like Everest, but far more accessible. For better or worse, millions seek it out today as some have for millennia. (Indians who wintered inland spent summers on these shores, though Europeans who immigrated to the New World much later failed to discover the delights of summer beaching for generations.) In the 1850s some New Jersey boosters convinced a railroad to run a line from Philadelphia all the way to the water at a place called Absecon Island. Thus Atlantic City was born, and within twenty years its boardwalk was built—to keep guests from tracking sand into the hotels! That ominous beginning recalls Lewis Carroll's beachcombers:

> The Walrus and the Carpenter
> Were walking close at hand.
> They wept like anything to see
> Such quantities of sand:
> "If this were only cleared away,"
> They said, "it would be grand!"
> "If seven maids with seven mops
> Swept it for half a year,
> Do you suppose," the Walrus asked,
> "That they could get it clear?"
> "I doubt it," said the Carpenter,
> And shed a bitter tear.

To my way of thinking, the beach is for people who take it as it is. There are still many without boardwalks, even some without condos and crowds, though these are becoming fewer and farther between. There are places of various degrees of wildness, and wildness must be taken on its own terms. There are special pleasures that can enhance any sandy sojourn. There are lessons to learn and lore to reflect on.

It is beyond this book's scope (and its author's ken) to discuss high-rise resort living. When I want all the comforts of home, I stay there. When I want a sense of the real world, an adventurous rest or just a thorough airing, it's beach time. When the hunger grows for a few self-reliant days—a sense of the need to know how to handle natural hazards alone—I find an island. When the city closes in and I need the perspective of being apart, I face an overwhelming ocean. Tiring of the urbane, I watch shore birds. I tend to go where and when other people don't. Some years I've spent more time on the shore in January than July because the easy-to-reach places are empty in winter. For several years running I swam in the Atlantic off the Delmarva Peninsula within a week of Christmas when the water still held a hint of summer's warmth and almost every summertime visitor stayed away. Between July Fourth and Labor Day, I generally walk an extra mile or drive an extra day to find some kind of solitude.

Why go to the beach? For reasons touched on before and hereafter. To see the critters, to taste the rose hips, to let a child reinvent castles in the sand again, to find a whale's jawbone. For isolation and the challenge of elemental living. For superb sea-fresh food simply cooked outside or in a cottage kitchen. For a lover's constant, quiet company. For the contrasts of a sweating run and then a surf swim; of a freezing, day-long walk, then hot chowder. For the slow, sensuous roller coaster of searing noons and sleep in salty air. For the certain fury of a gale, the glory of the burning sun's rise out of a calm sea, the miracle of diving birds and the rare wonder of walking naked in moonlight. For the itch of sand between the toes and glimpses of infinity.

CHAPTER NINE

Justly notorious: the Portuguese man-of-war

Adolph's and the Lion's Mane

The beach, like Rhett Butler, frankly doesn't give a damn. It doesn't care whether folks visit or not, even whether a visitor lives or not. This is not to say that the beach is a maliciously deadly place. It is impersonal, remote (and in another sense, the more remote the better). Since wild beaches lack telephones and First Aiders behind every dune, people visiting them are on their own and had better know what they're doing. Anyone going beyond the boundaries of a "protected" beach must be alert to the kinds of pitfalls that can appear. Of course it's best to avoid physical problems, but once encountered they must be addressed directly and on their own terms; you can't con a wave.

Urban sophisticates are adept at verbally resolving all sorts of difficulties, like talking cops out of traffic tickets. But the sun's ultraviolet rays have no interest in extenuating circumstances. They just burn, and seem to burn hotter in spring than autumn, though that appearance is misleading: It's a matter of one's having gotten used to sunshine. By the same token, because the body's temperature-control mechanisms function best after steady use, a winter's layoff means that sweat glands simply don't work as well the first week of summer as they will after Labor Day. Even fatigue is a matter of conditioning, not imagination or moral laxness. Keep in mind that the beach is a physical place and can be dealt with only in physical terms. The problems it presents cannot be disarmed by personal charm or pleas for sympathy: A Portuguese man-of-war has no ears.

This chapter will not deal with general first aid—like how to treat a flesh wound; there are specific manuals for that. Rather it will describe the special hazards of the beach, the various mechanics they involve and ways to anticipate them. These hazards involve matters as general as one's salt/water balance and particulars as nettlesome as jellyfish stings. First, the business of the surf itself:

Richard D. Baker, Assateague National Seashore's chief lifeguard for twenty-four years, says the first rule is to respect the water. He has seen arms broken, thighs fractured, vertebrae cracked, and both shoulders dislocated in people who were "just dumped by a wave." His first rule when entering the surf is simple: Don't do it yet. Wait a minute—wait five—and watch what's going on. With a little practice and experience, simple observation can show you a great deal about the water and the surface of the shallow ocean bottom.

First, study the breakers in order to gauge their power, which increases exponentially with height and "period" (or frequency measured in seconds). Along mid-Atlantic summer beaches, a seven-second period is about average, Baker reports; offshore storms can manifest themselves in longer periods, if not taller waves. This explains why today's waves might look no higher than yesterday's but pack more wallop. The greater the height and/or period, the greater the energy that must be released when the wave breaks. When you want to get in their way, there is no need to compute foot-pounds of force; just visualize the effect if one should catch you across the shoulders—or catch your child at the knees. Then anticipate just how far you and others with you can safely wade or swim. Keep these limits in mind, but if you forget and see you are about to get hit too hard, don't jump up; instead, duck *down* under a breaking wave's crest to escape the greatest force.

Next, look for currents and underwater sandbars. That sounds as if it requires clairvoyance or X-ray vision, but in fact it's easy to spot the location of unseen bars. Harkening back to the mechanics of waves, remember that they steepen dramatically when the water gets shallow. Obviously waves break in the surf zone near the beach (where the water depth becomes less than one-seventh the wave length, the distance between crests). Breaking waves are the ones to watch out for because they physically transport water and whatever's in it—including people.

Waves undulating up and down simply demonstrate the passage of energy through the water; you can float among non-breaking waves and bob around like a cork, even beyond the closest surf line. But look farther out as well; there's usually another line of cresting waves. Its location betrays an underwater sandbar, a fairly abrupt shallowing, which is responsible for the water's visible disturbance. Study that line of cresting waves that keeps appearing at the same place: It indicates the shape and extent of the bar, which lies roughly parallel to the beach. Since bars mean shallows, the water there may not be over your head, should you need to touch bottom after swimming through the deep water beyond the close-in surf zone. Often a bar offers a place to stand and rest.

Regardless of whether the tide is rising or falling, the water breaking on the beach must go somewhere; it seeks its own level in the sea. Thus it rushes away from the land and, combining with the seaward movement of the trough before the next wave, creates a mythological "undertow." Baker says there's actually no such thing. Call it "backwash." Certainly this rush of water can be strong enough to nudge a wader's feet out from under him, especially at certain tide phases on the steepest slope of a summer beach. If that happens and the wader falls down, more backwash tumbles him farther downhill. This is a simple phenomenon, but folks promote it into the fiction of a malevolent force apparently bent on dragging them off the edge of the continental shelf. It's simply backwash: the flow of water going its own way. Farther out is where things can get really perilous.

As waves cross a sandbar they can create discrete inshore currents, occasionally becoming alarmingly strong. Flowing between the surf and the sandbar, these currents are sometimes dangerous, especially to unsuspecting swimmers. They are strongest where they have cut through a bar, because the breaks in the bar act like funnels. The currents move seaward surprisingly fast, especially in relation to the nearby land-bound waves. Misnamed "rip tides," the most dramatic and disarming of these currents occur when they run perpendicular from the beach, heading straight out to sea. This is rare, says Baker, but when it happens the results can be terrifying. An unwary swimmer paddles happily along, then finds himself suddenly being swept away from shore. The swimmer panics, understandably, and tries to make shore via the shortest route, namely, by turning right around and swimming straight back. The result can be swift exhaustion and possible drowning, since few organisms besides fish swim faster than these currents.

Baker's suggestion—study the surf before entering it—can keep a swimmer out of a rip current in the first place. By observing where lines of breakers end, one can anticipate the location and direction of these currents. A sharp break in a surf line parallel to the beach means that's where a rip current is apt to pass seaward through the bar. The rip current has scoured out a deeper channel in the underwater sand; hence, incoming waves don't crest or break the way they do in the shallower water above the intact sandbar. Ergo, Rule One: Stay away from such currents by staying away from gaps in the lines of breakers. They are rarely more than several yards across and they are widely spaced. Swim somewhere else, within an unbroken sandbar.

Break Rule One and your life can depend on assiduously observing Rule Two: When you get caught in a rip current, don't fight it head-on because you'll lose. Stop. Tread water. Get your bearings. Then move at right angles to the current; swim across it (even though it's still carrying you seaward) until you are outside its influence. This will take only a few strokes since these currents are narrow. Alternatively, if you passively let it carry you past the bar, you'll find that a rip current dissipates beyond the line of cresting waves. Then drift into the crest line and let the breaking waves push you back toward shore. Use the ocean's energy to your advantage.

Instructions like these are easy enough to codify in my comfortable study in Washington on a quiet night when most locals are away and even the tourists have taken their groaning Winnebagos off to bed. It's an entirely different matter on a windy day in brisk surf 30 yards from an East Coast beach that threatens to vanish over the western horizon. Please remember anyway: Don't panic. Turn right or left ninety degrees and *swim across the current* to slower water that's moving the right way. And if you do get into trouble in sight of people on shore, don't try to wave both arms violently to attract attention. That just wastes energy and makes you sink besides. Tread water and raise one hand; it'll be obvious that something's amiss—should anyone be willing and able to help in time.

Rip currents running straight away from land are rare. Currents running obliquely through a surf zone are more common. They're more insidious too; more subtle and longer, they move away from the land less dramatically. But the same rules apply. If you see a surf line slanting away from shore, recognize that a current probably goes the same direction and avoid it. If you forget and it starts carrying you the wrong way, don't try to swim against it. Swim across the current to easier water before heading back to the beach.

Closer in, when you start playing in the water, notice which way you're being carried. The surf pushes everything a little distance along the beach with each wave. Almost every working day, Baker sees a parent bawl out some innocent kid: "Didn't I tell you to swim right *there?*" It's an impossible order to obey. The slight slant of the surf will always carry a swimmer or wader up or down the beach. It takes a conscious effort to stay in one place or return to Point A. Better to tell a child to walk back every few minutes, explaining that the water will naturally push him astray. For yourself, pick a reference point—a pile of driftwood or a beach towel—and keep in sight of it.

While rip currents dissipate beyond the offshore sandbar, seaward winds don't. This doesn't affect swimmers, but it can play havoc with people riding air mattresses. In fact, if the wind is blowing off the shore, don't even bother to inflate a raft. It can be a killer. The reasons are simple. Swimming out, most folks are aware they'll have to swim back and budget their energy. But with the crutch of an air mattress, there seems to be a greater degree of safety and a willingness to venture into deeper water. Then a moderate wind can push the raft and rider farther out to sea, taking them into very deep water indeed. Next stop, Spain!

Naming the exotic place recalls the Mediterranean beaches of the Costa Brava: Ruby sangria and snow-white sand; cold prawns and sweet clams no bigger than a thumbnail; hot sun and brisk water. It also recalls a drowning off Costa del Sol—the Coast of the Sun—thirty years ago. The train had brought hundreds of *Madrileños* to Malaga for the weekend. One young man wired his mother that he'd arrived safely: *"Dios me guarde. Tu hijo."* The public beach, bordered on the south side by a high outcrop of fossil-filled stone, was wide and hot. The underwater profile sloped very gently. The young man from Madrid waded out a hundred yards or more to the surf off the point, slipped and went under— perhaps hitting a rock. His friends and a score of strangers had a slow time carrying him to shore. A Scottish dentist offered artificial respiration by-the-book, but not speaking Spanish, he was turned down. An American student climbed the cliff barefoot and ran for a doctor, but the doctor wouldn't come without payment in advance. With everybody in charge and nobody in charge, the Spaniards tried to revive the anonymous swimmer several different ways. None worked, and now, covered with foam-flecked sand, he was dead. It was frustrating; all our efforts had been in vain. It was frightening; any one of us could have been the victim. It was infuriating; the doctor should have come. A pall fell along the beach. The Catholics crossed themselves. The Scot cursed. I shuddered in the sun. That evening the text of the young man's telegram home went round the quiet outdoor cafés. Bartenders repeated it and passed it on. People crossed themselves again and drank to the memory of that dutiful son.

The good news is that drowning is declining in America; it has slipped from the third to the fourth leading cause of accidental death, which is to say, the fourth most common cause of avoidable tragedy. The cause of death in most drownings is asphyxiation from water in the lungs. (The brain's oxygen supply is cut off and death follows fast.) However, perhaps 10 percent of drowning victims die of simple asphyxiation because a spasm in the glottis (part of the larynx) cuts off the air supply and prevents both water and air from reaching the lungs. Authorities beg statistics on near-drownings, but medical experts warn ocean swimmers about a particular peril: Near-drownings can kill after the victim has apparently recovered. Aspirating salt water is twice as dangerous as inhaling fresh water because of different physiological effects. Quantities of fresh water can be inhaled and actually absorbed by lung tissue without too much harm if the victim starts breathing again (with or without artificial help). But ocean water, due to its salt content, behaves differently in the lungs. It extracts vital fluids because of differences in osmotic pressure. When a semipermeable membrane separates salt water from fresh, pure water particles pass through the barrier until the two solutions are equally salty. It's the same problem marine fishes face. When this phenomenon occurs in the lungs, the secondary effects on blood chemistry as well as lung function are complex and dangerous. Anyone who survives a near-drowning episode in salt water should be hospitalized, medical authorities say, and placed under intensive pulmonary care until both the blood and lungs return to normal.

Underwater swimmers ask for trouble if they hyperventilate before testing their distance. Voluntary breathing in and out hard seems a good idea before taking that last deep breath and diving. But it's really a bad idea, because it abnormally rids the system of almost all carbon dioxide. The normal impulse to breathe is triggered by a need to expel CO_2, not to get fresh air. Oxygen hunger is only a secondary cause of the breathing reflex. Hence, hyperventilation before swimming underwater any distance risks exhausting the oxygen supply before enough new CO_2 builds up to warn that it's time for another breath. A submerged swimmer can suffocate that way.

Other dangers at the beach have equally simple origins, causes that are purely physical. A U.S. Navy installation once geared up for an epidemic when an alarming number of recruits displayed an irreversible eye condition that was supposed to be rare. The problem, which led to permanent blindness, involved tiny water blisters on the central retina, the rear inner surface of the eye. Fortunately it turned out that no new contagion was involved. Rather, these recruits had been taking LSD. Then, under its numbing influence, they'd do what normal reactions usually prevent: stare in fascination directly at the sun. Under ordinary circumstances, this quickly becomes intolerably uncomfortable. But LSD (and drugs like alcohol) can desensitize or raise the pain threshold. The result for the recruits was sunburn and blistering of the inner eye. Ophthalmologists suggest that people other than acidheads should be alert to the problem. Tired vacationers lying on a beach under a light overcast are apt to stare at the dim solar disk, risking retinal damage from visible and invisible rays.

Sunburn is well named. The slow effects of ultraviolet light on human skin are akin to that of a flame. Exposed skin reddens as blood rushes to it; blisters develop to protect deeper tissues; and under rare circumstances, skin can actually burn. Destroyed cells release organic components that irritate sensory nerves, which carry a message—"Pain!"—to the brain. A suntan is the natural protective reaction to sunlight. Biochemically it works this way: Cells containing a brown or black pigment called melanin are distributed evenly in the skin (or unevenly in people with freckles). The amount of pigment is genetically determined and is responsible for every individual's normal complexion. In theory a person could spontaneously turn dark overnight, since melanin production is usually in a kind of suspended animation; the potential for making more melanin is always there but held in check. Sunlight results in tanning but doesn't create it directly; rather, solar radiation relaxes natural controls. In summertime doses, the sun's rays neutralize inhibitors that control an enzyme, tyrosinase, which stimulates the production of melanin. This has a biological purpose beyond human vanity: Melanin absorbs harmful radiation, protecting deeper tissues beneath the skin. The inhibitors remain active in skin areas protected from the sun; in exposed areas the inhibitors become active again with less exposure to sunlight. Thus a suntan fades over the winter in people with normally light complexions as skin cells slough off, revealing new layers containing less pigment. In addition, body chemistry breaks down some pigment after it forms.

Now the bad news: Tanning can be dangerous to your health—even lethal in the long run. Until recently, the deep tan was fashionable among caucasian Americans, but in recent years the tan itself has been identified as a cause of malignant melanoma. This very bad form of cancer is on the statistical rise, thanks to the fashion of decades past. Says a medical expert, "We have no treatment except local excision for melanoma. It metastasizes all over the body, can be dormant for years and then riddle your liver. It is an ugly way to die." If there is no cure, there is easy prevention: the commercial lotions called sun screens and sun blocks. Available in virtually every drug and notions store, they are numerically rated as to the protection they provide from ultraviolet rays. They work—if you use them with common sense (i.e., reapply them after swimming) If not for chic's sake, then for your own longevity, don't try for that deep tan this summer; it could kill you.

Dire warnings aside, people visiting the beach get sunburned in novel places. I knew a year-round golfer who, on an unaccustomed visit to the beach, applied the approved lotions to all the usual places: face, arms and legs. But she forgot her feet, usually protected by cleats and socks. Not so when she followed the tide looking for pretty shells. After that barefoot walk she couldn't put on shoes for a week. People beaching in the nude for the first time should also take special care. Patches of skin that have been covered by a bathing suit in the past have no residual tan and are apt to burn very fast.

An immediate problem caused by exposure to the sun is called "heatstroke" by the American Red Cross and "hyperpyrexia" or "heat prostration" by medical texts. In the classic study of hot-weather health problems, *Physiology of Man in the Desert*, Edward F. Adolph defined it as "disorganized thermoregulatory ability." (Zoologists aren't the only specialists with galloping nomenclature.) This condition can kill by any name. It involves a malfunction of temperature-control mechanisms, which cannot reinstate themselves spontaneously. Once excessive heat throws a victim's thermostat out of kilter, he is apt to die unless artificial means are used to reverse a runaway heating trend.

Like the bimetal gadget on a dining-room wall, the human thermostat has two controlling elements. Both are located in the hypothalamus, a portion of the forebrain, but they are distinct and each responds to separate stimuli. When a person feels cold, a message goes from the skin to the brain, which then signals surface blood vessels to constrict in order to conserve body heat. Other signals then trigger shivering, which paradoxically helps warm the body. When a person gets too hot due to exercise or environment, the other brain center responds directly to internal temperature without the intervention of sensory organs. Then the hypothalamus signals surface vessels to dilate in order to let more blood flow through the skin; this lets the body eliminate more heat through simple radiation. At the same time, the brain activates the sweat glands to help cool the body by excreting liquid, which evaporates on the skin. For every gram of water that evaporates, .58 calories of heat can be released. Evaporation of any liquid releases heat and has a cooling effect.

Normally the human thermostat is set at about 98.6° F. But a number of substances in the bloodstream can re-adjust the setting and delay reactions until a higher temperature is reached. These include recent immunization shots, some bacteria and viruses; hence fever accompanies the common cold or flu. Alarmingly important, excess body heat affects the hypothalamus and interferes with its normal function. This is when the trouble starts—trouble that can compound itself into a fatal vicious circle. If the body gets too hot, the hypothalamus works less effectively; cooling mechanisms like surface blood vessel dilation and sweating are delayed or weakened. Then the body gets hotter and the hypothalamus works even less effectively. As the body heats up, it inhibits the brain from turning on the cooling equipment full blast, which results in the brain getting hotter until the cooling systems shut down entirely. This can continue until higher body temperature kills brain cells and causes brain damage. Needless to say, an overdose of sun can start this runaway reaction.

Heatstroke symptoms may include any or all of the following: vertigo, unconsciousness, very flushed face, a strong rapid pulse, elevated blood pressure and dry skin, since the sweating mechanism is blocked by the kaput body thermostat. These symptoms may lead to convulsions, coma and death. First aid—or better yet, fast hospitalization—is needed to reduce body temperature so that the hypothalamus can start working properly again. The experts recommend trying almost anything to reduce body temperature if it reaches 105°:

Take the victim to the coolest available place where humidity is low.

Strip him to increase cooling.

Aim fans at him to increase air circulation and evaporation.

Wipe him with cold, wet towels.

Sponge the body with rubbing alcohol, which evaporates (and cools) faster than water.

Apply ice packs, especially to armpits, neck and groin.

Put him in a cold bath. One standard medical text prescribes ice water baths; the Red Cross manual specifies cold water without ice.

But then the Red Cross also suggests that after undressing the victim, the First Aider should use "a small bath towel to maintain modesty"—whether the victim's or the First Aider's remains unclear. (Gentle reader, dear friends, passing strangers: If you find me felled by heatstroke and waste any time on "modesty," I'll expire from apoplexy at such rank stupidity. Don't worry about fig leaves in potentially fatal situations. If a spare cloth is available, use is as a sponge. Delay meaningful treatment too long and the victim will have a sheet over his head soon enough.) Concentrate on lowering the body temperature and keeping it below 102°, since it can quickly "rebound" to higher levels.

Adolph writes: "One of the peculiar features of man's metabolism is that when he is sweating rapidly he does not take enough water to keep up his body water content; in other words, his sensations of thirst are not strong enough to demand sufficient water intake to replace water losses." This phenomenon can cause heat cramps and heat exhaustion.

Though less serious than heatstroke, these common conditions can lead to it if ignored. Both involve the sweating mechanism and the body's salt/water balance. The cramps come first, typically in the legs and stomach muscles. They result from too little salt in the body. Nerve control of muscles depends on electrical connections made by salt ions in the blood. When an unacclimated person sweats profusely, he expels salt in unusual amounts. This robs the body of sufficient salt to make neurological connections; brain messages don't get through, muscles go into spasm, and the person gets cramps.

Salt depletion is most common when unacclimated people encounter unfamiliar heat. Disused sweat glands excrete such quantities of sodium and chloride that the sweat itself may be nearly as salty as blood. But once these glands get used to summertime work, their ducts reabsorb much of the salt constituents and recycle them. Hence, someone getting used to hot weather may add extra salt to food for a few days. After getting acclimated, the extra salt should be stopped because excess salt retains water, inhibits sweating, and creates other problems. Remember that a normal diet usually contains ample salt; when more is needed, people develop a special taste for salty foods.

When someone in a cool climate encounters the first heat wave of the summer he simply can't sweat freely at first; each sweat gland is like a rusty pump and takes time to work up to maximum activity. An acclimated person can excrete nearly five quarts of sweat an hour; a newcomer to the heat does well to expel a quart and a half an hour. Obviously, the extent of perspiration depends on ample water in the body. Loss of that water through sweating means a lower supply until it is replaced by drinking. When cells in the brain's thirst center—again, another part of the hypothalamus—get dehydrated, the person gets the message to drink. But the message may be repeated after drinking since it takes time for the water to be absorbed. As a result you can drink too much and experience "water intoxication." This occurs when body fluids become too diluted and there aren't enough salt ions to perform the body's electrochemical work. Thus, muscle cramps can be a symptom of salt deficiency in the form of dilute body fluids.

Heat exhaustion can occur after a few days in an unfamiliarly hot climate. First, blood rushes to the capillaries in order to dispel excess body heat through radiation. This can rob vital organs of sufficient blood, so the capillaries constrict, leaving the skin pale and clammy (since sweating has been copious). The net result is a drop in blood pressure. Fainting occurs when not enough blood carries oxygen to the brain. The fainting spell itself can revive a victim, since after falling down the head is lower than before, and lower blood pressure suffices to supply the brain. Here the body takes care of itself.

The lessons are simple enough: Overexertion and overexposure at the beach should be avoided until you are thoroughly acclimated. Unless you are absolutely fit, pamper yourself when planning to spend more than a few hours on a remote beach. If you intend to walk a few miles, pack along plenty of water or fruit juice and some salty snacks. When you are sweating freely, a quart of fluid an hour is not an excessive amount to drink. Remember that the last half of the distance may take a good deal longer than the first. For one thing, fatigue has set in. For another, if you set out with a falling tide, the walking will be easy along the wet sand; but return with a rising tide and footing is difficult in dry sand above the swash. If your tan isn't complete, carry some light cover-up clothes: a wide-brimmed hat, long-sleeved shirt, long pants, socks and sneakers. Loose, light-colored cotton fabrics are best because they reflect rather than absorb sun and permit air to circulate over the skin.

Don't sneeze at the idea of shoes on the seashore. For one thing, surface sand gets hot enough in the sun to blister bare feet. For another, rocks, shells and man-made trash (increasingly) can inflict nasty wounds. On wild beaches broken shells tend to collect in shallow drifts along the scalloped foreshore; avoid them by staying out of low parts of the swash zone. But at a place like Townsend's Inlet, New Jersey, broken shells litter the entire beach. This is because dredge spoil from the boat channel has been pumped all along its length to replenish the eroding sand. Alas, the channel was where shells naturally collected and where beach people never walked. Now boats have easy access to the bay and everybody wears shoes on the broadened beach. Elsewhere shoes are necessary so you can choose the surest footing. Exploring a breakwater barefooted at Salisbury Beach, Massachusetts, I couldn't step on the tide-bared barnacles, so I stepped on green algae and slipped. Falling on a patch of the barnacles that looked no bigger around than matchheads, my arm was raked from elbow to wrist. The minute cuts, too shallow to hurt (at first), measured 15 to the inch and didn't heal for a month. If I'd been wearing shoes, I might not have fallen in the first place.

Aside from mollusks, dead or alive, and stingrays described in Chapter Three, a variety of other animals can hurt—the cnidarians in particular. Call them jellyfish, members of a particularly ancient phylum that includes corals, sea pens and anemones. Formerly known as coelenterates (along with the sponges that later found their own phylum), this is a varied group of radially symmetrical animals. (To confuse the issue a bit more, some apparent jellyfish—the comb jellies—not only belong to yet another phylum, but are harmless to humans. Nearly transparent or luminous, they may have a single pair of long filaments with short branches to snare their prey.) To avoid a tangle of zoological distinctions, let a simple rule suffice: Beware of jellyfish with many tentacles. They're the ones that sting.

These animals' notoriety depends on a tiny, fundamentally mechanical structure called the nematocyst. Typically it is a hollow cylinder containing a toxin and a long, coiled, microscopically barbed thread. When anything touches its closed aperture, the thread springs out like a sharp, diabolical jack-in-the-box. One nematocyst doesn't do much damage, but in the Portuguese man-of-war (*Physalia physalis*) each tentacle may have 750,000 nematocysts. The cumulative effect of several thousand minute, poison-dipped weapons is painful and debilitating.

Notably sluggish and delicate, a jellyfish spends its life drifting through the water pulsing its dish- or umbrella-shaped bell and trailing its tentacles. Small animals get entangled in the tentacles, immobilized by the nematocysts and engorged in the central gut. Able to stabilize itself to some degree and to sense light, the jellyfish cannot distinguish between likely food and anything else. Its nematocysts simply explode at the touch—even if a tentacle has broken off from the rest of the animal. In his encyclopedia of zoological horrors, *Dangerous to Man*, Roger Caras analyzes the general problem and offers sensible advice:

> Jellyfish don't swim around attacking men, they pulse and float along their own stupid, blind way waiting patiently to bump into something they can eat. They sting anything they encounter. They are never in a hurry and have been floating around this way for untold years. It is obviously a successful way of life since billions of them are still around. While they can't very well make a meal of a man, they don't know it. They just bump and sting, bump and sting. To avoid the sting, man has only to avoid the bump. While he may be able to depend on the fear, quiet good nature, or the escape "reflexes" of other potentially dangerous animals, he cannot do this with the jellyfish. He must learn to keep out of the way.

When one has failed that and bumped into a cnidarian, the next problem is to remove the tentacles "as they continue to discharge venom," according to Bruce W. Halstead's enormous, lavish and definitive *Poisonous and Venomous Marine Animals of the World*. Wipe them off with a towel, sand or anything handy, he says. Then apply alcohol, household ammonia, vinegar, lemon juice, boric acid, hand lotion or sodium-bicarbonate paste; these are the standard salves. Ray Manning, a Smithsonian crustacea man and veteran of beaches around the world, recommends another: Adolph's Meat Tenderizer (or any other brand). He regularly carries a shaker of it to sprinkle generously on jellyfish (or insect) stings. It acts on the foreign body the same way it softens chuck steak: by breaking down the proteins. Assateague Island's Dick Baker suggests pouring on alcohol first—to anesthetize any nematocysts that haven't discharged—and then using the tenderizer.

In East Coast waters, jellyfish are not often lethal; usually they just hurt. Because the larger varieties have geometrically larger numbers of nematocysts to hurt with, they can be very painful indeed. In addition, the toxin can be a real danger when delivered in large amounts. Also these stings, like those of bees, can trigger allergic reactions, such as vomiting, sweats and difficulty breathing. For reasons not yet explained, Baker reports that such cases became more common in 1990.

Popular sources disagree about many details of specific East Coast jellyfish. Rachel Carson, in *The Edge of the Sea,* says one member of the *Cyanea* genus has 50-foot tentacles. Zoologist Donald J. Zinn writes of the same jellyfish that its "more than 800 trailing tentacles may extend 200 feet." More important, various authors differ in assessing the danger of some species to humans. The question is whether a particular animal has sufficiently strong nematocysts to penetrate skin. Differences of opinion may depend on the stingee; whether the individual is thick- or thin-skinned. In addition, some people are more susceptible to the toxins, which can have anaphylactic effects (hypersensitivity resulting from previous exposure).

One of the most common jellyfish from Greenland to the West Indies is the moon jelly, *Aurelia aurita,* a milky white, short-tentacled animal often distinguished by red, horseshoe-shaped internal structures, the male gonads. In the fall, moon jellies release gametes in the water. Miss Carson wrote:

> At this season the adults are carrying the developing larvae, holding them in flaps of tissue that hang from under the surface of the disk. The young are little pear-shaped creatures; when finally they are shaken loose from the parent (or freed by the stranding of the parent on the shore), they swim about in the shallow water, sometimes swarms of them together. Finally they seek bottom and each becomes attached by the end that was foremost when it swam. As a tiny plantlike growth, about an eighth of an inch high and bearing long tentacles, this strange child of the delicate moon jelly survives the winter storms. Then constrictions begin to en-

circle its body, so that it comes to resemble a pile of saucers. In
the spring these "saucers" free themselves one after another and
swim away.

This is a classic example of an organism whose generations alternate
between sexual and asexual reproduction.

Small specimens of *Cyana capillata* commonly drift into shallow water as far south as southern New England. This is the lion's
mane—a.k.a. arctic jelly, sea nettle, hairy stinger, hair jellyfish and
snotty. Halstead describes it as "large, repulsive . . . a mop under
a dinner plate." Carson rhapsodizes about its behavior:

> Young cod, haddock and sometimes other fishes adopt the great
> jellyfish as a "nurse," traveling through the shelterless sea under
> the protection of this large creature and somehow unharmed by
> the nettlelike stings of the tentacles. . . . Its offspring are the
> winter plantlike generation, duplicating in almost every detail the
> life history of the moon jelly. . . . Little half-inch wisps of living
> tissue represent the heritage of the immense red jellyfish. They
> can survive the cold and the storms that the larger summer gen-
> eration cannot endure; when the warmth of spring begins to dis-
> sipate the icy cold of the winter sea they will bud off the tiny discs
> that, by some inexplicable magic of development, grow in a single
> season into the adult jellyfish with 50-foot [or perhaps 200-foot]
> tentacles.

The Portuguese man-of-war, or bluebottle, is not a single animal, but actually a colony of specialized, mutually dependent organisms. A warm-water oddity, it is common along southern coasts
but often drifts from the Gulf Stream to beaches along the Outer
Banks, Nantucket and the Vineyard. When they're seen near shore,
word spreads fast. For one reason, the man-of-war's reputation for
inflicting pain is deservedly widespread. For another, the animal is
undeniably pretty. This long-tentacled organism stays afloat by
means of a triangular balloon that rides the surface of the ocean.
The gelatinous, translucent balloon or "sail" is an astonishing pale
electric blue with almost iridescent pink highlights. The animal
manipulates this sail to a degree in order to catch the wind and
move in a chosen direction—like a skillful windsurfer. However
nice they are to look at, a man-of-war is a drifter to be avoided in the
water. (One swimmer stung by *Physalia* off Florida died after the

encounter—of heart failure, perhaps induced by the pain of several thousand nematocysts.) Many other people have been scarred and hospitalized by the mindless creatures; however, they are not without merit in the natural world. They shelter some fish, and they are fodder for sea turtles and the giant sunfish. I've seen a calico crab make a meal of a little red jelly off Fire Island.

Another animal to beware is the spiny black sea urchin, which haunts the rocky New England littoral. Stepping on one barefoot will prove the point. It's like walking on a porcupine. The purple sea urchin (*Arbacia punctulata*) is the most visible on our coast. It lives on shallow, rocky bottoms and avoids sunlight. Like its starfish relatives, this five-part radial animal siphons water through a madreporite ("mother of pores") on its upper surface and pumps it through tube feet. In this manner it can move an inch a minute. What it lacks in speed it gains in mobility, moving in any direction with equal ease.

The greatest hazard to human life and health on the beach—in statistical terms—is the easiest to avoid: a hurricane. How? Get out of the way. Why? For the answer to that, try sticking your head out the car window the next time you drive down some interstate at seventy-five miles an hour. That's the wind speed of a puny hurricane on the Saffir/Simpson Scale, which categorizes these storms as follows:

Class	Severity	Mean Wind Speed	Storm Surge Height
Category 1	weak	74 to 95 mph	4 to 5 ft
Category 2	moderate	96 to 110 mph	6 to 8 ft
Category 3	strong	111 to 130 mph	9 to 12 ft
Category 4	very strong	131 to 155 mph	13 to 18 ft
Category 5	devastating	156 mph or worse	19 ft or more

A Category 1 hurricane packs the strength of the famous winter storm (a northeaster) that paralyzed New England in February of 1978. It was a Category 2 hurricane that reorganized Delmarva's coast in 1933 and opened up the inlet that stimulated the birth of Ocean City, Maryland, as a resort town. "Major" storms begin with Category 3, the sort that blow trash around at dangerous velocities, topple big trees, destroy mobile homes and damage even sound buildings. These come ashore along our Gulf or Atlantic coast about every other year. The high water that accompanied Hurricane Hugo in 1989 qualified it for Category 5, although its winds, which devastated Charleston, South Carolina, were only Category 4. Nonetheless, it has since been rated as the most destructive storm in American history. But you can bet your bottom dollar that a more costly one is coming before very long—if only because the values of beach properties keep rising out of sight.

The most destructive element in a hurricane is usually not the wind but the storm surge. Misnamed "tidal wave" and a host of other things, it is nothing less than a monumental movement of water that rises because of the extreme low pressure in a hurricane's eye, which acts like a vacuum. In fine weather, the atmosphere's high pressure presses down on the ocean's surface and physically keeps the water level down. Reduce that pressure and the water level rises to reach places on land it could never touch otherwise, especially when driven by these mighty winds. Nine out of ten fatalities in our hurricanes result from the storm surge, which can manifest itself long before the wind arrives; this is why authorities fear catastrophe the next time a major hurricane hits the Atlantic coast.

The National Hurricane Center warns, "some structural damage to small buildings" occurs in a Category 3 hurricane, which causes coastal flooding and damage from "battering waves and floating debris." But there's more to it: "Low-lying escape routes inland [are] cut by rising water 3 to 5 hours before hurricane center arrives. Flat terrain 5 feet or less above sea level [is] flooded inland 8 miles or more." Now adapt that wet scenario to a landscape like the Jersey Shore, where a chain of barrier islands has been camouflaged under pavement and ground level barely reaches 5 feet above mean high water. This means entire barrier islands from coast to inland marsh will be flooded before a hurricane hits. Ditto the barrier islands of the Delmarva Peninsula and Ocean City in particular. Ditto the Outer Banks, which has all of two bridges linking the islands to the mainland and the nearest high ground.

The havoc a hurricane might wreck on a barrier island was demonstrated in the fall of 1990. A storm with Category 1 winds barely brushed Pamlico Sound with gales strong enough to tear a dredge loose from its moorings. The dredge struck the bridge over Oregon Inlet and knocked out a 400-foot section, which effectively isolated Hatteras Island from the mainland and the world. Ferries sailed round the clock to evacuate tourists, an effort that took some thirty hours to move 500 cars. Now hear this: In summer and during part of hurricane season, the island may have 150,000 visitors. Should a hurricane threaten Hatteras, such a horde might be evacuated by all those ferries in 150 hours, or say about six days! Any Atlantic beach area that must be evacuated on the approach of a hurricane is going to face a mighty traffic jam. Consider also that hurricanes often move at thirty miles an hour and sometimes over the highway speed limit of fifty-five.

Hurricanes have happened with grim irregularity. Hugo, in 1990, brought a storm urge 17 feet high. In 1893 a storm of similar magnitude inundated the Sea Islands and killed more than 2,000 people. The hurricane that hit Galveston, Texas, in 1900 claimed more lives than the Chicago Fire, Johnstown Flood and great San Francisco Earthquake combined.

This may sound like doomsday stuff, but the rarity of hurricanes in recent years has encouraged beach development and made people complacent. And the long lapse just means we're due.

One final hazard on the beach is the occasional threat of lightning. The dimensions of these electrical extravaganzas stagger comprehension. Sometimes 5 miles long but rarely thicker than a pencil, a single bolt lasting less than one second can carry 100 million volts and reach a temperature of 70,000° F.

By all means get out of the water at the first hint of a thunderstorm. Probably the safest place to be on the beach is crouching down behind a dune—and keeping well below its crest. Since lightning often strikes the tallest local objects, don't hide under an isolated tree, bush or metal watchtower, which may just draw the next bolt like a magnet. (Seeking shelter in a forest is okay.) A source citing National Oceanic and Atmospheric Administration instructions says if "you feel your hair stand on end—indicating that lightning is about to strike—drop on your knees and bend forward, putting your hands on your knees. Do not lie flat on the ground."

Remember that a little rain must fall everywhere—even at the beach. Resign yourself to a good rinsing and enjoy the spectacle.

Driftwords: What's in a Name?

Having reached the shore and put down roots (perhaps as temporary as a tomato's but roots nonetheless) most summer people perform a certain rite: They christen the beach house. It may be a one-room hutch called "Shan-Grila" with trash cans on the torn-screen porch or the Newport mansion Vanderbilt built and plainly dubbed "The Breakers." But plywood or palace, it gets a name. Some are simple, some inscrutable.

In the last century my grandfather built a summer home large enough to become a boarding school later. (A residence again, it's now surrounded by split-levels and ramblers like an Arab steed among asses.) A civil engineer with a mathematical bent, he named it "Azimuth," a term astronomers and surveyors use to describe the apparent elevation of a star. His heirs never knew why. By the same token, a passing stranger hasn't a clue to the meaning of cottage signs in a squalid hamlet near the pristine expanses of Plum Island Wildlife Refuge: "Dartmouth" and "Gemini." A few years back Johnny Cash sang a song about "A Boy Named Sue." On the North Shore I've seen a house called "George." On Fishers Island there's a retreat called "Will o' Dale"—just a sweetly bucolic name, it seems, until one learns that the house was bought with a bequest from the Wall Street banker and art collector Chester Dale.

Most modern dwellings have self-explanatory names, like the remote and tidy fishing shacks along Nauset Beach: "Out of Reach" and "Tax Shelter." A colleague recalls a house on one narrow island called "Chateau Frontenback." At Sandbridge, Virginia, long-legged boxes on stilts are called "Seaduce" and "Mermaison." In one Fire Island town the locals call single folks who share their digs "groupers," a term only a little less graphic than the names of the houses they lease: "The Sensuous Bear" and "Inn the Bushes." These names would hardly be permitted in nearby communities, which are so proper that nonfamilies cannot be admitted. But then "groupers" might not be able to relax in a "Wee Kirk o' the Heath."

From one end of the coast to the other there must be a hundred "Driftwood" motels (each with a mandatory stump on the porch) and a like number of "Sea Shanty" restaurants, most of them overgrown huts charging mansion prices. There are more "Sandpiper" gift shops than shorebird species; more "Sea Breeze" cottages than directions the wind can blow. Yet the most unlikely cliché of a name applies not to a structure but a stripper. On a beach highway north of Boston a neon sign announced the appearance of an entertainer called "Sandy Shore."

Apropos of names, it's high time someone examined America's athletic totems. By that I mean the Chicago Bears, Baltimore Orioles, Princeton Tigers and the like. How the current menagerie evolved is a mystery. The University of Maryland fields team after team of able competitors called Terrapins, named after an indigenous reptile. The animal itself is rather lackluster. Not possessed of any particularly valorous trait, it's best known as the main ingredient of an epicurean soup. Does Louisiana State University go rah-rah for its Gumbo eleven? Of course not. Lions are ubiquitous sports symbols—not native pumas, but the imported kind, à la Phineas T. Barnum and MGM. Bears also show up on sports pages everywhere. Yet in the American west, where the Ursidae are most common, the ubiquitous black bear appears most frequently as a garbage thief, a pest—hardly Hall of Fame material. My alma mater identified with the bulldog, a member of the genus *Canis* that was bred by British gentry for pit fighting in an age when blood sports were considered amusing.

All this seems so biologically inept. I am not suggesting that every beastly icon needs to be replaced. Dolphins are swift, intelligent and aggressive, so the Miami team seems well named despite the animal's reputation for playfulness, a trait that has no place on the football field. The Los Angeles Rams is another well-totemed organization, given the amount of head-to-head contact that occurs on an NFL line of scrimmage. If *Ovis canadensis* does most of its butting when in rut, the football players don't seem to mind the association.

So let well enough alone where teams have traditional identities. But all the professional athletic leagues seem to be expanding and I submit that each new team has a golden opportunity to employ a degree of zoological sensitivity. Let them chose symbols with a brighter eye to accuracy and select animals noted for some trait that's useful in the particular game. Consider these characteristics and candidates:

For tenacity (useful in any sport) *Balanus* or *Crepidula*. Thus the Beaufort Barnacles and Savannah Slipper Shells. Yes, the latter do change their gender as they grow older, but most athletes retire before menopause. Nobody's perfect.

A capable foot is the prerequisite for skillful soccer, so a Pacific Northwest owner might enfranchise the Walla Walla Lightning Whelks. (The impression of speed is always desirable.)

Football is such an intrinsically territorial game it seems a shame not to recognize the proprietary determination of some *Sternidae*. Thus, the Salt Lake City Sea Swallows or Terra Haute Terns.

Speed and defensive acumen are valuable in hockey, so if that game spreads far enough south, Dixie might root for the Lauderdale Lobsters.

CHAPTER TEN

Before the beach feast

Delicacies de la Mer

There are few secrets to eating well at the shore—unless a new-comer thinks that fish and shellfish come from a frozen-food case and taste like their cardboard wrappers. The sea is where seafood lives. So catch it, net it, dig it, trap it. If all else fails, buy it from the local grocer or a skipper on the dock and tote it home. If there's no place to buy fresh seafood, you must be in Ohio. Pack up and drive east. (Another thing about catching and cooking your own: When the sea serves up dinner, it doesn't order you to "enjoy your meal").

Unless you are spectacularly sedentary, it's most rewarding to gather seafood yourself, whether from the surf with rod and reel, from the marsh with a baited string, or from a clam flat with your toes and muddy fingers. No license is necessary to catch fish from the sea. In many national seashores you can take reasonable amounts of shellfish "for personal use" without anyone's by-your-leave, though the most heavily visited seashores discourage this and many states and localities require permits. The best rule anywhere is to check first about local caveats with local authorities, whether wardens, rangers, troopers, the grocer or postmaster. Certain likely looking clam beds may be closed. Sometimes the reason for a ban is public health; nothing is quite as certain to make a person very low with a serious disease like hepatitis as bivalves fresh from a polluted bay. (Since these animals are filter feeders, which strain water continually to extract their own microscopic food, they retain and concentrate a number of toxic substances from a tainted environment.) Or the dread red tide may have passed that way—an inexplicable population explosion of certain plankton that can render fin and shellfish fatally poisonous for brief periods. In other cases clam beds are closed for a season to let depleted mollusks recover their numbers in peace.

Assuming it's open season, here's where you find dinner: Quahogs and cherrystone clams live in mud or sand. Hunt for them at low tide on sandbars, particularly in the protected waters of bays and tide-fed pools. On soft bottoms east of the Hudson, the traditional way to stalk a hardshell clam is with bare feet: Scuff slowly through the shallows, burrowing your toes into the sand. You'll soon learn to feel the difference between a clam, a rock and a broken bottle. Yes, this can be risky. Savvy Virginians wait for low tide to leave a mud flat bare, then walk the mire, looking for the southern quahog's telltale sign of an almost T-shaped hole that resembles a kind of antique key slot. North or south, you'll be surprised how many kinds of similar holes are made by dissimilar animals, including worms that only a bottom-feeding fish finds edible.

In New England particularly, softshell clams live in everything from the densest mud to rocky bottoms. Armed with 12-inch siphons, they may be too deep to feel with your toes, so the proven approach to these animals is with a clam rake. Walk around when low tide has drained an unpolluted clam flat. Look for jets of water shooting from the gravel or mud 10 yards ahead, then study the shape of the hole before destroying it. Since a softshell doesn't squirt continuously—but most visibly when first frightened by human footsteps—many holes without a fountain contain a sweet clam. With the rake's long, flat tines, dig around the hole to pry away a large chunk of mud, then finger through it. The critters may be hard to see because their shells are stained the color of the mud. Dig gently several inches from the most likely hole or you'll smash the quarry. (This does more aesthetic than actual harm, though broken clams don't keep well and should be eaten soon.) Find one clam and there's likely to be half a dozen within the radius of a foot. Harvest the large ones but leave those less than about 2 inches long for next year. Lightly cover them with mud so the gulls don't get them.

Depending on the kind of grounds they come from, softshell clams need anywhere from an hour to a couple of days in clean water to rid themselves of internal sand. I've heard of people grinding fresh pepper into the water to speed up the process, but I can't vouch for it. Clams from soft mud will flush out their grit fast in a dishpan of fresh water. Friends in Maine dig a few clams daily and keep them tied to the dock in a lobster car—a floating wooden crate with slits wide enough to let water in but not wide enough to let animals slip out. This assures a constant supply of sandless steamers.

Blue mussels live in active, wave-washed places, clinging to rocks and pilings with their byssal threads. Gather them there—again at low tide, of course. Better yet, at a low spring tide, the best time for any shellfishing on foot, since the water falls an extra distance to lay bare rocks and flats that have been covered for a fortnight, a month or half a year.

Low tide is also the time to find lobsters on the right kind of coast. Near Plymouth, Massachusetts a boy told me he hunted them on mud flats, seeking out their burrows, plugging the escape tunnel and digging them out! I didn't believe him, having lobstered only in Maine, where the animals are taken in sunken traps. Apologies, kid. I've since learned that lobsters do burrow in muddy bottoms to seek the same kind of shelter by day that their kin find in rocky caves and crannies off other coasts.

Hunting mollusks may be the easiest part of the prefatory process. Opening them is harder. Start with cherrystones if you've never done this before. All it takes to secure a small quahog is a dull knife designed for the purpose and a firm grip. Hold the clam with the hinge cradled in your left palm; with the right hand lay the knife edge in the slight, straight groove between the outer lips of the shell and squeeze with the left fingers. The knife enters—insinuates itself between the valves. Pivot it inside, snip the adductor muscles and presto! The clam opens with a twist of the right wrist. Toss one shell away and serve on the other.

Oysters are much more difficult. An oyster has an irregular shape. The valves are rough and their lips hard to find. Crooked and wrinkled, the hairline crack between the valves can't be widened with the blade of a knife; the point must enter first. Furthermore, a big Chincoteague doesn't fit the left hand. One must hold the animal slanting against the edge of the kitchen sink and poke around, seeking the slot by touch as much as by sight. It takes painful practice. When the knifepoint finds a purchase, push carefully and quickly before the oyster realizes what's afoot and gets a firmer grip on itself. Push in the wrong place—it's easy to mistake a growth line for the groove—and the knife takes on a life of its own. It can skid and open up your hand. This delicate work requires patient agility to find the groove, push the knife in, then slit the muscle and open the critter without losing too much juice. (Restaurants serve oysters on their flat shell. It's better to throw that one away and lay the delicacies on a bed of crushed ice in the roundest half-shell, which holds its delicious liquor. Sprinkle each one with lemon juice—a healthy oyster will wriggle the slightest bit at this to prove it's alive—lift the dishlike shell to the lips, and drink the oyster down. It's a delicious, addicting experience.)

A word about culinary/molluskan terminology. Most oysters marketed in America are *Crassostrea virginicas*, though they'll be called a multitude of names: Chincoteagues, Wellfleets, Blue Points and so forth. These names simply indicate where the beasts came from. Differences in appearance result largely from the kind of bed that nurtured them. Crowded beds produce rather contorted oysters that tend to be oblong, as the animal grew into whatever space it found. Open, well-culled beds produce more nearly round bivalves. To my taste the best are informally called "salt oysters" and the best of these are Chincoteagues. These come from beds in nearly undiluted ocean water, rather than from the uppermost reaches of long, protected bays.

Periwinkles can be found at almost any tide in their varied habitats and boiled. Live whelks wash up on beaches after storms, or you can dive for them in sheltered areas, like in the lee of Nantucket's Great Point. They make an interesting chowder.

Horseshoe crabs can be taken after they've come ashore and mated along a quiet, sandy coast near the mouth of a bay. Steam them like blue crabs, in a laundry tub—if your palate is more curious than discriminating. Slightly less adventurous epicures might take a leaf from a Yankee cook's book and serve slipper shells as escargots.

For people who prefer more cunning shellfish prey, the blue crab's the thing. "Hardshell" crabs can be caught in a variety of manufactured or homemade traps. This is the easy southern way practiced in Maryland and Virginia where the traps are 2- or 3-foot cubes of metal fabric like chicken wire (but sterner stuff to survive salt water). Each trap has an entrance to a large compartment, a straight-sided funnel, then another chamber. There's also a wire cylinder to hold bait of fish heads and the like. Attracted by the bait, the crab pokes around the contraption until it finds the entrance and enters the large chamber. To reach the bait, the animal enters the wide end of the funnel and follows it into the next chamber, where he's trapped, unable to escape again through the narrow end of the funnel. Ideally, you bait such a trap after breakfast, drop it in a bay and empty it for dinner.

For slightly more active crabbers, there's a wire cube or pyramid with sides that open when the attached lines are slack. Tie the bait inside it and drop it to the bottom from a dock, slackening the line so the sides fall open. Wait a few minutes, then close the sides with a jerk on the lines and pull the thing to the surface with a few crabs inside. Empty the trap carefully; blue crabs bite. Repeat. (This method also works for rock crabs much farther north.)

Crabbers with a sense of sport go armed with a ball of string, a mess of chicken necks and a long-handled net. Tie a neck to a string, toss it in the water and stay very still for a few minutes. Holding the string between thumb and forefinger, tug it very gently to feel if anything tugs back; or the string may move when a crab starts walking away with the bait. However you tell a crab's nibbling, pull the string in very slowly until the crab is close to the surface within netting distance. Then snatch with the net fast! Aim well below the bait, since the crab will flee as soon as it sees you move. This is a diverting pastime; moments of motionless waiting, then the quick stab for the wary prey.

Softshell crabs are taken by net alone from their hiding places in the shallows. Just walk along the shallow fringes of a bay looking for quarry that's just cast its shell (or is about to) and scoop it off the bottom with a net. Of course its easier said than done until you practice.

As for acquiring fin fish, my own experience is slim. I've caught a few and had them in a pan when the flesh was still cool from the sea, but it would be presumptuous of me to recommend methods of fishing, an avocation many people devote their lives to. Some go at high tide, some at low. The most serious fish only at night, and all night long at that, for species like striped bass. Ichthyological authorities Bigelow and Schroeder note: "The best advice we can give the surfcaster . . . is to go fishing whatever time of day he is free to do so." Amen.

Once you've acquired a finned fish, clean it as soon as possible, before the viscera—digestive juices in particular—taint the meat. On a wild beach, simply gut it on the spot (being careful not to perforate stomach or intestines) and toss the innards to the gulls. In the case of shark, which can be delicious when simply fried in butter, bleed your catch as soon as it's dead or the urea-laden blood will make it barely fit to eat—even after marinating in lemon juice. But whatever you catch, finned or shelled, don't take any more than you'll eat. If you fish for sport, put everything back that isn't bound for the table.

The best fish in the world is caught fresh and then baked, broiled, sautéed or poached without much fuss. Lemon or lime juice, herbs like thyme, rosemary or dill, a garlic clove and perhaps a little white wine are the only secondary ingredients needed. (Some finicky friends of mine, who live off the littoral when visiting Nova Scotia, pack seasonings along because no herbs fresh enough for their palates can be bought at that latitude. Most folks can find what they need in local groceries or gas station/general stores that serve even the smallest coastal hamlets. Bring your own wine to strange territory, however. Some seaside emporia only offer choices between Thunderbird and two flavors of Ripple.)

Generally speaking, as far as shore fare is concerned, follow Thoreau's maxim: "Simplify, simplify," as written. (If he meant it absolutely, he would simply have said "Simplify" and left it at that.) Utter simplicity is eating cherrystones as you pluck them from their bed without bothering to wade ashore. They're delicious that way, but I wouldn't want a crab uncooked, and my fondness for raw fish is limited to the confines of a good Japanese restaurant. So if some of the following recipes have a few twists of the *cordon bleu*, it's because even simplicity has its limits. But almost all of them can be followed in a simple kitchen—the kind found in a rented beach cottage. Most can be fixed on a camp stove. They were compiled with a couple of criteria in mind: They depend on fresh seafood that's easily found along the coast; they're easy to prepare; and they're part of the fabric of living along a beach.

You can do two things wrong to fresh seafood: overcook or deep-fry. The only reason to do the latter is to fix a dish worth smothering in catsup for anyone who likes catsup. Any fish is better underdone than overdone; no fish is harmed by being put back on the fire if it comes out rare the first time. One rule of thumb is to cook a fish no more than ten minutes per inch of thickness, then test with a fork. This applies to any kind of fish and any method: frying, baking in a preheated 450° oven or poaching. (Start timing when the water returns to a simmer after a cold fish is put in.) A fish is still underdone if it looks gooey-wet between the muscle segments. It's overdone when the flesh flakes at the poke of a fork. If a fish is big enough to handle a meat thermometer, serve it when the internal temperature is 140°; at 150° it's ready for a crematorium urn instead of a platter.

Fresh fish is more tender and juicier than frozen, and each species is more distinctive in flavor when fresh. The different fish and shellfish available at surf or dockside are so varied, even when cooked simply, that meat is easily forgotten as an inland oddity. For the uninitiated, here are some technical hints:

To clean a fish: First, sharpen a knife. Then slit the belly from vent (the anal orifice) to throat and throw out all the innards. (There is one notable exception to the gut-first rule: fresh-caught northern puffers, a.k.a. blowfish or, if store-bought, "sea squab." The flesh of this odd fish is said to be delicious and healthy, but the viscera—particularly roe, gonads and liver—are poisonous, as is the skin. If you catch a northern puffer (*Sphoeroides maculatus*), don't gut it at all. Just skin it, slice fillets from the back and throw the rest away. Fishing and food fish authority A. J. McClane suggests staying away from puffers entirely because "the flesh of the southern puffer is frequently toxic," and *Sphoeroides nephelus* looks very much like its northern cousin.)

After gutting a fish, scale it—if it has scales. Hold the fish firmly by the tail on a cutting board and use the back of a knife to remove the scales by scraping against the grain briskly. To remove the fins with their little bones down the roots, cut deep into the flesh around (or along) the appendage, then pull the fin toward the head with a quick jerk. Don't bother to skin a fish—unless it's a thick-skinned species or a puffer. Nor do you need to remove the head and tail if your pan's large enough; they'll keep more juices in.

To cut fillets: The object is to remove all the meat from one side of the fish in a single piece, cutting close to the backbone and wasting as little as possible. First find a slender knife that's longer than the height of the fish—that is, the distance from the belly to back. Lay the fish on a hard, flat surface, preferably a plank or cutting board. Hold it by the tail and work toward the head. Slice down into the fish just in front of the tail, then smoothly slant the knife parallel to the board and cut along the backbone all the way to the gills. In the smaller, softer-fleshed species, this can easily be done in a single slow stroke. With some bigger or tougher fish, a sawing motion works best. I know a veterinary surgeon who holds the knife steady and pulls the fish by the tail, wiggling it back and forth. Use any method that works comfortably; anyone who isn't all thumbs can master filleting in a week's vacation.

To fry fillets: Melt some butter in a pan over moderate heat (stir in some crushed garlic if you like). When the butter bubbles, lay the fish gently in it, skin (or outer side) up. Add lemon juice to taste, any chosen herbs and perhaps a little white wine. Having estimated the total cooking time—ten minutes per inch—leave the fish alone until two-thirds of the time has elapsed. Then turn it over for the remainder and test with a fork.

To bake or broil: Preheat the oven. Grease the pan or rack well and dot the top of the fish with butter. Sprinkle with lemon juice and any seasonings. Cook the total time without turning (except in the case of thick steaks if they threaten to burn).

Charcoal methods: Wrap the whole fish, dotted with butter and seasoned, in an aluminum foil cocoon. Place it as close to the coals as possible and cook 14 minutes per inch of thickness, since the foil reflects some heat.

If you have any large leafy herbs or rockweed handy, try this variation. Soak the herbs in fresh water (or rockweed in sea water) and lay them wet on the coals so that they smoke and steam. Put a piece of foil slightly larger than the fish on the grill with the edges curled up to catch the juices; place the fish on that. Then blanket the whole grill and fish with foil to hold in the smoke. Some will escape; don't worry about it. Make sure the coals are at their glowing peak when you begin and open the damper to allow a draft or it'll all smother. Allow a little extra time.

Clambake Supreme

This meal deserves a mob, a family reunion, a wedding on the beach or no excuse beyond a gathering of good friends organized by an energetic host and hostess with willing helpers. The preparations are complex and some odd hardware's needed, but complexity is part of the fun here. Special events take special work. This method is nearly foolproof, given enough firewood. (The hot-rocks-in-the-sunken-pit method can fail miserably and never be set right because the rocks cooled off before anything got cooked.) The best place for such a feast is an island, of course. Second best is a piece of Maine riverfront with cold tidal water to coddle the shellfish and chill the drinks. Third best is wherever you can build a roaring fire without setting a roof ablaze and spread out without tumbling the neighbor's carport. Here's the rite as it occurs on Chanterelle Island, Maine.

Two days before the feast, hard- and softshell clams are gathered around the island to fill the lobster car floating at the dock. Then they're left undisturbed while they contentedly siphon out their interior sand. Supplies are laid in with each boat: beer, white wine, net cooking bags, paper plates and cardboard bowls. Kids gather heaps of driftwood and deadfalls. One day before the feast, another car is floated with the one-and-a-half- to two-pound lobsters (one per person at least, kids included). There are two schools of thought about lobsters. Some folks like "shedders," which have recently molted and whose shells are still somewhat pliable. These devotees say that because the beast wears his shell loosely he'll be juicy, soft and tender. I prefer animals with the hardest shells, the ones that are ready to molt again. These may be a better buy since they have more meat. But they're firmer too, though some people call them tough. (And they're hard to find in summer.)

The morning of the event, all the accessory dishes are pre-pared in a kitchen: cakes baked, salads tossed, bread bought, and everything ferried to the island along with a watermelon that's tethered off the dock. Two hours before dinnertime the real work begins. A fire is lit in the antique stone fireplace by the old boat-house. Folks arrive to watch and work their share. The tide starts going out to make room for more on the pocket beach. The host says in vowels rarely heard west of the New Hampshire line, "Get it hot as the hinges of Hades and gradually increase the heat." When the fire roars, pile on more wood and make it bellow. The iron sheet across the hearth starts to take the heat, plus the weight of a huge kettle two-thirds full of sea water.

The last boat from the mainland brings the last guests and new potatoes. The latter were rolled in salted oil (one teaspoon of salt per half-cup oil), then partly roasted in a 400° oven for half an hour and oiled again. Sweet corn arrives now. It was picked minutes earlier since its sugar starts turning to starch as soon as it leaves the stalk.

An armload of rockweed from the shore is spread on the hot steel plate and starts to steam. Nestle the potatoes in it, cover with another layer of seaweed and an inverted pot, which later becomes what they still call "scultch bucket" here. The term, a variant of "culch," was more common in seventeenth-century England, where it meant the broken pottery, shells and other rubbish used to make an oyster bed. Now it means the remains of a sea feast, shells and other rubbish included. A pot of butter (half a stick per person, please) is placed where it'll melt without burning. The net bags are filled with clams.

Keep feeding the fire. Have a beer; this is hot work. Check the potatoes—heavy canvas or asbestos gloves are a must—and turn them as they brown. When the water is rolling like Vesuvius ready to surprise Pompeii, toss in the bagged clams and cover. Feed the fire; the water mustn't stop boiling volcanically. Wait three minutes and pull out the bags of clams, which should have just opened. Feed the fire.

Empty the bags, serve the clams, feed the fire, crack a beer, check the potatoes and fill the bags with lobsters. Feed the fire, down a couple of clams and toss the lobsters in. Cover and let boil, dividing the time between feeding clams to yourself and wood to the fire. About twenty minutes does it. Test a representative lobster by picking it up by an antenna and jerking. If it pulls out, he's done. Serve the lobsters (with melted butter of course). Serve the potatoes, breaking each one open with a gloved hand and lacing it with butter and salt. Bag the corn and toss it in for barely five minutes—or long enough to switch to wine and crack a claw. Let the fire die and feed yourself till dark, or dawn

Blue and Brew

Blue crabs make something more than a meal. Properly done, they become a delicious, difficult and messy ritual. I learned about it all in Baltimore from a native who was doing time in the Navy while I apprenticed at the local paper. When my college pal came home on leave, I'd wangle an evening away from the police beat and we'd go to one of the local crab houses. These were the only restaurants where two young men (on a cub reporter's pay and a lieutenant j.g.'s respectively) could hire a table for several hours of food and talk without being either fawned over by supercilious French waiters or hurried by sullen American ones. Sit down in one of these establishments and they didn't want you to leave until closing time—so long as there was another crab and another beer on the paper-covered table.

The best way to enjoy crabs at home is à la Frederick Road, with beer in the can, a length of 2-inch dowel, a dull paring knife and a fresh roll of paper towels. Here's how:

First haul or lay in some crabs. Catch them if possible; buy them if necessary. Next get some beer, a tin of prepared seafood seasoning—Old Bay is the only kind I know—and a large covered pot. A proper steamer is nice, a sort of huge double-boiler affair, but any big kettle with a lid does fine. Just put something solid in the bottom like a few old saucers or clean rocks to keep the crabs out of the liquid. These critters should be cooked by the rising steam, not boiled.

Open a beer, pour it in the pot to the depth of about an inch, and drink the rest. Set the stove on high. When the beer comes to an active boil, toss in a third of the crabs alive and kicking. Do this carefully; given the chance, they are as willing to bite you as you are them. (Chuck out any dead ones). As they pile up in the pot,

sprinkle seafood seasoning on them according to taste and/or directions on the label. By the time you've finished another beer the
crabs will be bright red. But cook them for at least a total of twenty
minutes. Spread Sunday's paper—all of it—on a table and tong the
crabs onto it in a pile. Then sit everybody down and get to work,
because work is what it takes.

Callinectes sapidus is a miracle of packaging. If you've never
eaten one before, don't be discouraged. You'll learn how with time
and practice. Pry off the apron—the pointed plate covering the rear
of the bottom shell. With this gone, the top shell will flip off to
reveal the gills. These feathery gray things should be scraped away
with the dull paring knife. Eat everything else that tastes good—
namely all the meat you can find, the yellow tomalley (spelled
"Tom Alley" in one restaurant) and the whitish fat in the body
cavity. Then go for the meat. This is easier said than done because
each morsel is diabolically encased in ectoderm and partitions. A
crab surrenders its meat one nibble at a time.

Using both hands, break the remaining crab in half along the
seam that runs front to back. Crush each half slightly. Break off
one leg at a time, doing your damnedest to keep a segment of
muscle attached. This is a little tricky; practice is the only
teacher. With thumb and forefinger, grasp both the inner joint of
the leg and the body segment to which it's attached, squeeze, and
twist the leg off gently. Start with the hind legs; it's easiest with
them and, when done properly, results in a legitimately bite-
sized piece of "back fin" meat jutting from the end of the leg.
After dispatching that morsel, nibble at each pliable leg joint; sort
of squeegee them between upper and lower incisors to get the
meat out.

To get inside the claws, tear off the entire appendage from the
body and lay it on the table. Hold the blade of the dull paring knife
across the claw and smack it gently with the dowel, broomstick, or
whatever's handy. (You could always tell if a crab house had pre-
tensions; it provided little mallets for this job.) Repeat with each
segment. The notion is to cut about halfway through the claw, then
snap it apart with your hands and nibble at the exposed meat. As
you proceed, pick out elusive bits of meat with the knifepoint. Go
back over your first crab, making sure you haven't missed anything.
Morsels hide in all sorts of nooks, crannies, and cubbyholes. You'll
soon know the animal's anatomy better than it did.

Needless to say, the entire procedure creates a good deal of scultch and beer cans. That's why you spread the table with so much newspaper. When things get out of hand, roll it all up in a few layers of classified ads, chuck the bundle and start fresh on the sports section. This cannot be a tidy meal, nor a delicate one, nor a fast one. A hungry man can eat a dozen jumbos—if he has the patience and a couple of hours. (One never gets sated on crabs; one gets tired first.) When the party is on the way to finishing the first batch of crabs, put another on to steam and fetch another six-pack from the fridge. The ratio of crabs to cans is sometimes on the order of one to one; peppery seasoning warms a thirst. Outlanders sometimes accompany crabs with french fries and/or coleslaw. Some people even drink good wine with this meal, though fingering a wineglass with crabby hands seems gauche, at least, and all that pepper dulls the palate. Beer goes best.

Discussing the corruption of the mother tongue, H. L. Mencken rather proudly observed that "in Maryland *crabfeast* has never yielded to *crabfest*." (He probably knew more about Maryland foodways and the American idiom than anyone of this century, and wrote about both at greater length.) A crabfeast traditionally includes she-crab soup, crab imperial, crab cakes, and sautéed softshells. Some Baltimore restaurants—the places that had moved from dowels to mallets and from newspapers to brown wrapping paper to gingham tablecloths—featured fried hardshells too: hard crabs covered with batter and cooked in deep fat. This practice is slightly more obtuse than gilding lilies.

Becky's Surefire Clams

Clams of any genus get tough as hawk's feet when cooked too long. Here's a way of knowing when to turn off the steam.

Put an inch of fresh water in a pot with a lid that fits loosely and fill the pot with clams (steamers or littlenecks—i.e., *Mya* sp.; cherrystones or quahogs—i.e., *Mercenaria* sp.). Cover and set on a high flame. When the water boils, the clams start lending their juice to make broth; then the pot boils over, literally flipping its lid in the process. Put the lid back on. When it pops off again the clams are done. Pour off the broth and serve the clams.

Rebecca of Chanterelle, who swears by this method, adds one word of warning: Make sure all the clams are alive. One bad one in the pot, like a rotten apple in a barrel, can spoil the lot. (Nothing tastes worse than a dead bivalve.) It's easy to tell a healthy clam. Touch a softshell's siphon and it flinches slightly, withdrawing into its shell. A quahog closes tight when handled.

Serve softshells with a cup of broth and a cup of melted butter on the side. To eat: Grasp the whole clam in the left hand (right for southpaws), peel the black membrane off the "neck" (siphon) like a sock and discard. Pull the whole animal from the shell, swirl in the broth, dip in butter, devour. Serve hardshells with butter or nothing. Pluck them from the shell and pop them down.

Eyeballed Clam Chowder

There are no eyes in this stew; they're what you measure with. Clams in the shell, plucked from a low-tide flat, are not labeled as to weight, volume or unit price. Yet the best chowder depends on the proper ratio of solid ingredients. Eyeballing (or using a measuring cup if you want to get fancy) is the answer.

Acquire some hardshell clams, a.k.a. quahogs of the northern or southern persuasion, and a few razor clams, if possible. Let them wash themselves out in cold water. If one isn't firmly closed, chuck it out; it's dead and hazardous to your palate, if not to your health. Put them in a good-sized pot over a high flame with an inch of water in the bottom and cover. Peek at them soon; remove them with tongs as they open. Remove the clams from the shells and toss out the latter. Strain the broth to remove sand and return the broth to the pot.

While you were resting you should have chopped some onions and sautéed them until translucent in a little butter and salt pork or bacon fat. You should also have diced some potatoes (without peeling them) and parboiled them until almost soft. Now, with a sharp knife, mince the clams into small pieces. Eyeball the amount of clams (or count handfuls) and put them back in the pot with the broth. Now add the cooked onion. How much? About one-third the amount of chopped clams. Pour in the pan drippings as well. Add potatoes—about two-thirds the amount of chopped clams or twice the amount of onions. Stir. Then double the whole mixture by adding an equal amount of milk or, preferably, light cream, or both. Add salt to taste— careful, it may not need any. Heat to the simmering point and dish it all out in bowls, being sure to ladle up a fair share of solids—half of which should be clams. Twist a pepper grinder once over each serving, add a pat of butter and serve.

Coquina Broth

This is a real beach treat, and a dish you simply can't get inland. I've never seen it sold anywhere. It is the simplest and purest fish soup in the world, a delightfully evocative first course or thermos drink. All it takes is the discovery of some coquina clams at the beach and a container to carry them in. If you're going back to a beach where you've seen coquinas the day before, pack a colander or a sieve along. Coquinas are the tiny, triangular, and sometimes varicolored clams that live in the swash zone, moving up and down the beach with the tides, always staying in the shallowest active water. You'll see them on the surface of the sand when a wave washes up the slope; as it recedes they'll start burrowing out of sight. Though they may be less than half an inch long, they're not hard to spot; when they're around there are literally millions of them. Since they're so small, the best way to take them is by the double handful, sand and all. That's what the colander or sieve is for. Fill it up with coquinas and sand, step a few feet to seaward and wash the sand out in the ocean like a forty-niner panning gold. Take them home in a bucket of seawater.

Now comes the easy part. Pour fresh water in a saucepan; add a handful of coquinas for each serving. (Some people gussy it up with various extras—onions, potatoes, spices—things this soup needs like a viola needs chrome.) Boil gently for about ten minutes. That's all there is to it. Strain into cups and serve a steaming marine nectar.

Deep-Fried Fish

Eschew it. Like rubber. Fish and seafood that come in naturally small pieces or thin slabs—fillets, picked crabmeat, shrimps, scallops—may be sautéed in butter, perhaps with a crushed clove of garlic, a teaspoon of basil, rosemary or thyme and/or a little white wine. Thick fillets or steaks can be baked, broiled or roasted over charcoal. Most fin fish are delicious steamed, baked or roasted whole, dotted with butter, laced with spices if you're feeling fancy,

and stuffed with a bread, mushroom, or crab stuffing if you're looking for a way to pass the time before dinner. But nothing good ever
came from taking a self-respecting marine creature from the sea and
drowning it in a boiling surf of deep fat. French-frying a fresh fish
is close to sacrilege. This is as certain as the promise that the tide
will rise again.

Mary's Miracle (or Breakfast in Paradise)

First, way ahead of time, learn to make a French omelet—the
light, fluffy kind that is nothing but eggs, butter and dexterity.
Practice before a beach weekend in a month with an "R" in it.
Saturday afternoon, beg, buy, borrow, or poach a dozen fat salt
oysters—six apiece, this breakfast being for two only. (If you're
uncertain about opening them yourself, buy them on the halfshell;
covered with cellophane wrap, they'll stay moist and firm in a
refrigerator overnight.)

Sunday morning brew a pot of real coffee, squeeze some fresh
orange juice and invite your best friend, lover or spouse to the
table. When all's ready, whip up the eggs and start making an
ordinarily exquisite omelet while, in another pan, sautéeing the
oysters with butter, a splash of white wine and freshly ground black
pepper. Do it briefly—don't cook them to death (literally), but just
until the edges start to curl. You will have timed this to happen just
as the omelet is ready to fold—it takes a little planning and luck at
first. When the eggs are still wet on top (but have that delectable
golden-brown on the bottom) slide the warm, buttery oysters onto
the omelet, fold the sides over gently, count to ten in any language,
and serve on the flip side. The results are extraordinary.

Correction: Don't bother with the coffee. Open a bottle of
champagne instead. You won't be going out this morning anyway—
it's too glorious inside.

Indoor Lobsters

Robert Lautman, the Escoffier of architecture photographers,
cooks seafood on the side—for the love of it. After building a new
kitchen at home, he christened it by having ten for dinner and
serving us a lobster. One lobster, shelled, sliced and served like a
turkey. Weighing in at twenty-some-odd pounds, it looked a yard

long and proved that the big fellows don't have to be tough. In fact, when you can get (and afford) a jumbo, it's likely to be sweeter than a runt, since these are the ones that grow slowest in the cold, deep offshore waters.

I've stopped eating chicken lobsters—one man's poor protest against our genocidal greed. The point is simple: A lobster in the one-and-one-quarter-pound class is probably a juvenile and never had the chance to mate. Because of shortsighted regulations and the inability of the Atlantic states to take a momentarily unpopular stand—people are eating the breeding stock of *Homarus americanus*. This kind of simple conservation, as traditional as tossing back little fish, is mandatory if our grandchildren are to eat lobsters and the lobstermen's grandchildren are to catch them. Otherwise there may be none left to speak of in another human generation.

The reason big lobsters have a bad reputation—one that's perpetuated by seafood stores and some culinary authorities—is that people overcook them. If a small lobster needs boiling for twenty minutes, they assume a five-pounder wants one hundred minutes. Nonsense. That might be the case if the critter were a perfect sphere, but he's not. He's built more like an eclair than a baked Alaska, and cooking heat penetrates through the narrower dimensions. Hence, Lautman uses a sliding time scale. Boil a one-and-one-half-pound lobster twenty minutes or steam it twenty-five if you prefer. Boil a ten-pound lobster thirty-five minutes, or steam it forty to forty-five. A monster in the thirty-pound range should be boiled no more than forty-five minutes at a rolling boil, says another friend with authority. For lobsters in between these benchmark sizes, extrapolate the cooking time. When you open up the lobster before serving, check the light greenish tomalley in the body cavity. If it looks runny, as it may one time in ten, toss the animal back. This isn't a cheese soufflé; nothing is lost in returning it to the pot.

How big a lobster should you buy? The biggest you can get, then divide its live poundage by two and invite that number of hungry friends to share.

Double-Bedded Mussels

Blue mussels are fine as hors d'oeuvres, as an entrée or as part of a seaside smorgasbord—a pastiche of whatever low tide offered for the taking. First scrub each animal with a stiff brush and pull out the "beard"—the clump of byssus threads. Then steam the mussels briefly, just until they open. In a separate pot melt a stick of butter, stir in two cloves of crushed garlic and ¼ cup of chopped parsley. Now the trick: Remove half the mussels from their shells, which seem too big to begin with. Put each animal in a half shell with another one. Double them up, as it were, like Ishmael and Queequeg in the Spouter Inn. Arrange the double-occupancy half shells on a cookie sheet, dab a little of the butter on each, and bake briefly in a hot oven until the butter bubbles.

Stuffed Fish

Dressing up a dish comes easier than putting on shoes after a week at the beach. There are many popular stuffings, each fancier than the last. Here's a hearty one made from simple ingredients.

Peel and chop one medium onion. Clean and slice a pound of mushrooms. Dice five or six new potatoes. Rough-chop four celery stalks. Sauté all the above for fifteen minutes with a half-stick of butter, two tablespoons of dry sage, salt and freshly ground pepper. Clean a fresh bluefish or striped bass and stuff the body cavity with the mixture. Lay two or three strips of bacon across the fish, bake in a 425° oven using the ten-minutes-per-inch rule, and garnish with lemon slices for instant class. Serve with the chilled white burgundy you brought from the city or, alas, bought in one of the all-purpose boutiques that are cluttering the coast increasingly.

Driftwords: Night Swims

Call me chicken. I don't swim at night when the moon hangs behind the beach because from beyond the breakers I cannot see the edge of land, the place where home begins. Facing the shore, the shining light turns sea, shallows and wet sand into a twinkling blur. Thirty years ago I swam out in that kind of moonlight, turned, and was lost suddenly in black and silver water that had no visible scale, no reference point. I turned, kicked and thrashed toward the unseeable shore so blindly my arms scraped bottom before I thought to wade. The beach still looked vague, far off. The next time I learned that the right time comes when a full moon hangs over the sea itself. It was a night that lingers in memory, in the perpetual present. . . .

Walking between Yankee villages late at night, our shadows fall inland up the slanting shore. The moon shines on the backs of breaking waves and their landward faces stay concealed. But the surface of the water shimmers, the moon's reflections reach the world's slightly scalloped rim and I'd swim beyond it if I could, knowing that the edge of land stays visible.

"Let's go in." Yes, she says. Even in midsummer the air chills a little as we strip on the empty beach, the water too at the very first. "Don't dawdle." Dive through the first breaker, into its black, curling, hidden face. Swim straight out; it seems warmer. Beyond the surf the sea grows gentle and supports, rocking in its swells. Seen from there, each wave toward land brightens as it grows, curls and breaks against the sloping land, its swash a bright line against the matte sand.

She hangs back, porpoiselike between the waves, her streaming hair a plume; then she surfaces and waves a shining arm. Waiting for my mermaid, treading water, I see the farthest breaker rise in a distant curl that hides the lower beach again; then a ribbon of sand, the fringing grass and salt-pruned trees beyond. Except for a bleached log and our bundled clothes, the beach lies empty as the Sea of Serenity itself high behind me. The grass along the dunes is gray and the sky a midnight blue behind counterpointing stars. She reaches me, we hug and sink laughing, to come up all coughs and sputters, holding each other afloat. It's time to splash the moonlight, then drift and float dead-man style (a misnomer of the first magnitude).

We were never so alive—fingers touching, rising with every swell toward the warm deep sky and easing back again, staring stars in the face, glimpsing the moon from the corner of an eye, fingers touching, almost out of reach, connected, moving, closing with the sky itself, floating down and up again. But we can't stay there forever. A jellyfish stings her arm; it's getting cold. We stroke away from the moon again, at last touching bottom waist-deep inside the outer surf. We wade ashore and dry ourselves, shivering together. On this perfect empty beach, the moon turning dark water bright and not another soul in sight or mind, the world seems ours alone. We two—we are the human race.

It's a little frightening the first time, a swim like that; as unlike land as space must be, a place and time of mesmerizing quality. Don't swim alone at night—that's dangerous, they say. And to swim together risks sudden overwhelming love on land again.

CHAPTER ELEVEN

Chanterelle Island, Maine

My Archipelago

Catching the Beach Bug—

I was born on an island, though one so drastically altered that it hardly counts. Suffice it that my delivery occurred no farther west of a certain tidal river than a fiddler crab could creep before running into a York Avenue bus. But if Mimi did her lying in on Manhattan, she says I was conceived on another island and my earliest memories involve summers beside salt water.

On special days the family went out toward Montauk, the eastern end of the land. Mimi took a snapshot near a dune out there of a human pyramid—well, more like a cairn of kin. Dad crouches in the sand, my brother kneels on his back, I perch on his, and our sister leans on the grinning lot of us. My parents must have prized that exposed and wild beach because gas was rationed and it was miles from home; there was a war on. Sometimes a khaki halftrack showed up—the army's hybrid of a pickup truck and a Caterpillar. Its helmeted crew would point an enormous machine gun at the horizon and wait. That's where the Axis lay, I understood; the world spun around Hitler and Tojo just as a birthday party revolved around the kid who had the worst tantrum. The patriotic gunmen stared out to sea for interminable periods, or longer than an after-lunch rest under a beach umbrella, then disappeared behind the dune again. I ran up the sand hill to see them go, but the beach grass had hidden spikes and hurt my feet. It seemed hateful stuff, so pretty in the wind and so painful.

The surf out there could be huge, or taller than me. But there were stout ropes strung from the beach to floating buoys a little way offshore. I'd grab a rope with both hands (unable to grasp around it with one) and inch my way out. The waves lapped my ankles, my knees in turn, my crotch and my belly. Then one got me wet all over and I went squealing back to the dry, hot sand to start again and get a little farther out. Melinda was my first love. (Her father was the doctor who delivered me, so you can guess the age we got together; we were both in diapers. It was an affair of convenience, our mothers'.) Melinda hated surf. When it rose any higher than a clam shell, she'd stamp her feet and scream bloody murder. I couldn't fathom how she'd stay away from the semifrightening waves that held such frothy excitement. After all, everything good could have barbs inside. The world was full of barking dogs, cross streets, two-wheel bikes, cozy bedtime and then The Dark, artichokes. My point is that every familiar thing in childhood can turn to terror—even elevators with bright brass gates (that jammed) or a doting cook (who went crazy when she drank once a year). And every fright could hold a laugh or a present, like Halloween or a Grimm fairy tale.

The world was a place that a four- or five-year-old forayed into, then came home from, washed his hands for supper and had a story. The beach was part of that outside world; a place to play in the water and get nipped by a crab. In childhood one takes what comes. Gold stars in front-room windows were normal;

didn't everyone have a neighbor die in the Pacific? One moved half way across the country for the war effort's sake, and then moved back again, as a matter of course. In childhood one learns that "saving the best for last" is risky in summer because ice cream melts. We did save gum wrappers and made huge balls of tinfoil. We had bonfires by the water and picnics and sang "America, the Beautiful" when the A-bomb lit up an unseen sky, in innocent childhood. So many things seemed of the same magnitude from a viewpoint 3 feet high: spiked grass, merry-go-rounds, the horseshoe crab, white margarine, Christmas, fear of drowning, rice pudding with raisins, grandma's cancer, Walt Disney's *Bambi*, Victory gardens, war, reading, parents' divorce, cotton candy and the beach itself.

Peace came for a few years, its bright promise overshadowed (for me) by the immediate siege of adolescence. White bucks outshone piano lessons; the new Gregory Peck epic at the Garden Theater surpassed a solar eclipse any Saturday afternoon. I was away from the beach for most of those years. I fled the familiar across the great plains' seas of grass to summer jobs on ranches in the Rocky Mountain West. The beach surfaced again, in college, as a place for terribly serious winter weekends in cold summer houses where herds of us would congregate like untimely turtles, then sneak off in pairs to talk about Camus and woo.

Life in several cities working in various corners of the fourth estate brought me back to beaches, older and a stranger, looking for joy or solace, not existentialism. I was briefly a born-again New Yorker who returned like the prodigal son to what people said was the center of the universe. But it couldn't be the hub—everything spun too fast and randomly for that. The reaches of Long Island offered freedom from artificial deadlines, cool clean air and a little quiet in the night. A Columbus Avenue grocer sprinkling salt on his sidewalk (to save customers from slipping in stab-wound blood) suggested that the margins of civilization might be nicer. By design I headed west again and got as far west as Baltimore before my trusty Chevrolet coupe slipped its rusty radiator like an ill-fitting denture. But a newspaper there offered the perfect job and I hired on before learning that a cub reporter's first duty tour was the solo, all-night, every night "lobster trick." The morning rewrite man who relieved me at 7 A.M.—he was a perennial old pro with all the tattered trimmings—offered counsel in psychological survival tech-

niques. Rx: nickel blackjack, bourbon and the Gayety Burlesque's
Saturday Morning Show.

The reward for surviving both "lobster" and its prescription
was a long weekend; I asked my mentor for new advice on where to
go for a change in scene. "Booze, gambling and girls?" he queried,
pouring half his carry-out coffee in the wastebasket. "Life," I answered. "I'm gray as a mushroom from not seeing the sun and
haven't touched a body of water larger than a highball since July."
Tomorrow was Labor Day. "Ocean City," he said, filling his paper
cup with rye from the bottle in his bottom drawer. He hadn't been
there since he was married the day before embarking on a free trip
to the beaches of gracious North Carolina, sunny California and
Guadalcanal. But in his day Ocean City was where young bloods
went, he said, tearing obits from the teletype.

I slept, packed the car and arrived at sundown. The place was
not as he described. It had aged and grown respectable with a
vengeance. No alcohol could be had in the entire county on a
Sunday; even most Communion services offered grape juice. The
only gaming was Thursday night bingo in the firehouse. And each
single female parading along the boardwalk sported as many plastic
curlers in her hair as she had years on this earth—between nine and
fifteen, depending on head size. I was glumly choosing between an
auction sale of "oriental" rugs (woven in the east of Belgium) and a
prayer meeting as the evening's entertainment when some college
kids staged the parody of a riot. It was an odd relief. I went to work
covering the inanities of young rowdies tossing empty beer cans at
a burly, brutal police chief who replied with something close to
martial law. He locked up twenty slightly soused jejune delin-
quents; they spent the night in two two-man cells and I got my first
by-line. Ocean City had a beach, but during the recess in a kan-
garoo magistrate's court the next noon I didn't see it for all the
beach towels, folding chairs, lotioned flesh and litter.

That experience taught me to save comp time for planned
vacations in Mexico, Puerto Rico, the Caribbean, Martha's Vineyard, Nantucket, the Maine coast, Cornwall—places like that. They
had two things in common: seashore and distance. Why not? It
seemed that anywhere closer to the eastern megalopolis had only
beery collegians, bullish cops and blue laws. These distant places
had (variously) friendly strangers, odd customs, rum, tides, scuba
diving, shells for the picking, clams for the digging, waves for the

surfing, sailboats, stunning scenery, whales, bikinis or less, fresh seafood, nesting birds in season, dunes to nap on, palm trees to read beneath, stretches of hard sand to run along, cliffs to climb, breakers to romp in and countless peninsulas to round, each one guarding another private cove that ended with another promising point. They had beaches.

In time I found some closer to home—by then the nation's capital, where I first chased fire trucks, wrote obits and covered suburban sewer plans. I crashed the White House press room at 2 A.M. when President Kennedy swapped an obsolete Russian spy for Ike's U-2 pilot, interviewed Commander-in-Chief-Emeritus Harry Truman on a railroad platform and covered Ocean City's Third Annual Labor Day Riot, which was sillier than the first. Jaded by stuff of such transient importance, I swaggered across the newsroom to the Sunday Department as a budding critic in search of real theater and significant cinema. After seeing too many movies before multiple martini lunches, I quit the paper to free-lance and found myself seeking out more beaches between assignments.

I even came to love Ocean City, as a twelve-year-old running back named Christopher loved pro football; that is, from a distance. One July Fourth the chamber of commerce proudly announced the number of people packing the beach there. It was either 100,000 souls or 1,000,000; the difference between 10^5 and 10^6 can be a typographical error. I love Ocean City because another beach not much farther from my desk has no neon-bright boardwalk by night, no people cluttering every horizon by day and no high-rise structures except a lighthouse. If Ocean City's pathologically popular playland weren't where it was, some of the hordes would appear on my empty beach and change it into a very different place. Not that I'm an anthrophobe. It's just that among organisms in vast numbers, I prefer nesting terns or even menhaden to man, who swarms so erratically.

The Racecourse

One island near the tip of Maine has a moral history. Those who've seen it say Great South Beach is mythically beautiful. Even a botanist's cold catalogue of its flora sounds lush and alive. The beach curves huge and smooth for more than a mile. The west end, close to an evergreen forest, hooks sharply and stops at the foot of a sheer rock bluff that rises 40 feet as it juts into the sea. Along most of the long, gentle crescent, which arcs through one-quarter of the compass, the sand is soft and white. At the east end the beach becomes gravel to reach a tall, sloping crag that runs at a right angle for another mile to the granite head. This beach is growing year by year. Protected from storms, it rarely receives the big waves strong enough to rob its sand. Instead the sea wastes its strength on outer islands and on the complex headlands that guard both ends of this sheltered, sandy stretch that's exposed only to the gentle southeast. Waves that reach into the cove bring sand from some offshore lode, break on the foreshore and, having spent their energy, sink into the beach face itself. And so it grows.

Punctuated by clumps of sea rocket and beach pea, uneven rows of beach grass slowly advance seaward each year, keeping pace with the sand. Behind the grass are raspberry briars, blueberries, mustard, orach, alder and yarrow. Indians shared this place and left the heaped shells of their camping feasts. That was before the Europeans settled, laying claim to "real estate" and enforcing notions of private ownership. Today the island is private—a pity in that more of us won't see it; a blessing since our heavy presence won't change it into something tamed and common.

The man who first described it to me—an aesthete and a runner—was awed by the place. That may be why another man who knows it well told him the story, which changes with each telling:

As I remember the tale, this was a littoral arena, a place of final judgment. When two Indians fell into a dispute that grew out of all proportion, when they couldn't or wouldn't settle it until the tribe knew no simple peace, they went to the island and this beach. Not just the antagonists—the whole nation traveled to witness a days-long contest. They went to the beach and the two men ran. Only one would leave it living. They ran back and forth along the shifting mile of soft, white, sloping sand until one was dead. No weapons, no furious combat. Just fatal settlement of a stupid quarrel that had gone too far. Whether the best man won, the fittest surely did—unless a weaker man strengthened by certain knowledge that he was right beat a titan who knew his cause was false. Either way, there was no room for further argument, no hope for a new decision, no complaint that the deal was rigged or the judges biased or the counselors drunk. No appeal. The test was hard, the verdict final.

Would the whole tribe gather for the start? Men, women, children gathered in a mass? Or were the young barred from seeing so serious a rite? One imagines some witnesses watching from start to finish, at least one silent, trusted elder from each side. Some solon calls the start. Setting an easy pace—but not too slow for the sake of pride—the enemies match strong, long strides over wet sand where the footing's firm above an outgoing tide. Back and forth uncounted times beneath a high summer sun. Then come dusty heats through softer sand after the tide returns to nudge the runners higher up the beach face. One tries the swash but the water sucks at his feet like the other's ally, and he too must move up to the hot, uneven sand. Some children peek, until their patience lags, then go off hunting hares and raiding bird nests. Women gather shellfish and tend the cooking fires. Night falls; the runners find second wind with the ebbing tide and the cooler offshore air. A chant rises from those waiting in circles around the fires beneath the pines. The sachems bear constant witness, old men with small appetites, judges who'd impose a ritual death on anyone who stains the sacred contest with a foul. The runners match stride for weakening stride into the night, one of them daring a pace a little too fast to tire his enemy under the rising moon. . . .

Wouldn't that be a way to settle arguments between two troublesome peers: "Put an end to this feud, you two, or one dies running an endless marathon. The tribe insists." If the gripe goes on, they hit the beach they called "The Racecourse" until one runs the other into the sand. A tradition like that would encourage peaceful settlement before things went too far. It might also end an argument once and for all.

But it wasn't quite that way. A single epic race ran its course here, according to a white man's much-later history of the island. Hunting Wolf, chief of the Abnachi Tribe, had a daughter, and Forest Flower had two suitors. Her father proposed a race—one lap down the mile-long beach and back—to win the bride. In the written account, the rivals sprinted from the west corner of the beach along the crescent coast on hard, wet sand by the loud surf "whose mighty intimations presaged either death or victory." Neither had an edge at the far end. They reached the towering rock beyond the

pebble stretch together, pushed off and started back, at a dead run
too. Halfway down the beach one pulled ahead by inches. The
other willed more speed, gained a narrow lead but couldn't hold
and faltered, then came abreast again for a few last strides. He
stumbled in the sand and fell, bleeding from nose and mouth, dying
not from too weak a heart but one too strong for its vessels. The
other panted on, ran toward the waiting princess, crossed the line
and tumbled at her feet—as dead as the one who dared to race him.
The runners each won remembrance but not the prize they sought.
Their names live on, if history doesn't lie.

I like the first version better—the one my friend heard—
embellished in remembering, "improved" in telling me and which
I, in turn, amended in remembering. But that says more about us
than beaches, history or Abnachis. Perhaps they did have simpler
ways to settle disagreements than us litigious moderns. But not
quite as simple as we hopefully construe according to our own
standards with each retelling of the saga that this perfect beach
deserves.

I said there was a moral. There are two. First, it seems that
even in simpler times people sought out islands for occasions too
important to suit the trackless mainland. Islands are special places,
more defined, more contained and hence better able to contain an
event of special feeling and significance. We pour the finest port in
small glasses. The other lesson is that we hunger both for heroes
and for more simply honest ways as desperately as Running Chief
and Eagle Wing sought a princess for a bride.

Chanterelle

Cradled in a cranny of the Maine coast stands an island called
Chanterelle—though it is not on any map or chart. It has another
legal name: one that suits it about as well as Frederick Austerlitz fits
Fred Astaire and Frances Gumm fits Judy Garland. (Called by any
other name a rose would smell as sweet, but it would take a bloody
while for another word to evoke the bloom.) Only a few miles from
open ocean, Chanterelle lies in what Maine calls a river—really a
twisted arm of the sea. Storm surges don't overwhelm it, but the
tides range 8 feet up and down its shores each day making a brack-

ish haven for lobsters, oysters, crabs, clams and fish. The river winds around steep land; tendrils of the continent and countless islands all covered with evergreens and hardwoods clutching bedrock through shallow soil of their own making. Parts of Chanterelle's little shores are sheer at high tide while at the ebb, dark sands strewn with rocks and rockweed slope gently out into the clear, cold water.

At the turn of the century these sixteen acres were owned by two sisters from "away"; genteel Philadelphians who contrived to have several small buildings erected and formal gardens sown. Paths were cut wide enough for the Victorian sisters and their gentle friends to stroll two abreast without snagging a hem. They dressed formally for dinner in their briefly tamed wilderness and left each year before winter locked them in. No doubt they read Sir Walter Scott aloud, emulated Evengeline's fidelity, held musicales and voted for William Howard Taft. Day lilies remain in profusion around the shingled cabins. About the time Calvin Coolidge frowned his way to the White House, the sisters began buying their fowl from an ambitious mainland boy. A chicken farmer by the age of eight, he sold his birds for 25 cents a pound—head, feet, feathers and viscera included. (It was expensive in those days. When Herbert Hoover promised "a chicken in every pot," he evoked luxury.) The boy left Maine, sought his fortune close to Boston and returned to buy the island during the Truman years. Perhaps he had a sense of Dickensian achievement: the distant goal grasped at last. Perhaps he just meant to preserve something special: a place for friends and scattered daughters, and their friends and grandchildren to spend particles of summer that lend savor to the winters passed in cities.

A friend of mine was one of those daughters, and I reached the place after a frantic, several-hundred-mile solo drive to join close friends who'd had time to settle in. The island is hidden from the landing at the end of a dirt road; the boat ride takes ten minutes. But climbing ashore in this strange sylvan place I felt suddenly unsettled. What if there wasn't enough food on Chanterelle? (The kind that comes from stores, I mean.) What if my hostess blew an appendix or one of the children split a chin running on the rocks? What if the water rose too high that night and swept the boat away? *What would I do all evening?* There was not a street nearby to stroll

down, not a telephone or cigarette machine in sight. And if I had
the itch, I couldn't just pat the Cherokee on the transmission and
be somewhere else by morning. Call it island fever.

The cookhouse was well stocked. A safari lamp did lose its
charge but there was a spare battery, and besides it was time for
bed. We ate raspberries and felt the wind.

Next day everyone went off sailing or shopping in the mainland
village, leaving me alone to work at a kitchen table in one cabin.
For a moment I snuggled in the peace, then sat up with a start. It
was not *quiet*. Not at all. A squirrel ran across the roof. Some
raucous birds began a debate that threatened to last till noon. Fishes
jumped with no discernible pattern. But what lured me from the
typewriter was a high-pitched cheep, a pure note that swelled so
briefly, then stopped. It was repeated a dozen times, then answered. The call came now and then from every side. I had to learn
its source and walked down to the island's southern point. Ospreys
were teaching their young to fly over the water and high above the
next island to the west. Soaring, gliding, diving, chasing each other,
disappearing behind the trees to swoop back again. Sometimes half
a dozen were visible at once; sometimes silent, sometimes singing
that piercing, delicate note. I walked around the island once lis-
tening to all the sounds before settling down to work.

After dinner that night the erstwhile chicken farmer's grand-
daughter was troubled by a sound: an engine close offshore. It
wasn't right, she said, knowing the night noises better than the rest
of us. It made her nervous, so she and her suburban girlfriend crept
through the woods to have a look. A large boat with no lights and
several men aboard moved about, then anchored in the channel.
Returning to camp, the girls urged me back with them. They imag-
ined the worse. But the men were not raiders, drug runners or
pirates (and the girls not fated Sabines). They were fishermen out
to net herring in the tide.

Another afternoon toward sunset we circumnavigated the island in the dinghy. One osprey stood watch on the branch beside
a treetop nest on the next island. Ten more came and went, not
fishing, just taking their constitutionals as the sister ladies must
have done. We saw great blue heron too and another wader—I've
forgotten which because of what happened next. Passing the
north end of the island, I rowed slowly east around the sunken

rocks. We were 100 yards from the mainland shore opposite a lush stand of hardwoods. The tide was high, the sun low, directly behind us and about to hide below the mile-distant evergreens. It appeared that a spotlight shone into the trees ahead. Broad daylight still, a half-circle shimmered brighter in the trees. The sun seemed a perfect hole in the pale sky through atmospheric haze; its light bounced off the water like a skipping stone into the trees and bounced straight back at us. There was nothing rare standing in that light; no primal deer come down to drink or bald eagle peering from a branch poised for prey. There was just bright phenomenon highlighting a half-round portion, a Giotto halo in the trees. A simple spectacle, beauty to the eyes of the few beholders blessed to be there and see it.

Lookout

Even fine weather batters the Outer Banks. While a hurricane too distant to notice whips the Caribbean, Indian summer warms the Great Lakes. Tomorrow is Halloween; tonight is windy on Ocracoke and the ten-minute task of pitching a tent becomes an hour-long struggle with the fly streaming out like a battle flag, pulling up stakes and tossing them about in the dark. Next morning one orange pennant flies from the Coast Guard flagstaff: Small craft stay in port. The ferry to Cedar Island cancels its three-hour run across Pamlico Sound. By noon a second orange flag whips the wind. Local radio stations interrupt their rock and gospel songs to announce the gale warning. That high-pressure system to the north is feeding air to the donut low beyond the Devil's Triangle. These islands lie in the middle, and winds rake in from the northeast rising to forty knots, then gusting toward fifty. The tide will crest soon after sundown. Fed by waters pushed abnormally high by this fair-weather frenzy, it may flood the islands.

By dusk the sea's gone mad off Hatteras Lighthouse at the easternmost corner of the land. For several hundred yards the shallow water churns white. As often as not six lines of breakers stand up to be counted, like a troop of mounted cops in riot gear waiting for orders. The waves in front rise and roll forward; one gallops in, breaks and crumbles. Another overtakes its swash, marches erect for several seconds further, rides up the narrow beach and strikes the scarp. Breakers beat beneath the long-gone foundations of the first lighthouse, undermining ledges of sand precariously held by tangled bayberry roots and beach grass. A half-foot slab of shore slides away with every twelfth wave. The next eleven splash straight up the scarps like geysers; some splash inland down a narrow road.

After dark the tide turns without major flooding, but the beach a few miles north becomes an eerie place. I approach it with care, as if one can walk carefully in wind like this. It slants across the island, driving and dragging the Atlantic to the base of man-made barrier dunes, cutting them back. Beneath an invisible sky the surf shows white as far as can be seen—a ghostly white that has no depth, no leading edge, no ending. The peculiar thing is that human eyes can see at all. There are no artificial lamps; the electric power lines behind the dunes have shorted out and the sky is overcast. There seems to be no source of light. But the furious surf writhes visibly in the dark. I crouch in the lee of a broken dune trying to see some order in the frenzy, but the wind whips tears from my eyes, replacing them with sand.

Hard to see, it's impossible not to hear. Each breaker makes its own sound, yet there are so many that the noise seems out of synch. Watch one specter of a breaker and the loudest sound comes from somewhere else. Wind screams through the grass beside me and from everywhere offshore comes a long, low groan of noise like a final phase of Inquisition torture. The whole beach is white and moving, but the sea doesn't eat my dune; nor does the berm sand reappear as it should between the flood and ebb of waves. This beach is covered with dry foam; no one ever drowned in foam. I walk toward where water must be. The surf rises more clearly. A wave charges in and breaks. Another overtakes it; distance and speed are impossible to judge. I turn and trot back from the invading white. After an hour or more, a spitting rain begins in fits and starts. I leave the beach and drive to a nearly empty campground. Too tired to wrestle with wet nylon in the gusting wind, I sleep in the jeep, which rocks gently in the gale, cozy as a cradle.

Days later, I reach an island that never suffered the construction of an artificial barrier dune line. Because prevailing winds don't cross it from the seaward side (but blow along its length), its

Cape Lookout, North Carolina

dunes occur in clumps of mounds anchored by sea oats. The berm is 100 yards wide—twice that in some places. It slopes away from a barely noticeable crest. Where spring and storm tides reach across it, only a few grasses take root. There is an expanse of natural pavement across the center of the island: shells, shards and coarse sand that have compacted into a glazed surface.

Toward the bay the marshes begin. A couple of clumps of land rise barely 5 feet above mean high water. These hammocks boast live oaks and pines. Even here whole and broken shells lie on the surface because storm tides inundate the entire island from time to time. Because there is no line of barrier dunes, the active beach remains very wide, so storm tides waste their energy over a large area. When they wash inland they carry sand, shells and nutrients across the island. These materials nourish the marsh behind the island and stimulate new growth. All the plants resist salt spray to some degree and can survive occasional flooding. After a storm has robbed the outer beach of some sand, normal wave patterns bring it back in succeeding seasons. Burial stimulates pioneer grasses like sea oats, and these plants collect new sand in young, temporary dunes that withstand the gentler storms. When a major tempest occurs, they succumb after retarding the storm surge awhile. The dunes "retreat," but the dynamic, "unstabilized" island survives pretty much in place, edging slowly west. The habitat survives too for uncounted centuries; this was Cape Lookout.

The drive along Cape Hatteras had been as boring as a turn-pike between a wall of American beach grass (which doesn't natu-rally occur this far south) and a barricade of bushes. Both ocean and bay are concealed. But on Cape Lookout, as on the islands of the Virginia Coast Preserve, the virgin views extend from shore to shore—a marvelous panorama of surf, foreshore, berm, dunes, grassland, occasional clumps of maritime forest, marsh and bay. It's a varied, vibrant place. Forty-two species of reptiles, amphibians and mammals live on this seashore's several islands among 188 kinds of plants. The catalog of resident and migrant birds reads like John James Audubon's life list.

Returning to the mainland, my boatman says, "You got away from the world there. That's why the fishermen come year by year. But now the National Park wants to take it away from us. They want it all for theirselves." A mixed blessing. The Park people are haul-ing carcasses of cars away and burning fishing shacks, most of them put up by squatters with no legal right to occupy the land even before it became public domain. Though plans are not final at this writing, odds are good that most of the island will be preserved in a wild state: no permanent camps, no roads, no more private ve-hicles of any kind, and possibly no public jitneys or park vehicles either. It's painfully obvious that cars can cause ecological confu-sion. Not only do they kill grass, they compact the sand, interfere with percolation and make ruts. But the ruts collect ribbons of rainwater and nurture native grasses. Are RVs good or bad or both? Certainly they allow hundreds to ride where only tens would walk, carrying everything on their backs. The fishermen will scream and I'll miss the convenience of a jeep, but this place would be better without beach vehicles.

Here is a National Park island that can be easily returned to a natural state. It is a rare opportunity to restore such a place that will be open to gentle human use by anyone willing to forego the "im-provements" found almost everywhere else. Call it Eden by the Sea.

Sandy Serendipity (Or Littoral Litter)

On a Yankee island just after World War II, three boys en-gaged in what an English writer calls "the gentle art of wrecking." That means to go see what the tide dragged in and tote it home for

fun or profit. Farmers used to harvest rockweed fertilizer that way,
along with horseshoe crabs for chicken or hog feed and sea-soaked
firewood. People with metal detectors do it now in search of Spanish gold but settle for loose change and lost car keys. Traditionally
one hopes for random flotsam (wrecked ships or cargo) and jetsam
(stuff thrown overboard to lighten a foundering vessel).

Looking for anything the Gulf Stream might deliver, my pals
and I found a large waterlogged crate on the empty beach. Its
stenciled letters indicated war materiel—treasure of the highest
price for kids whose generation barely knew peace and who yearned
to be fighting men when we grew up. We worked cautiously with
pocketknives and driftwood levers—in case the crate contained ex-
plosives or hand grenades for the French Resistance. But we
worked with zeal. It might hold bayonets or bullion for some fifth
column.

The job took hours. We had to move the leaden thing twice
from the returning tide. When the lid came off at last, our treasure
was this: about one thousand gross cartons of matchbooks. They'd
been destined for troops closer to the rear than the front because
the covers had cartoons of hussies leaning against lampposts and the
caption G.I. JOE KNOWS V.D. CAN BE PREVENTED. We knew wet
matches wouldn't light our grape-leaf cigarettes. As for V.D., we
hadn't a clue.

One beachcomber became a craftsman, one an oceanogra-
pher and I went into the word game. But I never gave up assid-
uous wrecking. In the subsequent three decades I have found two
nearly complete whale skeletons, a recently deceased porpoise
with lovely pearly teeth, a Chevrolet, three loggerhead turtles,
enough bleach bottles to launder the Sixth Fleet and enough
assorted barrels to fill a delicatessen, one rusty tricycle, a per-
ambulator, many gloves and boots (always filled with sand), an
18-foot sailboat with her back broken, an almost whole pilot whale
that couldn't be approached downwind without a gas mask, one
16-foot runabout with an outboard motor, uncounted pieces of
wooden hulls and decks, a barge large enough to carry six freight
cars, a hundredweight of antique iron ships' nails in worm-eaten
timbers, a yard of oyster-encrusted cable that looked like a sea
snake, one half-full squeeze bottle of Spanish pomade, innumerable bottles (never with a note), several fishnet floats, a gill net
with about a hundred pounds of spoiled fish, three jet-fuel tanks,

one anchor and chain, miles of hawsers, two willing girls, half a catamaran, and one loving couple.

Most of the objects I've come across had to be left behind. Once I negotiated a telephone cable reel more than a mile to a friend's bayside back yard where it became a breakfast table—a herculean labor stretched over several days. I have never found another sealed crate or anything closer to a piece-of-eight than a sand dollar. Now I kick those echinoderms aside and keep on looking for rarer things to carry home: a loggerhead shell, the rib of a wrecked whaler. Many folk are content with starfish, devil's pocketbooks, sand dollars. I envy such simple acquisitive tastes and have long since stopped trying to explain the 2-foot whale vertebra beside my fireplace. But guests understand the bowl of seashells on the coffee table and finger them like worry beads. That heap evokes the ineffable mysteries of the ocean and its infinite designs.

Shells may be the most sensible things in the world to collect. Easily handled and carried, they're light, little trouble to preserve, more varied than a herd of Pet Rocks, and free. They have nice names too: little white trivia, fighting conch, greedy dove, strawberry cockle, sunray Venus, Humphrey's wentletrap, false angel's wing. People gathering dead shells have an easy task: Walk, look and pick—with R. Tucker Abbott's field guide in a pocket or the American Museum of Natural History's *Guide to Shells* in a backpack.

The rules of beachcombing are easy enough: Anything washed up is fair game for anyone who wants to take the trouble to lug it away. That stated, there are exceptions. The one broken runabout I found had been "claimed" already by someone who left a note to that effect in the belief that it was common salvage. Local police didn't honor the claim, however, since the boat had been beached by a couple of drunks, who planned to fetch it after drying out in the local lockup.

Some National Seashores set limits on collectors. You can take as many seashells as you can lug on foot, for example, not as many as you can carry in a pickup truck. This is to discourage commercial collectors from picking a beach clean. As for living plants, leave them alone; the beach needs them far more than your arboretum. As for anything washed up on the shore that man has made and lost in the sea, it is a beachcomber's for the taking—but the taking can involve considerable effort.

Back to Basics

The beach moves different people in the same ways.

I knew a man whose life involved arguments, legalisms, and institutions. A cautious policy-maker in public life and a bachelor, he kept company with a distinguished career woman of esoteric tastes. They were both intelligent and urbane—he rather stuffy, she a little slim—the kind of couple welcomed at dinner parties, where his polysyllabic conversation through a deviated septum was as reliable as Muzak. In the city I never saw him unshaved, un-buttoned, or untied around the throat with rep silk and conven-tion—except in the sauna of a humorless club. She was a member too, but, more important, for part of every summer she visited an island that's long on simplicity and short on amenities like plumb-ing. She told me about it during a buffet.

Knowing my interest in natural places, the lady invited me to stop by if I was in that latitude. There'd be no way to phone and the mail would be haphazard, since days pass without anyone reaching the mainland to pick it up. "Come visit anytime," she said after the almond tart. It was the kind of vague invitation people offer in the happy belief it will be accepted but never acted on; the kind you accept with a certain postprandial enthusiasm because you'll cer-tainly never be in the neighborhood. What's "nearby" an island, after all? But months later it happened that I was in sight of that island and had time on my hands. It was closer than any other place I had to visit. It had the undeniable attraction of being a bastion that doesn't admit strangers without invitations. In a mainland harbor I found a boat that could head that way, and I hitched a ride to this limpet of bleak and rustic land.

Some colonists, as ubiquitous as George Washington, had slept here, so it has a place in the pages of history—if only a footnote. There are a dozen dwellings, some foundations dating back to the seventeenth century, some mansions that suffered the heavy hand of Victorian renovators. One house has running water and another electric lights powered by a home generator. The others don't. On this private island, people walk to their own rhythms. It offers no public facilities, but then the public wouldn't like it; there's nothing very public to do. You can visit the graveyard where a family is planted under white marble stones—except for one black slate set apart and bearing the same surname. You can draw water from the common well, visit where a founding father prayed by a rock big as a Winnebago, hunt coon oysters, listen to the poison ivy grow, chase wild rabbits, and count the gulls.

These three wild species—rabbits, gulls, and poison ivy—dominate this place of absurd ecological equilibrium that has no predators except hunters in the fall. The cottontails are so sure of themselves that they'll hop down a path 15 feet behind a person toting water. The gulls are eerie. They own one end of the island more certainly than the old families own the other, and they fill the air with constant, monotonous screaming. To cross the island at their end is startlingly strange. Herring gulls and great black-backs are everywhere, living, lame, deformed, dying and dead. They nest on the beach, under bushes, and in an ancient fallow orchard. The cripples of each year's brood, which elsewhere would die before they fledged, hide among the brush and briars to scrape a living off the carrion of their kin. This is the only place I've seen gulls roost in trees—perhaps because there's nowhere else to rest. It was also the only place I've been afraid of birds that weren't defending nests or young. In this chaos there was no apparent pecking order—except a lethal one. It was so crowded that the normal rules of avian behavior seemed to have been abandoned. Inland, beneath a flying flock so thick I saw two birds collide, the flightless ones ran into blind corners of bramble, then rushed past me almost rabidly within arm's reach. A one-eyed bird picked at a carcass undisturbed. It seemed an evil acre, as if that corner of the natural world had gone berserk. It is a place that all the islanders visit from time to time, to keep in touch with something.

Elsewhere there are mud flats full of clams, bays full of fish, sand beaches full of solitude, sheds full of firewood, and scattered houses bright at night with kerosene lamps. This island has the compelling attraction of the wild, the exotic, the remote—even of those birds themselves so obviously untouched by any man. But back to my host and hostess.

They would occupy "The Boathouse," she'd said. I took the term for one of those euphemisms in exclusive summer places where butlers in white jackets pass canapés and lapsed debutantes pick wildflowers in picture hats. I was not surprised to see a house commanding a well-trimmed yard big enough for Scarlett O'Hara's garden party. Certainly "The Boathouse" would be a renovated storehouse built to serve blockade runners in 1862 or a bootlegger's cache. Not so. It turned out to be a single room with a bottled-gas fridge and stove at one end; it was smaller than a slaver's cabin. The policy maker answered my knock in a five-day beard and cut-offs. The lady was reading Tolstoy barefoot. They greeted me with equal measures of warmth and surprise. After all, I was a man they saw at city dinners.

My host seemed as settled as a barnacle on a low rock at high tide—and equally aware of the rhythmic need to eat. He'd never soiled so much as a fingernail in a mud flat before first seeing this island a few summers before. But the tide was falling and he planned to dig clams at dead low, three hours hence, he said, with a glance not at a clock but at the water. If he missed the tide there wouldn't be much dinner. One thing he hadn't lost: his manners. Would I care to come along? He'd seen a new and likely spot for steamers and meant to try out a Yankee tool he'd bought by mail. In winter this man doesn't wield anything much more physical than a Dictaphone, I thought, but he hefted the clam rake deftly and called a halt when the bucket was two-thirds full. Leave some for tomorrow, for next year. Reading by hurricane lamp, bathing out of a bucket beside the privy (if at all), digging clams, bearding the mussels, catching fish, sharing the cooking and KP with his lady, he still talked through his nose. But the ideas were different. "I find I spend half my time gathering, preparing and eating food. I never give those things much thought at home. But out here they're important and I enjoy them."

There were moments over supper—a seafood smorgasbord with a bit of beef split three ways as an excuse to open a bottle of Bordeaux—that they were comfortably mute. We listened to the wind shift and, when the tide returned, went down to see tiny shrimp swarming near the surface of the bay.

The Oyster and the Marathon

Variously and simultaneously a beach can be seductive, disciplinary, evocative and unforgiving. One spring I decided to join a 10-mile foot race. For some serious competitors it was a preamble to the Boston Marathon; for many more it was a sweaty, panting test.

For the friend who egged me on, and for me, it offered a simple challenge: to finish a "marathon" after forty. To ice the cake of a short training stint, I went down to Assateague, where the wildlife refuge had always maintained mileposts along the dunes. If I could run a fast 5 miles on sand with a ten-pound pack on Friday, I could certainly double the distance over asphalt on Sunday morning.

Out on the beach I began to run, feeling good, feeling like the Athenian messenger himself ready to shout "Victory" when I saw the first milepost ahead. Then my spirits slumped: 1 KM it said. Assateague had gone metric over the winter. Remembering that a kilometer is 5/8 of a mile, I began computing and plowed on along the beach, past the dunes and the large-letter signs that mark dikes through the carefully managed marsh. My second wind arrived near the old pony fence, now a meaningless line of posts without wire stretching clear across the narrow island. I was still strong down the long, slow cove where the beach broadens to a quarter-mile of dry white sand before the dunes. Feeling good! I made the eighth kilometer at something close to a plodding sprint and stretched for a tape as impalpable as the laurels I meant to win. Time: forty-two minutes, which was good enough. Ambling back, I did a few wind sprints just to show off to the sandpipers. I was fit and ready. The 10 miles on pavement around the Tidal Basin and along the Potomac would be a snap.

My first oystercatchers of the year appeared, ostentatious as Easter Paraders with their beaks bright red for breeding season. I drank juice from my pack by the old fence that looked so desolate now without wires. When it was intact, with four cables strung post to post from ocean to bay, it had served a purpose: to keep a herd of healthy Chincoteague ponies safely apart from some quarantined horses suffering an infectious disease. Back then, a few years earlier, there had been an encounter:

I'd wandered up that beach mile after mile, fleeing something in the world of cities. Leaving lifeguards and children behind first, I passed surfcasters and a few scattered sun-seekers, then finally found unpeopled solitude. There were only the skittering ghost crabs, ceaseless shore birds and the sea bothering the shore. Warmth and stillness filled the early summer afternoon. I swam in the cold, gentle surf, then floated, looking up at an incomparably clean sky, arms outstretched, rocked by the easy waves until I thought I could fly. Instead I walked from the surf onto a beach that had no footprints but my own, momentarily feeling like Robinson Crusoe. I wandered back toward the dunes. The wooden deck of a wrecked boat lay on the flats, which are washed only by spring tides and storm surges. It had moved a hundred yards or so from behind the little hummock that hid it the year before—unless the hummock had moved. There was an enormous barkless tree trunk, its roots shiny in the sun, and a battered aluminum fuel tank jettisoned by some jet fighter-bomber on an unknown errand. It had come ashore during the winter; I *knew* this stretch of beach. Then, behind a barrier dune, there stood a little chestnut foal and her dam, eyeing me with gentle curiosity.

Though these stunted "wild" horses come from domestic stock somewhere along the line, tradition has it that the first horses came ashore from the wreck of a Spanish galleon. The more pedestrian historical truth is that Virginia farmers kept surplus stock on these barrier islands until this century. Also, the Chincoteague Volunteer Fire Department, which owns the present herd, culls sick animals (secretly selling them to slaughterhouses, so it's said) and brings in new horses from surplus herds of mustangs in the West. But none of that mattered just then; I was remembering my own summers in the Rocky Mountains.

I walked slowly toward the mare and her foal as I'd walked, with a halter hidden in one hand, toward countless ranch mounts on a sagebrush range land. The trick was to coax oneself within arm's reach, grab a fistful of mane, and slip the halter over the horse's head in the cold dawn, because morning was breaking and it was time to round up the night-scattered herd for the day's work. The halter rope served as a single rein; riding back to the corral without a bridle, a teen-age wrangler controlled the horse by legs and will, since halters have no bits.

So I walked toward this equine madonna—the pair of Chincoteague ponies—with nothing certain in mind but the sense of a distant memory and without so much as a string of whelk eggs in hand for a halter. The air was hot that far from the surf, the horses quiet and standing almost easy, flicking flies. The mare didn't move; the foal wandered toward me a little. It seemed to be twenty years or more before, the commonalities clearer than the differences, as I mounted the edge of a steep hummock. . . .

Then from out of the pages of history (or mystery) came the thundering hoofbeats of a runt horse rampant. Daddy! The dusty

stallion, minding a harem that ranged among the dunes, was running my way, head down, ears back, teeth bared. My reverie fled
at a gallop but I stopped in my tracks. He was 30 yards away, then
20. I might have stood taller than he eyeball to eyeball, but under
the circumstances I was no match for those brown incisors and
splayed, unshod hooves. I didn't even have a Stetson to spook him.
I leapt down the face of the dune, putting a fragile physical barrier
of sand between us. Out of sight out of mind? The alert stallion
didn't follow and I pursued my ramble a little chastened, somehow
very conscious of the fact that I was stark naked. Farther along the
flat I found a beautiful oddity, a talisman of sorts. It was a single
perfect mushroom, big around as a tennis ball, pure white across
the crown and fringed in silver gray. It grew atop a dry pile of horse
dung.

But all that was years earlier. Thinking about the race two days
away, I walked back to a crossing through a marsh where I'd once
found the skull of a sika deer, an exotic species imported from the
Orient decades ago by Junior Conservationists. I saw sikas alive
that day, whitetails too, and slept well in a motel on nearby Chincoteague, the settled, tourist-loving island that lent its name to a
tame children's story and to those sometimes-wild horses.

Next morning, feeling up to running another beach from end
to end, I fed on pancakes on the theory that lots of carbohydrates
the day before a race sates muscles with stored energy. The beach
and the amenities of its nearby town were standing me in good
stead for my rite of passage, the mini-marathon. If only I could have
ignored the coast's seductions. But no, before driving back to Washington I bought half a bushel of Chincoteague oysters on-the-hoof
for about the price of a dozen on the halfshell in a French restaurant. Mary was having several special friends to dinner and these
would be extraordinary openers.

John Benson would be there: calligrapher, stonecutter (viz.,
inscriber of the Kennedy graves at Arlington), windsurfer, fiddler,
earthy aesthete and epicure. In town to carve some words on I. M.
Pei's wing of the National Gallery, he'd appreciate Chincoteagues.
He'd also help open them, being as deft with an oyster knife as a
stone chisel. Also, Arnost Lustig was invited: professor, writer,
Auschwitz survivor, catalyst of *The Shop on Main Street* and author
of several novels about the Holocaust as seen from within the Nazi
flames. Knowing life's fragility so intimately, he takes more kinds of

joy in living than most men can enumerate. He might not know Chincoteagues by name, as Benson would, but he'd relish them. I bought champagne and arrived in time to start opening the tenacious oysters.

Just as the remoteness of a beach relates directly to its beauty, the difficulty in securing a bivalve from its shell is an index of its excellence. A steamed softshell clam opens easier than a softboiled egg. But oysters? *Crassostrea virginica?* They're harder. Hardest to open and best to eat. Especially Chincoteagues. I only ventured to buy such a big basket of them because I knew I'd have capable help.

Benson arrived first and joined me in making a midden. We couldn't help it: For every two or three we put on ice, we ate one. When the other guests arrived, the party grew in the kitchen. We finally got far enough ahead so that a silver tray covered with shining ice was filled edge to edge with opened oysters and quartered lemons. We all adjourned to the living room and champagne. We laughed, we drank the dry bubbling wine that set off the slippery shellfish like diamonds against blue velvet. It was a noisy party almost, without many articulated paragraphs just then—only declaratives and sounds of delight. In the middle of it the Professor had something to enunciate, an inspiration.

"You know how oysters taste?" he said in his thick accent—and everybody else shut up. When he speaks the words are worth hearing, imbued with contagious feeling. But caught up in the moment he'd started to talk without thinking. How do oysters taste? Who can say? Now we wanted to hear the pregnant simile. He was stuck, hoist by his own palate, his effusive mind trapped by an Eastern European tongue.

"Oysters taste like . . . Oysters taste like . . . the universe!" It made no more sense—and none less—than our appetite and glee.

I don't remember what happened to the entrée or dessert. I do know we ate oysters until I couldn't pry any more. Then Benson, whose forearms are like hawsers from carving stone for two decades, opened another trayful. We saved only a dozen or so, for breakfast perhaps. We stayed up too late, sated and strong, energized by Chincoteagues, euphoric with good company.

Next morning I woke up alert and in plenty of time to run the race. A thousand people gathered near the Lincoln Memorial: curious spectators, slightly nervous unofficial runners and the long-limbed racers, who sat on the dewy ground bending heads to knees, stretching tendons, breathing, meditating. It was an inspiring crowd, and as the racers shed their sweatsuits they looked like heroes ready for an Olympiad and limber heroines of sagas yet unsung. But warming up, I felt sacks of wet sand hanging from my knees. My feet felt like clamshells, my legs like kelp, my stomach like the crest of a breaking wave.

The challenge of Friday's beach run had led to easy seduction by delicacies from nearby waters. I'd celebrated too soon. The oysters had wanted champagne—only there were so many oysters they'd demanded too much sparkle, and I hadn't had the will to resist. The beach had been there, 30 miles of it or so. I'd needed only five of them. I'd met the challenge of that day, rested the next and forgotten about tomorrow, today, Sunday and the marathon. I couldn't have jogged 10 miles to see a whooping crane hatch out triplets or the fabled phoenix nesting atop the Washington Monument.

So instead I ran the mini-mini-marathon, the race for ladies, kids and some handicapped folks who hopped and hobbled 2 miles with the fighting, glorious will of that Athenian messenger. Two young friends ran it too, and eight-year-old Andrew finished ahead of me.

Next year, older and wiser, I'll run without oysters.

The Beach Road

The Atlantic comes closest to our house at the shoulder of Delaware, a couple of hours' drive due east. At Cape Henlopen the Beach Road turns south and runs straight down Fenwick Island(s) between ocean and bay. Barely a decade ago this stretch of road was a pleasure itself, as breaks in the reeds to the right offered glimpses of wild marsh. To the left at miles-long intervals, round cement watch towers still stand, relics of World War II; they overlook the ocean beyond the line of man-made dunes that lath fences have collected grain by grain until the laths are barely stubs. Now this tidy highway more resembles the nouveau chic suburb of some sandy metropolis, a costly series of security-conscious condominium clusters—if by security one means gates and locks. (If security from a storm tide was your desire, you wouldn't settle so close to the shore on a barrier island in the first place.) At Indian River Inlet, where fishermen cast from the rock breakwaters that guard the channel, the road arches across a bridge tall enough to let charter boats pass with their outriggers erect in the sockets.

Then a political boundary splits this island of shifting sand. Across the state line the gargantuan towers of Ocean City rise with a vengeance, as if an entirely different ecosystem lies south of the line in Maryland, as perhaps it does. Here are pyramids, monoliths and hexagons of prestressed concrete, rambling malls and truss-roofed arcades—a conglomeration of structures that one might find a thousand miles inland. Only along the shore does the real location make itself felt, though years ago the beach had to be armored with groins and jetties and later bulldozed into steep dunes, which melted like sugar each time a wave nibbled at their feet. Now this beach is being "replenished" with slurry pumped from offshore through a 3-foot pipe. Until this latest engineering effort, which seems to be working despite its extreme ugliness, the beach was retreating; nay, it was fleeing in a rout. The surf at high tide had come so far as to bare the footings of many buildings and lead one prominent geologist to wonder which condo attacked by an abnormally high tide would be the first to "fall seaward like a Douglas fir." (Ocean City's boosters say these towers won't collapse; they're designed to stay erect in 110-percent-saturated sand. So if the island ever gets washed away, as many have, or nudged a little way west, like many more, these buildings will remain standing in high-rise splendor slightly offshore. Then picture-perfect tenants can fetch up at their apartments in motorboats instead of Mazdas.

Ocean City's streets number into the hundreds, all of them dusted with a little sand. This is a city of synthetic amusements: roller coasters, arcades, pizza parlors, rent-a-bikes, auction houses selling 'art,' a few turn-of-the-century hotels and assorted honky-tonk facing the beach across a boardwalk stout enough to carry trucks. The most wild thing may be the purple moose head on the wall of its namesake saloon. In a bar at sundown several years ago, a pretty PR gal and handsome CPA told me they loved the town; they'd just come all the way from Seattle and Philadelphia respectively "just to have an affair," which was going swimmingly and they hadn't even gone to the beach once. For people who like people in numbers, who seek the anonymity or opportunity of crowds, this must be the place.

Just south of Ocean City lies Assateague Island, which is in sight of the boardwalk but a world apart. Now an outdoor recreation and wildlife enclave jointly overseen by federal and state authorities, this 35-mile island was once destined to have houses, condo clusters and cul-de-sacs with cutesy names. Only few short stretches of broken pavement remain and all the planned house lots are under the Atlantic now, because the very things that "improved" and "secured" Ocean City's island made Assteague move (as discussed later). It migrated, thanks to natural processes hastened by human doings. "There'll always be a beach," says an expert. "It just won't be where it was and may not stay where someone wants it."

A beach is a sometime thing. It constantly shifts and moves as countless grains of sand answer the ceaseless prodding of winds and waves. The motion of the sea is fascinating, mesmerizing, like firelight certainly or a TV tube perhaps, but that motion makes the ocean's edge a most difficult thing to nail down. And as much as the beach is the land's edge, it is also the sea's. Wild inhabitants of this dynamic realm are wiser than people who hope to draw permanent property lines in shifting sand. The dumb native critters and plants don't try to beat a wave on its own mobile turf. Their ways suit the place and they roll with each oceanic punch.

In any case, the Beach Road to Assateague splits. The short way leads to the island's near north end. The long way makes a loop west through farm country again, then south beyond another state boundary, the Virginia line, and only then east once more on two-lane blacktop past the hi-tech, weird machines of a NASA tracking station. Then the road curves due east over miles of marsh to Chincoteague, another island that was better off before prosperity. (Can one fault people from elsewhere for coveting here? Or blame locals for preferring the soft and surly work of tourist industries to the hard lives that made their parents proud?)

Formerly a waterman's town (the "salt" oysters called Chincoteagues are justly famous), Chincoteague is the jumping-off place for Assateague Island National Seashore and the adjacent wildlife refuge. The ramshackle village itself gives way to a road lined with motels and souvenir shops, then the marsh begins again, patrolled by "cranky birds" (as herons are called) afoot and a-wing. Crossing a tidal gut, there used to be a low, loud, rickety board bridge that somehow emphasized the breadth of the water and stressed the fact that an island lay at the other end. Predictably perhaps, the powers that be replaced it with a designer span, an arching thing on concrete piers to ease access to this nearly wild island. That's a pity; well-connected islands lose their special aura.

At one time or another I've walked every foot of Assateague, which by geological and historical rights belongs to Fenwick, the barrier island(s) running all the way up to Delaware Bay. It has dunes of all sorts, some rising steeply around artificial fences, others mere hummocks reared in the course of gentle-weather years by natural phenomena that I've come to wonder at. Beach grass grows on their seaward side, and the dunes in turn cast a "wind shadow." A bit to landward the flora become thickets of alder, holly, bayberry and loblolly pine, most of them growing in tortuous shapes, pruned by salt spray blown by the sea wind. Where a chunk of dune has slid away, it reveals layers of dark sand: garnet, magnetite and such. These minerals become concentrated in layers when winter winds blow away the lighter grains of quartz that were parts of mountains geological ages ago and which make up most of the beach today.

By the water along the outer beach are the ever-present birds: laughing, herring and ring-billed gulls, busy sandpipers and their vocal kin, all pecking livings from the sand. There are the remains of many marine animals: crabs, clams, snails, fish both finned and jelly, lost feathers and random bones. Like any beach where wild species outnumber *Homo sapiens*, this place is both alive with the former and cluttered with their dead remains, each bit of which contributes to the living place. But what lies on the surface is only icing on the cake, so to speak. Ocean water is a cold soup of tiny nutrients. Microorganisms live in the open sea and in the tiny channels of water between the sand grains wherever the beach is wet. The living is easy for small creatures fed by the tidal caterer. Because the ocean is an endless source of small meals, many slightly larger animals learn to put up with the oceanic headaches of constant pounding. They'd grow complacently fat if they didn't spend their lives evading the larger animals that feed on them. Each animal lives and dies, eats and is eaten. Each generation's success is measured by a single standard: Did it create another generation? As Samuel Butler said, "A hen is only an egg's way of making another egg." As sociobiologist Edward O. Wilson updated the notion, an "organism is only DNA's way of making more DNA."

From time to time there are oddities. As my notes from years ago indicate, a harbor porpoise came ashore here on Assateague; it is an animal rarely known to come so far south, the wildlife guides say. A fluke perhaps—though the brown pelicans I first saw in the middle eighties were the start of something new, or really the return of something very old. Pelicans, like the raptors, perch atop a food ladder where they suffered from DDT and its chemical relatives. When their population shrank, so did their range, but now that such pesticides are disused, pelicans are coming back and even moving north. Welcome, I say.

In past years, birds have been welcome here to the detriment of other biological classes such as predatory mammals. War was once declared on foxes, though at the height of it I saw a red fox; he was a saucy prince trotting down the road one night as if he owned the right-of-way. The Chincoteague National Wildlife Refuge is managed for the special benefit of birds by the U.S. Fish and Wildlife Service; the National Park Service, which has its own precinct here, prefers hands-off policies to let nature mediate between *Aves* and *Vulpes*. In any case 250 species of birds benefit from this place year in and year out; it's another migratory bottleneck and wintering ground. None are more welcome than peregrine falcons, the fastest birds on earth, who pass this way each fall in growing numbers as they too recover from the effects of DDT.

Botany time. Marsh alder grows down to the high-tide line in the marsh. So does salt meadow grass (*Spartina patens*), which farmers used to mow for hay that cost them only the price of labor. Where the salt hay stops, its cordgrass cousin begins. *Spartina alterniflora* is hinged near the ground and falls in a high wind to create mats like mattresses of reeds. The fiddler crabs live below it, their million burrows ventilating the mud at low tide and irrigating the mud when the water rises. There's phragmites too, hollow reeds of the sort the ancients carved into the first pens. Saltwort (*Salicornia*), which adds zest to salads, thrives in the tide flats, its spikes shiny from expelled salt. Snails creep up and down the flat grasses eating algae and keeping above the reach of the water whence their ancestors came. Seemingly sterile salt pans—flat areas of empty mud—are actually alive with different colored algae that migrate up and down as conditions change by the hour.

Sometimes in June the marshes will be kept nearly people-free by mosquitoes. Why not annihilate them? Because their larva is prime food for the shell- and fin-fish that spend their youth in shallow marsh waters. Without the eggs of these bloodsucking pests, three-fourths of the fish we eat would go hungry before growing large enough to go to sea. Raymond B. Manning, a Smithsonian Institution crustacea curator, offers this datum: Recent catches of marsh-dependent seafood amount to 535 pounds per acre of estuary. This is nearly twice what a well-managed and heavily capitalized Maryland farm can grow in livestock. Comparative agronomists say that acre for acre, a marsh is the most productive land on earth except for a well-fertilized pineapple field. And it does its fecund work alone—cleaned and fertilized alike by diurnal tides—if it is left alone.

Closer to the beach there's poison ivy, a plentiful source of berries for at least sixty species of birds. Sea lavender and seaside goldenrod grow on the dunes. "Terns used to nest here," a ranger says during a walk on the beach near Tom's Cove, where some vehicles are allowed now. But the odd mating rite of the tern, which includes paired flights across the rookery and gifts of ritual food, must be seen elsewhere. Their rites have the same surprising purpose as the heron's ungainly spring dance: for one individual to discover another's gender from its role. These birds must *act* male or female since both sexes look alike, even to their own kind.

The Beach Road leads farther south to a fishing village with the engaging name of Oyster, where a retired waterman, George West, Jr., waited in his boat. West had plied Virginia waters as an oysterman and as a boy, as his father and grandfather had before him. He was old enough to be a grandfather himself—the better to find a way around these treacherous bays. Here the shoals wander about like sad boors at a cocktail party; creeks open and close without respect for charts. We headed for the 35,000-acre Virginia Coast Preserve, a dozen islands bought by the Nature Conservancy, which had pledged to see that they're left alone in perpetuity. These islands include Metomkin, Cedar, Cobb, Wreck, Hog, and others.

Going outside the islands to the edge of the Atlantic, West's boat is surrounded by a herd of romping porpoises. Minutes later he says, "I owned a thousand acres right about here." The islands once lay farther east; the course he steers crosses where his family lived before the hurricane of '33. "All got in safe except my grandfather and old Mr. Cobb. We didn't know anything about hurricanes then—called them northeasters. Nobody could conceive a tide could come that high. . . . Any man says he can build something the ocean won't tear up is overlooking a whole lot. He's a damn fool pure and simple. And that covers it all."

Much of the coat once looked like these islands now: low, with broad beaches that slope gently to a short dune and, behind that, grassy plains, salt marshes and fresh ones where rainwater lies in a convex "lens" on top of the heavier saltwater table. There are a few wrecked ships and the bones of stranded whales and stuff that drifted all the way from Spain to these beaches. In the spring there are rookeries and later, no doubt, more man-eating bugs than grains of sand when the summer wind is wrong. These islands appear modest—so unimposing and unimposed on.

Smith Island, the southernmost, lies even with Cape Charles, the tip of the Eastern Shore. I rounded that point one hot afternoon in order to have the luxury of a beach walk that didn't backtrack over the same ground. I'd walked south down the bay side and climbed an imposing fence that announced NO TRESPASSING: U.S. GOVERNMENT PROPERTY, an offensive statement since the government is not properly the owner of anything, just a trustee. I'd seen thunderheads crossing the Chesapeake. When they reached the narrow land again—it's barely a sliver there while the bay mouth is 20 miles wide—their forward edge began rolling up like sterile cotton into its blue paper. It was an extraordinary sight, as I stood almost at the base of an invisible column of air that rose straight up forcing the moving cloud to twist itself up seemingly tighter and tighter like a magazine rolled into a bat. The leading edge stayed bright and fluffy in the sun as it rolled, and the roll itself stayed right overhead. But the rest of the cloud, spreading back across the bay, turned from a gentle gray to sooty black.

There was no thunder or lightning, just sudden rain. It blew horizontally in gill-sized drops, and the sun went out as if snuffed by the wall of wind that bent every tree and carried spring leaves away. I'd just passed an old artillery bunker from a nearly forgotten war, and I stumbled back to it as the rain turned to hailstones big as mothballs. Drenched and stung, I hid in the dark, dank, man-made cavern with a dripping ceiling and rusty rails running across the oddly even floor. The storm passed, leaving the land veiled with rising mists and sparkling sunlight.

Below Chesapeake Bay the Beach Road leads to Virginia Beach, another summer metropolis with motels offering all the comforts of home. But take a detour. Go to the water at Sandbridge, turn south between myriad summer homes on stilts (the better to see over the dunes, unless another house is in the way) and continue on to Back Bay Wildlife Refuge. Although he was nearing retirement, my guide there some years ago was still a child of the place. "My forefather was shipwrecked on the dune," explained Ronnie Water-field, who knew every beast and bird by name. The "hell diver," or pied grebe, sinks to hide underwater when frightened. The snowy egret is showy; "when he jumps up, look on his yellow dancing slippers," said Waterfield. "Puddle ducks" feed on the surface; "dabbling ducks" forage below it. "Ditty birds" include everything from sparrows to mocking birds. "There are those that think ducks was created for hunters to shoot. It couldn't be farther from the truth," says Waterfield, pointing out species with every length of neck to feed on every kind of aquatic plant in the marsh. While eating, a bird is "tearing roots up, knocking seed off and covering it up. What he's doing is cultivating better than a man can. Other than that you wouldn't have nearly as good a crop of aquatics," the food of water birds. That's ecology.

Steering a battered pickup along the beach, Watefield re-marked, "I remember when the birds nested on this side of the dune." But it hadn't happened in years, and he blamed the traffic. The beach "used to have lots of birds and few cars. Now it has lots of cars and few birds," he observed. He drove near a doomed gannet that was sitting immobile just above the swash, looking like a judge; its feathers were clotted with bilge oil, its sharp beak was pointing down and its frost-blue eyes were unblinking. "There's nothing to be done," Watefield said. But he had found his first killdeer nest of the year. The robin-sized bird rushed him, all puffed up like a cartoon turkey, and then fled, feigning a broken wing.

Another Beach Road two hours south crosses a causeway that leads to Kill Devil Hills, where the Wright Brothers first flew, and Roanoke Island, where Virginia Dare was born. Cape Hatteras National Seashore lies to the south. Eddies of the Gulf Stream sometimes launch flying fish near shore and roll heaven-knows-what along the bottom all the way from the tropics. There are bottlenose dolphins, grampuses, pilot whales, sea turtles, a few otters, even fewer and shyer water moccasins, all sorts of crabs, bivalves and innumerable fish.

"You should have been here yesterday," they said south of Nags Head. The bluefish had been running; corpses of bait fish, each with a piece of flesh missing, cluttered the beach. Light rain began an hour after dawn, and most of the surf casters went in for breakfast. Only one young man stayed, with his child, Shannon, while the mother slept. Then, very quickly, the shallow surf was alive with shiny fish, 8 or 10 inches long, swimming in tight-packed schools to the top of the wash. Then sloping fins sliced among them: the tails of big blues at an orgy. They'd take one bite from a silver-side and go for another. They took Shannon's father's lure on almost every cast. He'd reel in, cut the hook loose and run down the beach to cast into the swarm again. Other fishermen returned quickly until they ranged the beach 10 yards apart, sharing the spoils. They must have been watching from the porches like the gulls.

The bait fish came in such tight schools that I could wade among them in the water and slap a few ashore. The fishermen couldn't say whether they were shoaling to spawn or fleeing their hunters. "I don't know much about this," said Shannon's dad. "I just like to catch the big blues."

From a fishing pier where the kill seemed greatest, it appeared that while one bluefish fought the hook another swam below, veering in counterpoint. Judging from caps and coveralls, many major corporations were represented: Exxon, Caterpillar Diesel, even your Orkin Man. Four buddies from Norfolk carted off eighty blues load by load in a little red wagon. Beach vehicles are popular here because when the blues are running fishermen can cast until the school passes, then drive a few miles ahead and fish again. So the 58 miles of broken beach are rutted like a race-track between the wet sand and the dunes.

The Beach Road here is narrow, as the islands are narrow, and at the corner of Cape Hatteras the road turns to west—the direction of the distant mainland. Here stands the headiest proof of nature's dominion in this place. Built 500 yards from the surf in 1870, Cape Hatteras Lighthouse now stands less than 50 yards from breaking waves. Tides, currents and wave after wave have carried the shore away; now the lighthouse will be moved. Nearby at notorious Diamond Shoals, waves meet from diametric directions on stormy days. The waves crash head on and fly straight into the air like two-story fountains. Ashore, local folks' accents sound strange, more like Liverpool than Carolina and probably most like Elizabethan England, linguists say. At the lower end of this island, ferries shuttle farther west, followed by swarms of laughing gulls. The next island, Ocracoke, is stranger still, with a single village at its nether end and an inhospitable innkeeper: "You want a room, for one? Can't take you." Not when the last boat might bring couples enough to fill all his rooms at double rates.

Alta VanLandingham, the shell seller of Ocracoke, had a shop by the side of the road, and in her living room were aquariums housing pet spider crabs, which she fed by hand. To collect live shells, she worked at low tide, and in warm weather she preferred the early morning ebbs. That was because fewer tourists were there to interrupt and ask what she was doing. The answer was simple: She was digging the beach her way.

Finally, driving north, I knew that Prufrock was wrong:

I shall wear white flannel trousers and walk upon the beach . . .
I have heard the mermaids singing, each to each.
I do not think that they will sing to me.

Mermaids are found only on camper doormats and mirrors behind condo bars. There are better, living things to see and hear: choirs of gulls, ghost and hermit crabs, migrating clams in migrating sand, fastidious grasses and the ocean's endless energy. Just take the Beach Road to find them all.

Driftwords: Flashes

Two days ago a northeast gale carried seas 100 yards beyond the berm along Core Banks and left the beach crest clean. Tonight at dusk I stopped between two steep round dunes, the closest to the shore. Only one set of tires had marked the sand since ebb tide; the fishermen left a dead dogfish and a cow-nosed stingray, nothing more. The surf is always visible from where I sit. It looks higher than the nearly level sand, though of course it cannot be. It seems threatening to swamp my little plain and carry everything away to sea, except the inevitable sand. I know the tide will peak at 8:02 far below the beach crest—but I wait to make camp until it has. At home I'd been reading randomly before this trip; some notions come to mind:

- E. M. Forster: "Under cosmopolitanism, if it comes, we shall receive no help from earth. Trees and meadows and mountains [and waves and dunes] will only be spectacle, and the binding force that they once exercised on character must be entrusted to Love alone. May Love be equal to the task."
- George Steiner: "The widening gap that separates most of us in the antiseptic West from a normal, active religiosity not only cuts us off from grasping the life forces still primary to much of the Third World but divorces us from much that is elemental to our own past. . . . The seasonal pulse and segmentation of the year, the articulations of the day . . . and feasts both fixed and movable derive their meaning from precise religious occasions." The essayist's elliptical elegance boils down to this corollary: Mankind evolved knowing God(s) and acted accordingly. But that's all passé.
- The antique *Book of Common Prayer* speaks of "the peace of God which passeth understanding. . . ."

A soft wind rattles the sea oats on either side. I can see only one human light, the beacon 156 feet above Cape Lookout, 15 miles away, blinking shyly four precise times a minute at anyone wanting to know its whereabouts. The quarter-moon set soon after the sun, but I've known far darker nights. No clouds hide the November sky. So many stars appear that the constellations seem pale among them; my star map is a puny thing, like a connect-the-dots rendering of a Winslow Homer seascape. These stars are beyond counting, yet astronomers have presumed to identify them with anonymous numbers. Every few minutes—after a dozen waves or so—a truly unnamed gleam appears: a meteor dying as it brightens. The night is cold, the surf alive. It is as quiet as it ever gets here, but nothing close to silent. The sea oats rattle; the waves growl; the wind murmurs.

The tide rises with rhythmic waves, then at last retreats, and I relax again, hungry from the vigil of waiting for a sea that never rises unaccountably. After supper I see that all tracks have been erased, the shark and the stingray gone with them. The sand is smooth except where I have walked. The surf washes shoreward despite the tide's retreat. Polaris hasn't budged.

I wonder about Forster's "cosmopolitanism" and regret it. I think of "feasts both fixed and movable," the benchmarks of our years. Didn't every famous ancient culture observe the solstices, the promise of spring, the threat of winter death, the ebb and flow of life on land? Our word for equinox comes from a dead language. Then I get the joke I've played on myself: This trip—the last before my deadline—began the day the clocks were turned back to repay the hour stolen in the spring. What a way to mark a season! The Druids would call it blasphemy, and they might be right.

Osprey

A dying meteor flares and fades high above the west horizon, somewhere beyond the continent, over another ocean. Something suddenly comes clear on this wild and utterly empty beach where I am the only man: The act of dying may be full of private pain, but death itself holds no fear for me—nor should it for humankind until we cut all natural ties. Like those shooting stars, vanished to remain invisible and changed, we are a part.

Acknowledgments

In more lyrical times than these, every writer worth the sand to blot his ink began by invoking the Muse. Now it is more fashionable to finish a work, then list the people who provided help or inspiration and wedge thanks up front between the dedication and the table of contents.

This tradition, once sincere and gracious, has fallen on hard times. Some academic writers acknowledge a benefactor and slap him in the next breath: "My esteemed colleague, Dr. Jekyll, read Chapter X . . . but the views expressed therein are the author's alone." Other writers go to such lengths to share credit that they finally take responsibility only for whatever gaffes got into print. Then there are those authors whose grateful thanks read like a starlet's Academy Award address. They mention absolutely everybody's contribution in painful detail until the reader wonders who was mostly highly regarded: The all-suffering wife? The dogged dictationist who typed all nine revisions of the entire book? Or the brilliant grad student who quantified the stool of 4,000 laboratory animals for seven summers? In hopes of finding a better way, I wish to make some things uncommonly clear: I freely acknowledge sole authorship of any errors. Nay, I claim each skewed speculation and dubious datum—not that anyone else wants them. I happen to have done most of the typing, too. These admissions out of the way, let's turn to more important matters.

First, a number of organizations helped. Having complained for years about taxes, I was repaid in part during 1978 through the good offices of the National Park Service and the Library of the Department of the Interior. The Smithsonian Institution also provided bibliographic and human resources, even unique access, whether to handle a black skimmer's bill or to borrow a goosefish's corpse.

Turning to individuals, a number of authorities gave advice, and some offered thoughtful criticism on sections of text. The scientists named below also offered something beyond information, namely, insight, encouragement to a nonscientist, or infectious enthusiasm for their specialties. Two companions in the world of letters read the entire text in its nearly final and most cacographic form. One stranger provided a motor vehicle for a summer. Several faithful friends gave moral support. Others provided stimulating ideas when my view became too narrow, others a well-aimed toe when my problem was lethargy or hubris. Were these contributions more or less important than a private tutorial or a guided tour? Is a pomegranate as red as rare porterhouse? I'll beg such issues and try to obviate any ranking of my benefactors—as soon as I specify the roles three people played.

Behind every writer who doesn't go nuts (and some who do) stands a singular sustainer, a person who performs what Wordsworth called "little nameless, unremembered acts of kindness and of love." Mine listened to complaints, dared to offer unwelcome advice, shared a few travels but settled for tales of many more. She was there when I needed relief from writing and out of sight when I had to work alone. A part-time miracle worker, once she produced fresh raspberries on an island where none grew; another day she found the first aid kit just in time. The very versatility of her support makes a summing up next to impossible. This book is dedicated to her with love and gratitude.

I cannot thank another person personally for her crucial role. Two years ago Marion Clark, legendary editor of *The Washington Post*'s magazine *Potomac*, accepted my proposal for a natural science survey of nearby summer beaches. The project she commissioned and published became the springboard for this book. An airplane accident took her life too soon, and Washington journalism is the lesser for that.

Neither can I contain my incredulity at hearing of one Anne E. Lacy's work at the Smithsonian a year ago. She was then in the process of drawing the genitalia of every North American water beetle known to science, which is on taxonomic terms with some 1,500 species. It sounded peculiar but the reason turned out to be simple. These insects' bodies look so much alike that the best way to distinguish all the species is by microscopic examination of their minuscule private parts, which differ remarkably. And the only way to record the results for a definitive taxonomic catalogue is with exact line drawings. Hence, her odd preoccupation. Anne calls herself an illustrator. Her work, which illuminates this book, speaks for itself. But it cannot reveal the perseverance and joyful presence that this gifted artist of science brought to our collaboration.

The people named below know how they contributed. The

reader need only know that their gifts of time, knowledge and caring enriched these pages. I have the happy honor to thank them publicly now for early help, for sustained support, for scientific counsel. These were my tutors, mentors and Muses:

Donna Ari; Richard D. Baker, Assateague National Seashore; Maxwell Boverman, M.D.; Anne Buchwald; Daniel H. Crowley, Esq.; Robert F. Dolan, University of Virginia; Molly Friedrich; Paul J. Codfroy, University of Massachusetts; Mary Hallett; Mary Anne Harrell, National Geographic Society; Jill Johnson and Maryanne Gerbackis, Fire Island National Seashore; Col. Robert J. T. Joy, M.D., Uniformed Services University of the Health Sciences; Stephen P. Leatherman, National Park Service; author Charles R. Larson, American University; Irene E. Magyar and Raymond B. Manning, Smithsonian Institution; John R. Pichurski, American Motors Corporation; J. W. Pierce, Smithsonian; Aaron Priest; Theron Raines; Joseph Rosewater, Smithsonian; Carl N. Shuster, Jr., Federal Energy Regulatory Commission; George E. Watson, Smithsonian; Charles L. Wheeler, National Marine Fisheries Service; Austin Williams, National Marine Fisheries; and Richard Zusi, Smithsonian.

Washington, D.C.
February 14, 1979

Addendum to the Second Edition

Now, a dozen years later, I am pround to acknowledge the following men who found time to read parts (or all) of this original manuscript and comment on it critically. Their charge was to spot errors in the original and suggest new directions. It goes without saying that any errors herein—new or perpetuated—are mine exclusively. It also goes without saying that I am very grateful to these friends and associates:

Thomas B. Allen, novelist, biographer, natural science writer, editor, my coauthor in a previous venture, neighbor;
Dr. David Pawson, invertebrate zoologist at the Smithsonian Institution's National Museum of Natural History;
Dave Masch, steward of Penikese Island, Massachusetts;

Dr. Austin Williams (again), invertebrate zoologist at the National Marine Fisheries Service Systematics Laboratory;

Dr. Tom Monroe, ichthyologist at the NMFS Systematics Lab;

Richard D. Baker (again), chief lifeguard at Assateague Island National Seashore;

Dr. Robert J. T. Joy (again), USMC (ret.), physician and professor of medical history at the Uniformed Services University of the Health Sciences, Bethesda, Maryland;

Dr. Kenneth Towe, research geologist at the Smithsonian's Museum of Natural History.

In the botanical realm, the gifted landscape designer Rachel Lambert Mellon taught me the surprising lesson that beach grass is worth cultivating in both natural and urban settings.

I am also grateful to Charles B. Everitt, President of The Globe Pequot Press, for enabling this, my first book, to have a second life in this revised edition.

In addition, I thank my son Timothy Dana Bruce Kopper for his company, cooperation and observations on many a beach trek— even for inspiring some. (Please know that he took me camping at seaside for Father's Day when he was barely three.)

Finally, with love and special gratitude I again thank Mary, née Carll, now my wife, to whom this book will always be dedicated. I thank her for her continued patience, wise advice and stimulating support.

Chevy Chase, Maryland
November 22, 1990

Index

Note: Page numbers in italics indicate illustrations.

About the Author

Philip Kopper has written for the *Baltimore Sun, The Washington Post, The New York Times,* the National Geographic Society, *Down East, Smithsonian,* and a host of other periodicals. Trained as a newspaper reporter, he is also the author of six books that reflect his interest in science and humanity. These are: *The National Museum of Natural History, A Christmas Testament, Father's Birthing Book, Colonial Williamsburg, The Smithsonian Book of North American Indians,* and *America's National Gallery of Art.*